Word of Mouse

Word

of

D'YOUVILLE COLLEGE
LIBRARY

MOUSE

The Marketing Power
of Collaborative Filtering

John Riedl and

Joseph Konstan

with Eric Vrooman

WARNER
BUSINESS
BOOKS™

Published by Warner Books

An AOL Time Warner Company

Copyright © 2002 by Professors John Riedl and Joseph Konstan
All rights reserved.

Warner Books, Inc., 1271 Avenue of the Americas, New York, NY 10020
Visit our Web site at www.twbookmark.com.

An AOL Time Warner Company

Printed in the United States of America
First Printing: August 2002

10   9   8   7   6   5   4   3   2   1

Book design by Ralph Fowler

Library of Congress Cataloging-in-Publication Data
Riedl, John.
    Word of mouse : the marketing power of collaborative filtering / John Riedl
and Joseph Konstan.
        p. cm.
    ISBN 0-446-53003-4
    1. Consumers—Research. 2. Marketing research. 3. Consumers—
Research—Data processing. 4. Marketing research—Data processing.
I. Konstan, Joseph. II. Title.

HF5415.32 .R54 2002
658.8'34—dc21   2002016838

HF5415.32
.R54
2002

Contents

AUG 19 2002

Foreword

by Malcolm Gladwell
Excerpted from "The Science of the Sleeper: How the Information Age Could Blow Away the Blockbuster" (*The New Yorker*)

In 1992, a sometime actress named Rebecca Wells published a novel called *Little Altars Everywhere* with a small, now defunct press in Seattle. Wells was an unknown author, and the press had no money for publicity. She had a friend, however, who spent that Thanksgiving with a friend who was a producer of National Public Radio's "All Things Considered." The producer read the book and passed it on to Linda Wertheimer, a host of the show, and she liked it so much that she put Wells on her program. That interview, in turn, was heard by a man who was listening to the radio in Blytheville, Arkansas, and whose wife, Mary Gay Shipley, ran the town bookstore. He bought the book and gave it to her; she loved it, and, with that, the strange and improbable rise of Rebecca Wells, best-selling author, began.

Blytheville is a sleepy little town about an hour or so up the Mississippi from Memphis, and Mary Gay Shipley's bookstore— That Bookstore in Blytheville—sits between the Red Ball Barber Shop and Westbrook's shoe store on a meandering stretch of Main Street. The store is just one long room in a slightly shabby storefront, with creaky floors and big overhead fans and subject headings on the shelves marked with Post-it notes. Shipley's fiction section takes up about as much shelf space as a typical Barnes & Noble devotes to, say, homeopathic medicine. That's because Shipley thinks that a book buyer ought to be able to browse and read the jacket flap of everything that might catch her eye, without being overwhelmed by thousands of choices. Mostly, though, people come to Mary Gay Shipley's store in order to find out what Mary Gay thinks they ought to be reading, and in 1993 Mary Gay Shipley thought people ought to be reading *Little Altars Everywhere*. She began ordering it by the dozen, which, Shipley says, "for us, is huge." She put it in the little rack out front where she lists her current favorites. She wrote about it in the newsletter she sends to her regular customers. "We could tell it was going to have a lot of word of mouth," she says. "It was the kind of book where you could say, 'You'll love it. Take it home.'" The No. 1 author at That Bookstore in Blytheville in 1993 was John Grisham, as was the case of nearly every bookstore in the country. But No. 2 was Rebecca Wells.

In the book business, as in the movie business, there are two kinds of hits: sleepers and blockbusters. John Grisham and Tom Clancy and Danielle Steel write blockbusters. Their books are announced with huge publicity campaigns. Within days of publication, they leap onto the best-seller lists. Sales start high—hundreds of thousands of copies in the first few weeks—and then taper off. People who buy or watch blockbusters have a clear sense of what they are going to get: a Danielle Steel novel is always—well, a Danielle Steel novel. Sleepers, on the other hand, are often unknown quantities. Sales start slowly and gradually build; publicity, at least early on, is often nonexistent. Sleepers come to your attention by a slow, serendipitous path: a friend who runs into a friend who sets up the interview that just happens to be heard by a guy married to a bookseller. Sleepers tend to emerge from the world of independent bookstores, because independent bookstores are the kinds of places where readers go to ask the question that launches all sleeper hits: Can you recommend a book to me? Shipley was plugging Terry Kay's *To Dance with the White Dog* long before it became a best-seller. She had Melinda Haynes lined up to do a reading at her store before Oprah tapped *Mother of Pearl* as one of her recommended books and it shot onto the best-seller lists. She read David Guterson's *Snow Falling on Cedars* in manuscript and went crazy for it. "I called the publisher, and they said, 'We think it's a regional book.' And I said, 'Write it down: "M.G.S. says this is an important book."'" All this makes it sound as if she has a sixth sense for books that will be successful, but that's not quite right. People like Mary Gay Shipley don't merely predict sleeper hits; they create sleeper hits.

Most of us, of course, don't have someone like Mary Gay Shipley in our lives, and with the decline of the independent bookstore in recent years the number of Shipleys out there creating sleeper hits has declined as well. The big chain bookstores that have taken over the bookselling business are blockbuster factories, since the sheer number of titles they offer can make browsing an intimidating proposition. As David Gernert, who is John Grisham's agent and editor, explains, "If you walk into a superstore, that's where being a brand makes so much more of a difference. There is so much more choice, it's overwhelming. You see walls and walls of books. In that kind of environment, the reader is drawn to the known commodity. The brand-name author is now a safe haven." Between 1986 and 1996, the share of book sales represented by the thirty top-selling hardcover books in America nearly doubled.

The new dominance of the blockbuster is part of a familiar pattern. The same thing has happened in the movie business, where a handful of heavily promoted films featuring "bankable" stars now command the lion's share of the annual box-office. We live, as the economists Robert Frank and Philip Cook have argued, in a "winner-take-all society," which is another way of saying that we live in the age of the blockbuster. But what if there were a way around the blockbuster? What if there were a simple way to build your very own Mary Gay Shipley? This is the promise of a new technology called collaborative filtering, one of the most intriguing developments to come out of the Internet age.

If you want a recommendation about what product to buy, you might want to consult an expert in the field. That's a function that magazines like *Car and Driver* and *Sound & Vision* perform. Another approach is to poll users or consumers of a particular product or service and tabulate their opinions. That's what the Zagat restaurant guides and consumer-ratings services like J. D. Power and Associates do. It's very helpful to hear what an "expert" audiophile has to say about the newest DVD player, or what the thousands of owners of the new Volkswagen Passat have to say about reliability and manufacturing defects. But when it comes to books or movies— what might be called "taste products"—these kinds of recommendations aren't nearly as useful. Few moviegoers, for example, rely on the advice of a single movie reviewer. Most of us gather opinions from a variety of sources—from reviewers whom we have agreed with in the past, from friends who have already seen the movie, or from the presence of certain actors or directors whom we already like—and do a kind of calculation in our heads. It's an imperfect procedure. You can find out a great deal about what various critics have to say. But they're strangers, and, to predict correctly whether you'll like something, the person making the recommendation really has to know something about you.

That's why Shipley is such a powerful force in touting new books. She has lived in Blytheville all her life and has run the bookstore there for twenty-three years, and so her customers know who she is. They trust her recommendations. At the same time, she knows who they are, so she knows how to match up the right book with the right person. For example, she really likes David Guterson's new novel, *East of the Mountains*, but she's not about to recommend it to anyone. It's about a doctor who has cancer and plans his own death and, she says, "there are some people dealing with a death in their family for whom this is not the book to read right now." She had similar reservations about Charles Frazier's *Cold Mountain*. "There were people I know who I didn't think would like it," Shipley said. "And I'd tell them that. It's a journey story. It's not what happens at the end that matters, and there are some people for whom that's just not satisfying. I don't want them to take it home, try to read it, not like it, then not go back to that writer." Shipley knows what her customers will like because she knows who they are.

Collaborative filtering is an attempt to approximate this kind of insider knowledge. It works as a kind of doppelgänger search engine. All of us have had the experience of meeting people and discovering that they appear to have the very same tastes we do—that they really love the same obscure foreign films that we love, or that they are fans of the same little-known novelist whom we are obsessed with. If such a person recommended a book to you, you'd take that recommendation seriously, because cultural tastes seem to run in patterns. If you and your doppelgänger love the same ten books, chances are you'll also like the eleventh book he likes. Collaborative filtering is simply a system that sifts through the opinions and preferences of thousands of people and systematically finds your doppelgänger—and then tells you what your doppelgänger's eleventh favorite book is.

John Riedl, a University of Minnesota computer scientist who is one of the pioneers of this technology, has set up a Web site called MovieLens, which is a very elegant example of collaborative filtering at work. Everyone who logs on—and tens of thousands of people have already done so—is asked to rate a series of movies on a scale of 1 to 5, where 5 means "must see" and 1 means "awful." For example, I rated *Rushmore* as a 5, which meant that I was put into the group of people who loved *Rushmore*. I then rated *Summer of Sam* as a 1, which put me into the somewhat smaller and more select group that both loved *Rushmore* and hated *Summer of Sam*. Collaborative-filtering systems don't work all that well at first, because, obviously, in order to find someone's cultural counterparts you need to know a lot more about them than how they felt about two movies. Even after I have given the system seven opinions (including *Election*, 4; *Notting Hill*, 2; *The Sting*, 4; and *Star Wars*. 1), it was making mistakes. It thought I would love *Titanic* and *Zero Effect*, and I disliked them both. But after I had plugged in about fifteen opinions—which Riedl says is probably the minimum—I began to notice that the rating that MovieLens predicted I would give a movie and the rating I actually gave it were nearly always, almost eerily, the same. The system had found a small group of people who feel exactly the same way I do about a wide range of popular movies.

Riedl and Joe Konstan are two co-founders of New Perceptions, a firm specializing in collaborative filtering. One of Net Perceptions' clients is SkyMall, a company that gathers selections from dozens of mail-order catalogues—from Hammacher Schlemmer and L. L. Bean to the Wine Enthusiast—and advertises them in the magazines that you see in the seat pockets of airplanes. SkyMall licensed the system both for their Web site and for their 800-number call center, where the software looks for your doppelgänger while you are calling in with your order, and a few additional recommendations pop up on the operator's screen. SkyMall's system is still in its infancy, but, in a test, the company found that it has increased the total sales per customer somewhere between fifteen and twenty-five per cent. What's remarkable about the SkyMall system is that it links products from many different categories. It's one thing, after all, to surmise that if someone likes *The Remains of the Day* he is also going to like *A Room with a View*. But it's quite another to infer that if you liked a particular item from the Orvis catalogue there's a certain item from Reliable Home Office that you'll also be interested in. "Their experience has been absolutely hilarious," says Steve Larsen, the senior vice-president of marketing at Net Perceptions. "One of the very first recommendations that came out of the engine was for a gentleman who was ordering a blue cloth shirt, a twenty-eight-dollar shirt. Our engine recommended a hundred-and-thirty-five-dollar cigar humidor—and he bought it! I don't think anybody put those two together before."

The really transformative potential of collaborative filtering, however, has to do with the way taste products—books, plays, movies, and the rest—can be marketed. Marketers now play an elaborate game of stereotyping. They create fixed sets of groups—middle-class-suburban, young-urban-professional, inner-city, working-class, rural-religious, and so on—and then find out enough about us to fit us into one of those groups. The collaborative-filtering process, on the other hand, starts with who we are, then derives our cultural "neighborhood" from those facts. And these groups aren't permanent. They change as we change. I have never seen a film by Luis Buñuel, and I have no plans to. I don't put myself in the group of people who like Buñuel. But if I were to see *That Obscure Object of Desire* tomorrow and love it, and enter my preference on Movie-Lens, the group of people they defined as "just like me" would immediately and subtly change.

Collaborative filtering underscores a lesson that, for the better part of history, humans have been stubbornly resistant to learning: if you want to understand what one person thinks or feels or likes or does it isn't enough to draw inferences from the general social or demographic category to which he belongs. You cannot tell, with any reasonable degree of certainty, whether someone will like *The Girl's Guide to Hunting and Fishing* by knowing that the person is a single twenty-eight-year-old woman who lives in Manhattan, any more than you can tell whether somebody will commit a crime knowing only that he's a twenty-eight-year-old African-American male who lives in the Bronx. Riedl has taken demographic data from the people who log on to MovieLens—such as their age and occupation and sex—but he has found that it hardly makes his predictions any more accurate. "What you tell us about what you like is far more predictive of what you will like in the future than anything else we've tried," he says. "It seems almost dumb to say it, but you tell that to marketers sometimes and they look at you puzzled."

None of this means that standard demographic data is useless. If you were trying to figure out how to market a coming-of-age movie, you'd be most interested in collaborative-filtering data from people below, say, the age of twenty-eight. Facts such as age and sex and place of residence are useful in sorting the kinds of information you get from a recommendation engine. But the central claim of the collaborative-filtering movement is that, head to head, the old demographic and "psychographic" data cannot compete with preference data. This is a potentially revolutionary argument. Traditionally, there has been almost no limit to the amount of information marketers have wanted about their customers: academic records, work experience, marital status, age, sex, race, Zip Code, credit records, focus-group sessions—everything has been relevant, because in trying to answer the question of what we want, marketers have taken the long way around and tried to find out first who we are. Collaborative filtering shows that, in predicting consumer preferences, none of this information is all that important. In order to know what someone wants, what you really need to know is what they've wanted.

Collaborative filtering is, in effect, anti-blockbuster. The more information the system has about you, the more narrow and exclusive its recommendations become. It's just like Shipley: it uses its knowledge about you to steer you toward choices you wouldn't normally know about. I gave MovieLens my opinions on fifteen very mainstream American movies. I'm a timid and unsophisticated moviegoer. I rarely see anything but very commercial Hollywood releases. It told me, in return, that I would love *C'est Arrivé Près de Chez Vous*, an obscure 1992 Belgian comedy, and *Shall We Dance*, the 1937 Fred and Ginger vehicle. In other words, among my moviegoing soul mates are a number of people who share my views on mainstream fare but who also have much greater familiarity with foreign and classic films. The system essentially put me in touch with people who share my tastes but who happen to know a good deal more about movies. Collaborative filtering gives voice to the expert in every preference neighborhood. A world where such customized recommendations were available would allow Shipley's well-read opinions to be known not just in Blytheville but wherever there are people who share her taste in books.

Introduction

We always want what is advantageous to us but we do not always discern it.

—JEAN-JACQUES ROUSSEAU (1712–1778)

A woman orders a diet book over the phone. The call-center operator responds, "Today we've got ten percent off on a barbecue set. Would you be interested in that?"

The customer answers, "Yes, I would!"

The operator then says, "Well, ma'am, we also have ten percent off on a ham."

"I'll take that, too."

At a different company, a woman orders a pillow. The call-center operator asks if she wouldn't also be interested in a padded bra.

She is.

If these were your call-center operators, you might consider firing them. Recommending a ham to someone who ordered a diet book? That takes gall. Suggesting underwear to a customer? Impudence! But these recommendations were successful. They resulted in sales. And, in the case of the diet-book customer, the cross-sell value of the ham and the barbecue set was considerably more than the initial purchase.

So who are these operators? Seers? Psychics? Savants? Or were they just plain lucky?

None of the above. We know, because these orders and recommendations really did happen. These call-center operators weren't operating on their own volition. They had behind them the power of a new technology: collaborative filtering .

In his *New Yorker* piece "The Science of the Sleeper," Malcolm Gladwell called collaborative filtering "eerily accurate." ABC News described collaborative filtering as having your own butler—someone who knows your tastes, your sizes, and your history of past purchases. This analogy doesn't quite do collaborative filtering justice, however; because collaborative filtering uses data culled from many different people, not just one, it can predict what you'll like in the future better than a butler ever could.

GroupLens and MovieLens

At the 1992 Computer Supported Cooperative Work conference in Toronto, Shumpei Kumon delivered a talk about the information economy. People create valuable information all the time, he said, much of which escapes into the ether. Today, this information includes: clicking on a site, checking out a link, adding an item to a shopping basket, sending an E-mail asking about the availability of a product in a certain color, and even the length of time customers spend on a single page. This information is sometimes called *meta information* because it is information about other information. Meta information suggests larger patterns of interest, and often hidden ones.

Back at the University of Minnesota, we set to work, along with Paul Resnick who was working with us from MIT, developing a system that would collect meta information and turn it into something useful. Many months and balled-up pieces of paper later, we had it.

Like the robot inventors on Comedy Central's *Battlebots*, we were anxious to test our results in front of a live audience. In 1993, that opportunity arrived.

In the space of several months, we built the first Usenet news recommender system called GroupLens. Initially designed as a research prototype for students, GroupLens monitored user ratings of news articles. After a user had rated several items, GroupLens was able to make recommendations about other articles the user might like. The results were astounding. Users read articles that we recommended highly three to four times as often as those we didn't.

Later, we applied the GroupLens technology to another non-commercial site, MovieLens. MovieLens asks visitors to rate movies they've seen on a five-star scale. We pair their ratings with people who have rated movies similarly. So if you gave *Titanic* four stars, *Pretty Woman* three stars, and *Raising Arizona* five stars, you will be placed in a community of people who feel the same way. They're called your *nearest neighbors,* although they may live thousands of miles away. It's hard to imagine, but these people, complete strangers, are better predictors of whether you'll like a movie than Roger Ebert or Gene Shalit, better than your close friends, better than your loved ones, and better than your own hunches. On average, MovieLens recommendations are closer than one star to your own opinion (after you've seen the movie, of course).

Net Perceptions

After releasing GroupLens to the public in the winter of 1996, we started getting cold calls from companies that wanted to license our software or hire us. Instead, we decided to form a company of our own with Steven Snyder, Brad Miller, and David Gardiner. After all, if we could tell you what articles and movies you'd like, why couldn't we tell you what products you would like as well?

Net Perceptions has since become a leading provider of personalization and precision-marketing software solutions for Internet and multi-channel retailers. Our software is designed to help retailers understand customers individually; optimize product assortments, prices, and inventories; and offer the right product to the right customer. Today, Net Perceptions' customers include: Best Buy, Brylane, GUS (Great Universal Stores), JCPenney, Kmart, and Tesco.

Personalized Recommendations

You have probably used collaborative filtering. Amazon.com, one of our earliest clients, employs this technology. You may remember their doughnut-shop ad where the person at the counter recommends glazed doughnuts to a customer who ordered a cinnamon roll because people who liked glazed doughnuts demonstrated a higher propensity for liking cinnamon rolls. Amazon makes book recommendations the same way (now using their own software), as do many other sites.

Even if you haven't used collaborative filtering, you've probably experienced personalized recommendations. On the back of a Blockbuster Video box, you'll find a list of three other movies to try if you liked that particular movie. The banner ads you see on many Web sites are personalized for you based upon information that companies like DoubleClick have collected. Content sites get in on the action too. My Yahoo! and many other news sites offer you the opportunity to customize their pages so that articles about dolphins, the San Diego Padres, and John Coltrane are the first you see. MIT's Nicholas Negroponte calls it the "Daily Me."

The Internet is the perfect medium for collaborative filtering and recommender systems. Internet shoppers want ease, information, and immediacy. With information gleaned from page views, searches, purchases, and followed links, companies can present offers and products that are on target for each individual customer. Customers don't have to page through each item in their inventory or perform blind searches. And customers can participate in and modify their own profiles, so that they don't feel like recommendations are being done *to* them, but rather *for* them.

Collaborative Filtering vs. Friends and Experts

Everybody has friends or acquaintances they go to for advice. On *Who Wants to Be a Millionaire,* contestants call phone-a-friends based upon their knowledge of history, geography, pop culture, and other subjects. Or they poll the audience. Both strategies can help when the contestant doesn't know the answer. But what happens when the phone-a-friend doesn't know? Or when the audience doesn't provide a definitive response? When faced with these dilemmas, contestants either guess or take the money they've won and walk away.

Experts are often as unreliable as friends or a collection of strangers—if not more so. When it comes to taste-based products, like clothing, expert salespeople may know their products intimately, but they can't know their customers as well. A salesperson might mistakenly assume that, based upon a customer's interest in a polka-dot blouse, she might also like a retro-style bathing suit (when, in fact, she prefers single-color tankinis). With taste-based products, customers trust themselves most of all. More than experts. More than friends. More than a randomly selected audience.

Collaborative filtering succeeds where all else fails. It makes recommendations not from experts, friends, or random people, but from the people who most precisely share an individual customer's tastes. As a result, customers feel like they're seeing products they would have chosen for themselves.

GUS

In March of 1999, Lee Gerdes, our friend and colleague at Net Perceptions, started a collaborative-filtering pilot at Great Universal Stores (GUS) outside of Manchester, England. GUS's recommender system was already generating sales on 20 percent of their offers. Lee had never seen a ratio higher than 8 percent in his twenty years in the business. He soon discovered the reason behind their success: a staff of 45 full-time professional shoppers who studied GUS inventory and recommended product pairings to their 4,600 call-center operators.

At the time, GUS took over 30 million phone orders a year, maintained nine sites, and distributed eleven catalogs. They sold and continue to sell mostly personal items: clothing, consumables, home products, sporting goods, and general merchandise. In 2000, their sales totaled nearly $4 billion. They're good at what they do, which is why they wanted to see if they could improve their results.

Lee had six weeks to install a collaborative-filtering prototype and get it up and running. With collaborative filtering, data and algorithms can be tuned and optimized for the particular business. "Data is always the key," Lee says.

Businesses are naturally leery about product recommendations that might make them look bad. If the recommender doesn't properly interpret the data, it may recommend a bib to a customer whose child is now in her teens or an item that's not available in the customer's size. Good algorithms prevent this from happening.

The rules used to create these algorithms can be quite sophisticated. For instance, if a customer buys a six-inch drill bit, you shouldn't recommend a four-inch bit. If part of an ensemble is purchased (one drill bit instead of a collection of bits), there's generally a reason why the rest of the ensemble isn't, so you're better off recommending another item. For soft goods (like clothing), product recommendations should include the color of the item. That way you can capitalize on the customer's demonstrated color preferences. With hard goods (like sofas), however, color shouldn't be included because often the color is prescribed by outside factors (size and color of a particular room, for instance). In GUS's case, recommendations also had to come from the particular catalog the customer had in hand. Needless to say, Lee had his work cut out for him.

It took Lee five weeks to develop the prototype. That left little time to train the forty-eight call-center operators chosen to participate in the pilot program, but all he needed was one day. He found the operators with the most in-depth purchase histories at GUS and had them place an order for something they liked while the other operators looked on. He then asked them to hit the recommender button. "We were in like Flynn," Lee said.

At the end of the six-week pilot period, collaborative filtering had generated a 27 percent conversion rate on 93 percent of the orders. Using their traditional recommendation system, GUS had gotten 20 percent on only 60 percent of the orders. In addition, orders that included a personalized recommendation were 23 percent larger than those without. Perhaps the greatest indicator of collaborative filtering's success was the average upsell value. It increased by a whopping 60 percent. On one £50 order (approximately $85 U.S.), a customer was recommended a living room suite. That customer wound up spending an additional £1800 (approximately $3,060 U.S.)—thirty-six times the initial order!

"The results are a clear hat-trick," said David Main, commercial director of GUS's Home Shopping Division. "We increased our upsell acceptance rate, boosted the average value of each upsell item, and showed that personalization technology, when properly applied, is significantly more efficient and effective than a more manual intensive approach. In addition, we also found that our sales advisers were enthusiastic about discussing personalized recommendations with their customers."

Because collaborative filtering uses knowledge about all of a customer's purchases, not just one, the terms *cross-sell* and *upsell* aren't exactly accurate. When you cross-sell, typically, you recommend a cheaper product based upon its relationship to a purchased product (recommending socks to someone who just purchased shoes, for instance). When you upsell, you encourage a customer to purchase a similar item at a higher cost (more expensive shoes). Collaborative filtering combines the best of both—additional purchases, often at higher prices. By using a customer's entire purchase history, collaborative filtering has the confidence to recommend products that are more expensive than what's in the customer's shopping basket. It's not cross-selling, or upselling, it's just selling. Period.

Filtered vs. Unfiltered

Despite the impressive results, collaborative filtering has its critics. Cass R. Sunstein, a professor at the University of Chicago Law School and author of *Republic.com,* complains that filtering devices such as TiVo and the "Daily Me" narrow our horizons. If you get just the things you want, won't you miss out on experiences and information that lie outside that purview? In other words, if you were to read a traditional newspaper, you might stumble into an article about Liberia, read it, and thereby expand your horizons.

But collaborative filtering *is* a connective technology. It introduces you to new products, articles, and people. With Launch.com, for instance, you can create your own radio station—one that mixes in artists and songs you've never heard before. And those songs are more likely to be ones you like than the ones conglomerate-owned radio stations play, because with Launch they're recommended by people who share your taste in music. You don't have to listen to ads or a Mariah Carey song playing over and over again; you listen to music you want to hear. (For more about Launch, see our site profile in "Principle 4: Box Products, Not People").

Without collaborative filtering, someone else chooses what you see (what catalogs, products, articles). You're at the whims of an editor or marketer, or perhaps a team of editors or marketers. Either way, you're lumped into a demographic that will fit you like a mitten, not a glove.

Privacy

Does collaborative filtering misuse privileged customer information? Amazon was chastised when it failed to announce changes to its privacy policy in the wake of Toysmart's bankruptcy proceedings. A bankruptcy judge not only permitted Toysmart to sell its customer profiles, it required them to list the profiles as an asset. The FTC filed suit, but it was only able to restrict the sale of

Toysmart's profiles to one company. In response, Amazon changed its policy so that it, too, would be able to sell customer profiles, including purchase histories, in the event that it went bankrupt. Customers were understandably concerned. Customers were similarly concerned when Amazon created purchase circles, which allowed anyone to view which books were best-sellers in certain geographical regions, companies, or colleges. If, for instance, you wanted to find out what employees at Microsoft were reading, you could—without Microsoft's permission. As a prospective employee or stock purchaser, you might be curious to learn whether Microsoft employees were reading *Spending Your Wealth* or *Time to Get Off the Gravy Train*.

We don't advocate selling or publishing private customer profiles. Nor do we condone unwanted solicitations. Reputable sites have opt-in programs for customers. These allow customers the opportunity to determine if they want to be contacted with offers or information updates. Amazon learned this the hard way and now allows companies and individuals to decide whether they want to participate in purchase circles.

Wherever data is stockpiled, there is the potential for misuse. Fortunately, collaborative filtering doesn't need to know who you are. Names aren't important. Neither is your age, gender, or race. Collaborative filtering doesn't need to know anything about you except what products you want to buy. Because privacy issues are raised by some of the companies we examine, however, we'll provide you with tips to ensure customer privacy throughout the book.

Lifetime Learning

The more data there is available, the better collaborative filtering works. It learns from your behavior and adjusts to subtle changes in your taste and preferences. This is technology that listens. It provides real value for the data you provide, both explicitly and implicitly. Naturally, this value increases over time, building customer loyalty. Collaborative filtering is like a personal shopper who remembers all your purchases and preferences—someone you can trust to make decisions for you. With such an asset, why would you go to someone who doesn't know you from Adam?

Inventory

In addition to being a customer-friendly technology, collaborative filtering can help companies avoid inventory nightmares. Depth of product inventory can be a sticky issue if you're recommending the same product to every customer. Do we have too much in stock? Do we have too little? Collaborative filtering recommendations can be tuned to your inventory. As you'll see in The Children's Place profile in "Principle 4: Box Products, Not People," when a mistake or great deal leads to excess inventory, collaborative filtering can help you target just the right customers for marketing campaigns.

Why Now?

So why read this book? Why not just buy collaborative filtering? Well, for one thing, this book not only introduces you to recommender technology, it also shows you how to apply it so you can best articulate and accommodate customer taste. We give you insight into what technologies and interfaces work best for different businesses. We teach you how to create, manage, and maintain the right recommender systems for your business. Until recently, recommender technology was for techies only. Many major businesses are now creating personalization departments, and they're often loath to talk about what they do. We're not.

Word of Mouse—Overview

We begin by giving you a brief history of recommender technology. The technology is new, but its inspiration is age-old. There was a time, before Wal-Mart and minimum wage, when small merchants knew their customers well enough to make insightful product recommendations. They knew what you had already purchased and wouldn't try to sell you something you didn't need or want. Collaborative filtering and other recommender systems are designed to re-create the unique knowledge and service of these merchants.

In *Word of Mouse,* we examine thirty-six companies. Some of them we chose because they're industry leaders, others because we worked with them at Net Perceptions, and some because we know they can do better. Most of these companies use recommender technology in interesting and innovative ways. From their challenges and successes, you'll learn how to approach and respond to your customers.

Eight Principles

Personalized recommendations are revolutionizing business, especially on-line, where data can be tracked easily. In *Word of Mouse,* we tell you not just how to personalize recommendations, but how to personalize your site as well.

Web sites can change overnight. Some, if not most, of the businesses we discuss will have changed their sites by the time this book goes to press. The eight principles to personalize your business we describe in this book, however, are timeless.

We'll teach you how to:

1. Demonstrate product expertise
2. Be a customer agent
3. Maintain excellent service across touchpoints
4. Box products, not people

5. Watch what I do
6. Revolutionize knowledge management
7. Use communities to create content
8. Turn communities into content

Future Shock

In 1992, we developed collaborative filtering. In 1996, we brought it to the public via Net Perceptions. In 1997, we applied our patented technology to retail call-centers, outbound E-mail campaigns, and knowledge management on corporate intranets. In 1998, we created filterbots (intelligent agents that both learn from and create purchasing data). In 2001, we brought recommenders to handheld devices. What does the future hold? In our final chapter, "The Future of Collaborative Filtering and Recommender Systems," we'll give you a sneak preview.

Word of Mouse

Every click and comment from your customers provides information, but you need to know how to harness it. Otherwise, it's like having a mouse in your walls: The scratching and clicking will keep you up at night.

With *Word of Mouse,* you'll learn what your customers are saying. Maybe more important, you'll be able to *tell* your customers what *they're* saying. By establishing previously unconscious connections about what customers like and why they like it, you'll gain their trust and keep their business. You'll have the crystal ball.

Word of Mouse

The Insider's Guide to Collaborative Filtering and Recommender Systems

> Any sufficiently advanced technology is indistinguishable from magic.
>
> —ARTHUR C. CLARKE, *PROFILES OF THE FUTURE* (1962)

> Man is a tool-using animal. . . .
> Without tools he is nothing, with tools, he is all.
>
> —THOMAS CARLYLE, *SARTOR RESARTUS* (1833–34)

A Brief History of Collaborative Filtering

Collaborative filtering is at the same time very new and very old. At its core, collaborative filtering is any mechanism whereby members of a community collaborate to identify what is good and what is bad. Even in prehistoric days, our species relied upon informal collaborative filtering. When a tribe encountered some new berry or root, they didn't all eat it simultaneously. Some people watched to see if the others became ill. If those who had eaten did get sick, the others would use this strong negative recommendation by avoiding that food (e.g., the deadly nightshade); if not, they would eat it themselves.

All sorts of knowledge was gained through observation of our neighbors. We learned which animals were dangerous and which were tasty. Then, as we developed into societies where people had time for art, philosophy, and science, the same process of collaborative filtering helped us decide which creations and theories were worth our time and money.

We imagine that many listeners sat transfixed by Homer's stories. Others might have considered him overrated and lobbied for their own favorite storyteller. These people, though they may not have known it at the time, were critics. As early as we had choices to make, we found critics to guide us. Today, as then, we can choose from among a variety of critics. Film critics help us decide which movies to see, theater critics lead us to the right play, and restaurant critics suggest a place to eat beforehand or afterward. In the financial world, analysts, brokers, and advisers recommend places to invest our money, and then members of the press critique the critics, helping us to better select our analysts, brokers, and advisers.

In addition to critics, we have editors and publishers to filter material for us. Because printing and distributing information can be expensive, commercial editors and publishers assess the marketability of a submitted work. On the opposite end of the spectrum, university presses, religion-affiliated publishers, and other not-for-profits are charged with forwarding an agenda. In either case, the editor and publisher work to identify content that they feel is worth distributing and, by implication, worth reading.

All of these—editors, publishers, critics, and even cave people—are examples of collaborative filtering. Collaborative filtering exists wherever people help filter out the wheat from the chaff, so the rest of us don't have to. In return, we reward them (all except the cave people) with our patronage and purchases.

The examples we've described above are all *manual* processes of collaborative filtering, however. Editors, publishers, and critics pick products based upon their expert opinions. In other words, *by hand*. They don't use automated systems to make these decisions for them. As a result, these editors and critics can't tailor their products and reviews for each individual customer. The *New Yorker*, for instance, doesn't publish a different magazine for each customer based upon his or her fields of interest. Instead, the *New Yorker's* audience is *universal* (their entire customer base and beyond).

Sometimes, though, people want and need personalized material. This is where automated information-gathering systems come in: namely, collaborative filtering and its two predecessors, information retrieval and information filtering.

Information Retrieval

Collaborative filtering is not the only, nor even the most prominent, technology for helping people find what they want. As soon as large collections were created, people organized them for better search performance. From the Great Library at Alexandria to the Library of Congress, organization and cataloging have made content more accessible. Through combinations of author, title, and subject indexes, library patrons can quickly and easily find books that match explicit search criteria.

Indeed, the problem of information retrieval—finding information in a large catalog—lent itself well to computerization. Gerard Salton's seminal 1968 book, *Automatic Information Organization and Retrieval*, set forth the mechanisms for automatically indexing documents by examining the terms used within them (or within titles and summaries). Once a collection of documents is indexed in this way, a user can search for specific terms and retrieve documents of interest. Today, we see wide proliferation of such systems, including the widely used Web search engines. As the demand for search continues to grow, the quality of information-retrieval systems escalates as well.

Information Filtering

Information-retrieval systems address a particular information niche: cases where users have ephemeral information needs and want to meet those needs by using a relatively stable, indexed collection. In addition to Web searches and library catalogs, this niche includes a wide variety of search tasks from finding a file on your computer's hard drive (when you've forgotten where you stored it) to searching through newspaper archives or corporate records.

Sometimes, however, the situation is reversed. Users may have a relatively stable information need, and want to check new information content to see if any of it meets that need. *Information-filtering* systems address this niche by either being told or learning the user's need, and then examining a stream of new content to select items that meet it. The simplest information-filtering examples are clipping services. A corporate executive may want to see any newspaper articles that mention his company or its competitors. More sophisticated information-filtering systems help travelers find out when flights to a particular city go on sale, or avid readers discover when a favorite author has published a new book. Internally, information-filtering systems look like the mirror image of information-retrieval systems. The database stores a wide range of user profiles (or queries), and each new document gets passed through this database to see which profiles are triggered.

Computerized Collaborative Filtering

Both information retrieval and information filtering help people manage the problem of information overload by directing them to items that match their interests. Until recently, that seemed like enough, but the quantity of content available keeps increasing. In 1970, it may well have been possible for a corporate officer to read every article mentioning his company. By the year 2002, with the wide distribution of content on the Internet, it would take a team of officers to keep up. Something needed to be done to help people find items not only by topic, but also by quality or taste—and that something was the automation of collaborative filtering.

Automated collaborative filtering sprouted in three directions in quick succession, resulting in three different but compatible systems: pull-active CF, push-active CF, and automated CF. Since the three systems perform different tasks, you might even find all three on the same Web site.

PULL-ACTIVE CF

Tapestry is widely recognized as the first computerized collaborative filtering system. Developed at Xerox PARC as a research project, Tapestry was designed to help small workgroups team up to figure out which articles (usually electronic-bulletin-board articles) were worth reading. Tapestry users could annotate articles, for example, by marking them as "Fred should look at this" or "Excellent!!!" Other users could ask the system to find articles that met specific criteria, including the keywords in the article (*à la* information retrieval and filtering), the annotations left by others, and even the actions others took when seeing the article. For example, a user might say, "I want to see all the articles that Mary replied to, since if Mary replied to them, they must have been interesting." This type of collaborative filtering has become known as *pull-active collaborative filtering* because a user takes an active role in pulling recommendations out of the system (by forming queries).

PUSH-ACTIVE CF

Soon afterwards, David Maltz and Kate Ehrlich at Lotus Research developed a prototype *push-active* collaborative-filtering system. In their unnamed system, users who read interesting messages could easily "push" the content to others who might also value it. In some ways, this resembles today's joke-distribution chains, where jokes are forwarded to friends who (hopefully) share the same sense of humor. In organizations, a select number of people share the responsibility of gathering information and distributing it to the right people. These people, either officially or unofficially, serve as information hubs. Push-active CF made their tasks much easier.

AUTOMATED CF

At about the same time, the GroupLens project was developing *automated collaborative filtering*. The major difference between active and automated collaborative filtering is that active collaborative filtering requires human effort to establish the relationship between the people making and the people receiving recommendations. Accordingly, active solutions work best in small communities (workgroups, friends, or family) where people already know each other and their tastes.

Automated collaborative filtering uses each individual's history of interaction with the system to identify good recommenders for that individual. In the simplest form, automated collaborative-filtering systems keep track of each item a user has rated, along with how well the user liked that item. The system then figures out which users are good predictors for each other by examining the similarity between user tastes. Finally, the system uses these good predictors to find new items to recommend.

Soon after GroupLens appeared, a number of other automated collaborative-filtering systems emerged—clearly systems that were developed in parallel. MIT's Media Lab debuted the Ringo (later Firefly) music recommender, which used collaborative filtering to help people find music. And Bellcore created the Video Recommender, in which people rated movies by E-mail and received recommendations in reply. The number of independently generated collaborative-filtering systems suggests that its time had surely come.

The Role of Today's Marketer

With all this new recommender technology, some marketers are understandably concerned about their future. Will they be replaced the way tollbooth operators are being replaced by E-ZPass? Or as assembly-line workers have been replaced by machines? No. Recommenders need the right data, placement, and follow-through. They need human insight and direction. And they're only part of an overall marketing strategy. Recommenders are like tools on a carpenter's belt. So can marketers sleep easy? Yes, provided they know how, when, and where to employ recommenders.

This book examines many different recommender systems, in addition to collaborative filtering, so that marketers can initiate, update, or overhaul their recommendation practices. First, though, we should explain what we mean by marketing. The role of marketing and the marketer has evolved to keep pace with technological advances. Now, when we think of marketing, two separate fields emerge:

1. Manufacturer and wholesale marketing
2. Retailer marketing

Manufacturer and wholesale marketing refers to the efforts undertaken by manufacturers and distributors to promote products to merchants and the public, increase brand awareness, and generally position, price, and otherwise define the brand identity of a product. This is not the type of marketing we're addressing here.

Retailer marketing, which for small marketers has often been synonymous with merchandising, focuses on the smaller, more local decisions of how to promote, price, bundle, and sell products. Because this type of marketing can engage individual customers, it is the most ripe for recommender systems. This has been our area of study.

For small retailers, sales and marketing may overlap. A bike-store owner might decide that she needs to sell more Cannondales because of their high profit margins, so she advertises a free helmet with the purchase of a Cannondale mountain bike. When her customers come in, she can recommend the bike-and-helmet specials based upon biking preferences they've demonstrated in the past. And if she knows that the customers prefer recumbent bikes, she won't waste their time on Cannondale's Jekylls and Scalpels.

Marketers for large retailers have lost touch with the customer; they make decisions that guide and drive sales from a distance. To deliver the personalized service customers demand, they need to narrow the gap. We're not here to suggest that marketers become salespeople. We simply want them to deploy marketing techniques to serve each customer personally, the way good salespeople do.

The first step away from sales was mass marketing—the idea that a catalog, advertisement, or flyer could be sent to an extremely wide audience to get them to come buy. These marketing tools were necessarily untargeted but relatively cheap to produce. In an age of few alternatives (Sears or Montgomery Ward?), mass marketing works fairly well. But generic advertising doesn't reach out to people who are different from average. And it doesn't work when customers have many shopping alternatives to choose from.

The chinks in mass marketing's armor revealed themselves as media became more specialized. In the latter half of the twentieth century, a media explosion allowed marketers to *narrowcast* to audiences described by income, age, sex, race, religion, geography, and interest area. An advertisement for a product in a young women's magazine, for example, could address a different audience than an advertisement in a men's or parents' venue. In addition, the availability of categorized mailing lists made it possible to send different mailings and offers to smaller groups of people. Instead of getting a generic message, people received messages they were more likely to identify with.

Even demographic-based marketing has its limits, though. Real people don't fit cleanly into catalogs or simple categories. Some people reading young women's magazines are those young women's parents—people unlikely to be reached by the same advertisements. Some people in wealthy neighborhoods are cash-poor. Other "millionaires next door" live in modest neighborhoods and have no characteristics that reveal their wealth. These people fall through the cracks when using simple demographics, like wealthy neighborhoods, age, race, or sex, to determine marketing strategies.

Two things happened, largely in parallel, as technology continued to advance. Customer-relationship-management software and computerized record-keeping tools made it possible to pursue one-to-one marketing. This marketing model, first popularized by Peppers and Rogers in their 1993 book *The One to One Future,* makes an effort to treat customers individually, if only by tracking and remembering their preferences. At the same time, the Web and improvements in printing technology created cheaper delivery mechanisms. The Web, unlike physical stores, could present each customer with unique interfaces and tailored products—at virtually no extra cost. And efficient custom printing allowed each customer to get a semi-custom catalog, newsletter, coupon book, or offer. The convergence of these technologies resulted in the ability to deliver personalized messages. The only thing missing was the knowledge. One-to-one marketing still relied too heavily on human use of information. Determining what offers or products to display to each customer—especially on a mass scale—takes a lot of effort.

That's where automated recommender systems come in. They close the gap between the goal of one-to-one marketing and the reality of limited sales effort. With recommender systems, marketers can now set up general promotions (whether on-line sales, cross-sales by telephone, E-mail or physical mail campaigns, or in-store coupons and suggestions) and allow the technology to grind through the process of matching individual people with products and offers.

Rather than crunching numbers to figure out which income level gets which advertisement, today's marketers decide which recommender technology and interfaces to implement and where. The variety and appeal of recommenders are growing rapidly. At Amazon, we discovered over twenty distinct recommenders! Marketers everywhere (not just on the Web) are boning up on the potential applications. For one thing, recommenders draw customers in like one-to-one merchants because they demonstrate knowledge of individual preferences. But by studying recommendations, marketers also learn more about product relationships and purchasing patterns. As they do, promotions and customer interests dovetail together in a way that mass marketers can only envy.

Recommender Technology and Interfaces

In our "Introduction," we explained in general terms how collaborative filtering works. Now we'll go into a little more depth and also introduce you to the other recommenders we examine throughout the book. In addition, we'll explain how customers participate in the exchange of preferences and recommendations— the *interfaces*.

At the end of each company profile in Principles #1 through #8, we'll remind you what recommenders these companies used and how the interfaces operated. With that in mind, you may find it helpful to refer back to this chapter for more detailed descriptions of these recommenders and interfaces.

Automated Collaborative Filtering—The Technology

Automated collaborative-filtering systems depend on one thing: customer preferences. Customer preferences not only illustrate the taste of an individual customer, they also build the mountain of data necessary to establish effective nearest neighbors. So how do you collect these preferences? Obviously, sales are a good indicator of what customers prefer (especially if a customer purchases an item repeatedly). By studying how long a customer spends on a Web page, companies can establish whether or not the customer was interested in the products displayed there. If a customer prints or forwards a Web page, that indicates her preferences, as do items placed on a wish list or in a shopping basket. Customers might also tip their hand with reactions to recommendations that they're given: Do they click on the product, do they buy it, do they ignore it, do they rate it poorly after having purchased it?

Once we have a set of ratings and/or preferences for a population of users, we can start making recommendations and predictions.

Predictions

My wife said I should really go see the movie *Beaches*. I ask MovieLens, the personal movie recommender, "How well will I like *Beaches*?" The system then fetches my history of ratings (also known as my *profile*) and compares it to other users', trying to match their profiles against mine. Profile matches can be scored in two ways. The *correlation* is the degree to which, for movies we both saw, we rated them similarly. The *overlap* is the number of movies we both rated. Ideally, I'd like to find a set of people who have a high correlation with me and who also have a high overlap. The high correlation means that we agree, and the high overlap indicates that our agreement isn't just a fluke—it is based on a lot of information.

Next, we take the people who agree best with me (my nearest neighbors) and who have already seen *Beaches*. We then average their ratings for that movie to make a prediction for me. If these people liked it, I've got a date. If they didn't, I have a discussion.

It's that simple—almost. There's actually a lot of math behind these calculations. In part, we do this because people rate differently. On a scale of 1 to 5, many people rate almost all movies 4 or 5—they either like it or love it. Others rate movies all the way from 1 to 5. To help match these people together, we *normalize* their ratings, which is a mathematical way of adjusting them to a similar scale. If, for example, someone uses only 3's, 4's, or 5's when they rate movies and their mean rating is 3.7 (User #1), we might match them with someone with a lower mean rating (User #2). A movie rating of 4 for User #1, in other words, might be a 3 for User #2.

Then things get complicated. We give different ratings different *weights* based on the correlation and overlap of that person. Then come the business rules. We want to suggest items the customer doesn't know about, products and inventory, and products that are likely to lead to customer loyalty.

Recommendations

If, instead of a prediction question, I asked a recommendation question ("What movie should I see?"), the collaborative-filtering system would again gather a *neighborhood* of people who agree well with me. It would then combine their ratings on *all movies* to determine which ones are best liked among people with tastes like mine, and would return that list of movies to me. Often these lists will be ranked based upon how strongly my nearest neighbors rate them. It's interesting to note that movies that are "best liked" by my nearest neighbors are more useful to me than movies that are "most popular" (seen by all my nearest neighbors but not liked as strongly). "Best liked" movies may, in fact, not be popular at all. They may be very obscure and little seen, which makes these recommendations more valuable; after all, I may never have learned of their presence without the help of my nearest neighbors.

Tuning Recommendations and Predictions

We should hasten to point out that there are dozens of research papers exploring specific details on how to tune collaborative-filtering algorithms to make them work best for particular applications. Tuning can be quite complicated. It's affected, in particular, by the density of ratings (what percentage of items a person rates) and the number of people and items.

There are also both research papers and unpublished trade secrets about making collaborative-filtering algorithms fast. Most commercial systems store all preference information, and do their best to use that information. They may settle for a "good" neighborhood if it is faster than the "best" one, however. And there are lots of trade-offs about how many neighbors to consider for different questions. In practice, we suggest leaving these factors to the professionals. A commercial-strength recommendation engine will be tuned already, and experts can adjust it to match your application even better.

Complete List of Recommenders

A *manual recommender* provides recommendations that have been hand-generated by sales or marketing staff. These may be broad, impersonal recommendations (e.g., our editor's picks) or manually crafted personal recommendations (e.g., the salesperson's suggestions to a regular customer).

A *searchable database* isn't a recommender per se, but it may appear like one to a customer. When the database is indexed in meaningful ways (with categories like clothes for toddlers or winter clothes), customers may be able to narrow their search significantly just by following the categories. Indeed, the category descriptions are a form of recommendation—they recommend sets of items the marketer thinks are useful to view together.

Segmentation is the division of customers into groups. Stores may decide to suggest different products to people based on their age, where they live, their income, or other criteria. Often segmentation is the result of extensive off-line data mining to determine statistically different populations. Segmentation recommendations are, therefore, group recommendations.

Statistical summarization is the presentation of ratings data in aggregate, rather than an attempt to turn that data into a personalized recommendation. Examples include displays of the "average score" for a book or the "number of people who liked" a particular movie. Statistics are generally most effective when they are simple and when they can be presented visually.

Social navigation includes a variety of technologies that make the behavior of other customers visible. In the bricks-and-mortar world, we can see customers clustering around a bargain table. In the virtual world, this can be done by displaying markers of past usage or indicators of current customers.

Custom proprietary recommender systems take advantage of expert knowledge of a domain to evaluate candidates. Ticketmaster, which recommends seats at a concert or sporting venue, and DoubleClick, which recommends ads, are two examples. They employ a set of confidential strategies based on extensive data and preference analysis.

Machine-learning techniques build a model of customer behavior from a set of data and then apply that model to future data. The techniques vary widely. Some techniques, such as neural networks, build a usable model that humans cannot directly understand. Others, such as rule-induction learning systems, produce sets of rules that humans may read to understand what has been learned.

Information-filtering techniques allow users to specify or demonstrate their preferences. The filters then scan vast quantities of material, looking for matches. In content domains such as news, an information filter might be instructed that the user wants to read any news about Chinese telephony, or might learn that the user tends to read articles with terms such as "telephone switches." In product domains, these systems may learn or be instructed that the user tends to buy men's clothing, in extra large, and is partial to short-sleeved shirts.

Collaborative filtering refers to a set of algorithms that uses the preferences of a community to recommend items to specific individuals. While there are manual collaborative-filtering systems that depend on people explicitly making or requesting recommendations, most commercial applications use automated systems that gather customer preferences, identify customers with similar tastes, and use their experiences to recommend products for each individual.

Combination recommenders can employ a variety of the above techniques. Sometimes different techniques are used separately and the results are merged (e.g., a list of ten recommendations may include five generated manually and five more from automated collaborative filtering). In more sophisticated systems, the techniques are combined based on how much evidence there is of the correctness of a particular technique for that use. Hence, a customer with a detailed profile may get mostly machine-learning recommendations, while a new customer may get mostly statistical summaries.

Interfaces: Inputs and Outputs

Naturally, we don't expect customers to know or even recognize all the recommenders we've just described. What's important from the customers' vantage point is what preference and product information they need to supply, and how recommendations are presented to them. In this section, we'll describe the three different types of inputs (explicit, implicit, and community-based) and four outputs (suggestion, prediction, ratings, and reviews).

Input Types

EXPLICIT AND IMPLICIT

Inputs are simply the ways customers demonstrate their preferences. These inputs can be *explicit* (specifically elicited for the purpose of building a profile) or *implicit* (observed inputs generated from a customer's natural interaction with a site). The most common explicit inputs are *ratings,* numerical or symbolic assessments of a product, and *keywords/attributes,* declared interests of the customer. The most common implicit inputs are *purchase history* and *navigation.* Purchase history tells which products a customer found valuable, and navigation (including both products and information viewed and items placed in shopping carts) helps identify the customer's current interests.

COMMUNITY-BASED

Other inputs reflect the community. These include the ratings, purchase history, and navigation of others, as well as reviews those others may have written. The classification of products itself (films and books sorted into genres, for example) often is derived from community-wide standards. And *popularity* measures such as box-office sales or best-seller status help customers understand what the community finds valuable.

Output Types

SUGGESTION

The simplest output type is a suggestion; this is just the mention of a product, possibly not even explicitly identified as a recommendation. For example, when a product appears in the "would you like this while you're checking out" area, it is usually a suggestion, as would be a product selected to appear on the home page.

PREDICTION

Some systems go farther than simple suggestions by actually attaching a numerical or symbolic prediction of how well you'll like the product. The Zagat restaurant guide, for example, posts numbers in the food, service, and décor categories.

RATINGS AND REVIEWS

A number of systems allow their customers to view directly the ratings or reviews entered by other customers. This is particularly common in venues where there are many different items to rate. Amazon.com, for example, encourages its customers to rate and review books; this information is then made available to other customers. eBay encourages buyers and sellers to rate (and review) each other, presenting both a summary of the ratings and the complete set of reviews for others considering doing business with the same party.

Output Delivery

As we discussed earlier, recommendations can be proactively *pushed* to a customer, made available for the customer to *pull,* or simply placed in a natural location where they will appear *passively.* Examples of pushing recommendations include the variety of E-mail interfaces where businesses promote a set of products as well as the obnoxious pop-up windows that force you to acknowledge a suggested product before continuing. Annotations (starring recommended products in an unpersonalized listing, for example) are a far more subtle means of securing the customer's gaze. Query interfaces or links (to a top-ten products list, for example) allow customers to pull recommendations actively, giving them even more autonomy.

As recommendations become more pervasive and less novel, marketers are moving toward more passive displays. Just as supermarkets don't put a sign on the eye-level shelf saying "These products were placed at eye level because we think you'll buy them,"

Web sites, too, are finding that they can simply place personally selected products in appropriate spots and increase business.

Recommenders in Action

Now that you've been introduced to the types of recommenders out on the market, we'll examine them in their natural habitats. With the number and variety of companies we profile, you will be sure to find personalization strategies that fit your business.

Demonstrate
Product Expertise

1

> The function of the expert is not to be more right than other people, but to be wrong for more sophisticated reasons.
>
> —DAVID BUTLER

> We are generally the better persuaded by the reasons we discover ourselves than by those given to us by others.
>
> —BLAISE PASCAL (1623-1662)

F YOU SEARCH for "expert" on Google, you will find over 5 million listings: expert marksman, expert skier, expert witness, talk-show expert, and on and on. When you hear someone describe himself as an expert, though, aren't you a little bit skeptical? Does that person really know all there is to know about the subject? You probably don't want to doubt an expert marksman, or else you'll wind up thirty paces away with an apple on your head; if the co-author of *The Rules for Marriage: Time-Tested Secrets for Making Your Marriage Work* gets divorced just weeks after the book is published, on the other hand, you might question that person's credentials.

In Reputation We Trust

So, as a customer, when do you trust experts? Well, for one thing, when you trust the venue in which they appear. Whom would you be more likely to trust: a chemical-dependency expert on *Jerry Springer* or a chemical-dependency expert on *Nightline*? If the *Wall Street Journal* describes someone as a mid-cap expert, you're apt to believe it because you trust that the *Wall Street Journal* has investigated her credentials. After all, they don't want to look foolish and their reputation is at stake.

Reputation. That's the problem with the Internet. Reputations take a long time to build. How do businesses establish a reputation in a medium where people are allowed to have, and are in fact encouraged to have, more than one user name? Larry Lessig addresses this issue in his great book *Code and Other Laws of Cyberspace*. Chat rooms thrive because people like to pretend to be someone else. At least on TV talk shows you get to see the experts in action. You can look into their eyes, pick up clues from the tenor of their voices or their postures, and make value judgments. Online a lot of that is missing, even as video and audio players get more sophisticated.

Expert Tastes

There's another reason why customers don't trust experts: poor performance. When it comes to taste-based products, experts often fail miserably. Some people like the sports jacket and T-shirt look, some prefer muumuus. If a customer goes into a store wearing a sweatshirt and jeans, clerks will probably peg him for casual apparel or mid-tier products. He might have much more expensive tastes, but he was dressed for a softball game.

Tastes can be fickle. People who like three-piece suits might also like bell-bottoms or lawn ornaments. Or one day they may change their mind and decide they don't like Wheaties™ anymore.

With limited information, no matter how good the experts, they won't be able to detect all the subtleties of a customer's palate.

At a Loss

People rely most on experts when they know next to nothing about the topic. When it comes to thermodynamics, open heart surgery, hieroglyphics, and other specialties, we admit we're lost. So what do we want from experts in these arenas? We want some assurance that they are a current and respected member of that community. We want them to speak the language. And yet we want to be able to understand that language, otherwise we might as well be getting our information in Latin. It's a paradox many experts have trouble solving.

Experts vs. Expertise

Experts are often bad predictors of customer taste, they don't speak our language, and they're only as good as the venue in which they appear. The very term *expert* elicits feelings of mistrust and doubt. So why did we title this chapter "Demonstrate Product Expertise"? As a marketer, how do you deliver material customers will respond to?

Expertise is what customers covet, not experts. It's the goods without the swagger. It's hard facts, presented in easily digestible ways.

Internet shoppers are more demanding than mall shoppers. They expect deep and personalized content. They want reputations and brands to put their minds at ease, and they want to know prices, histories, service records, and much more. Bricks-and-mortar companies have an advantage, largely because their reputations imply safety and convenience, but that doesn't mean they can rest on their laurels.

Your site has to demonstrate product expertise—above and beyond retail stores. Wine.com by eVineyard offers customer and employee reviews; *Wine Spectator, Wine Advocate,* and *Wine Enthu-siast* ratings; wine-related articles; food-and-wine pairings; and descriptions of wine, wineries, regions, and types of wines. Spend enough time on the site and you, too, could become a master sommelier.

In this chapter, we study sites like Wine.com by eVineyard and Priceline.com that are packed with product expertise. It's no coincidence that they're not bricks-and-mortar companies. Businesses that start on-line know that they need to provide extra value to on-line shoppers. A number of bricks-and-mortar companies would do well to follow their example.

Here's what we've learned from studying innovative industry leaders. When it comes to demonstrating product expertise, they follow these three rules:

1. Use expertise and recommenders to build customer trust.
2. Provide deep product data, so that customers can make informed decisions.
3. Make it fun.

1. *Use expertise and recommenders to build customer trust.* Building customer trust is essential. You want customers to perceive you as Ted Koppel, not Jerry Springer. Unfortunately, you can't just will customers into trusting you. To paraphrase the old Dean Witter ads, "You have to earn it."

Here are five ways you can build customer trust:

1. Use recommenders to show you know how your products fit different customers' tastes.
2. Create and display brands.
3. Install a parametric search engine.
4. Display customer testimonials, industry awards, and celebrity endorsements.
5. Cite sales figures.

Use Recommenders to Show You Know How Your Products Fit Different Customers' Tastes

Universal recommenders like featured products, seasonal specials, and best-seller lists help customers navigate your site. Recommenders that integrate individual customer purchases are more likely to build customer trust, however, especially when product inventory is cumbersome.

Create and Display Brands

There are entire books dedicated to branding, so we won't get into the intricacies of the subject here. Suffice it to say that in a medium where trust is the central issue, on-line shoppers want to see brands they recognize (yours and others').

Install a Parametric Search Engine

Every site has a basic search engine. It is a sign of a company that cares about its customers. Show your customers that you understand your products better: Develop a search engine that lets customers search by the most important attributes of your products, not just by text labels. The message is simple: We want you to find what you're looking for.

Don't lean too heavily on search engines, though. If customers don't know the search terms that will help them find what they're looking for, you need to have enough links so that they'll find the product category within two clicks. Site maps also help in this regard.

Display Customer Testimonials, Industry Awards, and Celebrity Endorsements

Don't claim to be an expert: Nobody likes a know-it-all. Let others attest to your qualifications and quality instead. Customer testimonials, industry awards, and celebrity endorsements go a long way, especially on the Web, where customers don't have your products or store in eyeshot.

Also, don't be afraid to use customers as your salespeople. You can even use recommenders to choose which customer testimonials to present to individual customers. If a customer knows the testimonial is coming from someone who also bought the *Gone with the Wind* collectibles or rated Sassy children's products highly, they are more likely to appreciate these testimonials.

Cite Sales Figures

The days of having customer odometers on your site are long gone because the number of visitors isn't important (especially since those numbers can be easily rigged). Sales figures are, however. That's the kind of assurance customers want before handing over their credit-card numbers, especially with Internet-only businesses. Priceline.com, whom we analyze in this chapter, is one of many sites that make effective use of these figures; they boast over 4 million hotel nights sold.

2. *Provide deep product data, so that customers can make informed decisions.* One of the main strengths of the Internet is its ability to display content. In retail, you don't have the space to provide deep content. Places like Office Depot print and post flyers describing the features of printers and other electronic equipment, but retail stores aren't exactly designed for comfortable reading: You get bumped from behind, the flyers don't match the products on the shelves, and not every product has a flyer. But there isn't an excuse on-line. Still, an amazing number of high-profile sites neglect to create additional content, let alone personalized content.

It's one thing to know that customers expect deep content. It's another thing to deliver it. Do you know all there is to know about your products? More importantly, do you know what information to pass along to your customers?

To help answer these questions, we've divided product data into three categories:

INTRINSIC—Color, country of manufacture, materials, size, supplier

COMMERCIAL—Cost, time-in-inventory, stock, retail price

TRANSACTIONAL—Customer ratings or reviews, patterns of purchases (across time and product fields), customer profiles (with or without actual identities)

Intrinsic Data

The hard lines on a box of Tide can't be felt. Two sets of speakers appear the same size. The physicality of products, in many senses, is lost in cyberspace. Nonetheless, it's important that the customer *sees* the product—its color, size, and shape. If customers don't get a visual image of the product, they may suspect the product is chintzy and click out. Give them what they want: swatches of color, opportunities to enlarge images of the product and see it from different angles, and bullet points of information that are easy to digest.

"People don't think in words. Windows is proof of that. People think in pictures," our colleague Lee Gerdes says. People don't read contracts from start to finish. They sign at the X if you look and sound trustworthy. They don't read product manuals. They skim *Windows for Dummies*. They want the quickest, easiest, and most effective information. And they want it in seconds, not minutes.

Since time is vital, don't swamp customers with intrinsic information. Country of manufacture, for instance, is only important if it's a selling point (e.g., identifying diamonds from "approved" countries). Sprinkle facts judiciously and allow the customer to dictate the pace and depth of information through links.

Commercial Data

A virtual shopkeeper must identify products that are unusual values (e.g., substantially below usual cost). It's an age-old way to establish trust and rapport with customers. In the virtual age, it's easy to underestimate the product and cost knowledge of customers. Don't fall into that trap. If customers don't get accurate cost data from you, they'll get it from someone else. And they'll more than likely buy the product from your competition.

Customers can't try out your vacuum cleaners. They can't hear the sound of dirt being picked up off their carpet. They may know the dimensions of your leather sofa, but they can't sink into it and put their feet up on the coffee table. Since they can't experience your products, they are more likely to buy on cost. Recognize this with pricing and shipping discounts.

Don't be afraid to reveal commercial data. And don't be afraid to reward repeat customers.

Transactional Data

Products don't sell themselves; people sell them. More specifically, customers do. If a couple likes the Subaru Forester, they will likely tell their neighbors and friends. But how can you harness this power?

There's almost no end to the value of customer feedback and buying patterns. Customer reviews on your Web site will induce others to buy your product. If you identify best-selling products, both overall and within demographic groups, you can use these products to attract new customers or to offer "safe" rewards to loyal ones. More importantly, you learn how particular products segment your customer base. After discovering customer-taste indicators, you can leverage this product knowledge to increase customer knowledge and sales.

3. Make it fun. Just because on-line customers want deep content doesn't mean that they want to scroll through page after page

of text. Visiting your site should be fun. Customers want to be wowed by new technology. They want new displays, loads of sensory input, and the feeling that the company they're buying from is reaching out to them.

Your customers will be able to tell if you're holding back. If you're trotting out the same catalogs they get in the mail or in your retail stores, they'll be disappointed—and then you'll be disappointed.

Identifying Expertise

In this chapter, we examine four sites: Wine.com by eVineyard, Priceline, Godiva, and See's Candies. We remark on their ability to leverage product information and establish expertise. As you read, ask yourself, "How would our site or company perform under this kind of scrutiny?"

WINE.COM BY eVINEYARD

FOR SOME, WINE is an all-consuming passion. They build wine cellars rather than a workbench or an exercise room. They handle fifty-year-old bottles as if they were newborns. They monitor the temperature and humidity. They go to wine tastings and let wines decant, then swirl them in their glasses and wave the aroma to their noses. Finally, they close their eyes and let the wine settle on their tongues.

But what about the rest of us? Is a wine that has "a surprisingly smooth floral cherry finish" and "a little coffee and cola [that] wafts through on the nose" something we'd like?

Wine.com by eVineyard is a classic business-to-consumer E-commerce Web site. They make money by selling products to consumers. The more products they sell, and the more high-profit products they sell, the more money they make. The difference between Wine.com and other E-businesses is that Wine.com's product can be intimidating.

Having the right wine with a meal, or bringing an appropriate wine for a gift, shows the social ability of the wine purchaser. Since there are so many varieties of wines, however, the choice can be daunting; in order to avoid embarrassment, consumers may choose other products for gifts.

So how does Wine.com by eVineyard take a product as sophisticated as wine and make it accessible to people who have little or no experience? The answer: by simplifying the wine-buying process. In short, Wine.com by eVineyard transforms wine buying from an art into a science, using product expertise.

USE EXPERTISE AND RECOMMENDERS TO BUILD CUSTOMER TRUST

Wine.com by eVineyard employs several different recommenders. On the home page, you'll find a universal pick-of-the-week recommendation. On the Wine Shop pages, three top sellers appear on the right-hand side. And when you click on a specific bottle of wine, you are presented with a list of three other wines that customers have purchased who also purchased that particular wine. These recommendations could be based on expert opinions, like Jim Gordon's, the editor at large (who writes articles for the site). Expert recommendations for taste-based products like wines aren't as good as recommendations from other customers, however. That's because experts develop tastes that are different from "regular people." Also, expert opinions are based on only one wine, rather than on the entire history of a customer's interaction with the wine store. Wine.com by eVineyard does well to offer both expert opinions and customer-generated recommendations.

Wine.com by eVineyard's Pick a Wine feature is somewhat disappointing by comparison. Customers just get to select the kind of wine and how much they want to pay, and Wine.com by eVineyard returns with wines in their catalog that fit those criteria. A customer-focused version that asked questions about what you want the wine to be used for and what kinds of wine you like in general would be better. A sophisticated recommender would also be sure to remember your preferences the next time around.

PROVIDE DEEP PRODUCT DATA, SO THAT CUSTOMERS CAN MAKE INFORMED DECISIONS

Here is where Wine.com by eVineyard really excels. They allow customers the opportunity to drill down to multiple levels of detail on each wine. For a Blackstone 1999 California Merlot, Wine.com by eVineyard offers links to more information about Blackstone, California, Merlot, other Blackstone wines, other California wines, and other Merlots. They also provide customer reviews whenever possible, a picture of the label, and ratings from six different entities: *Wine Spectator, Wine & Spirits, Wine Enthusiast, International Wine Cellar, Wine Advocate,* and Wine.com.

Wine.com by eVineyard also ranks seven attributes of a wine's taste: intensity, sweetness, body, acidity, tannin, oak flavor, and complexity. Then Wine.com by eVineyard's experts rate each wine on each attribute across a fifteen-point scale. A 1998 Buena Vista Merlot from California, for instance, was ranked low for tannin, acid, and oak, in the middle range for intensity and body, and on the dry side.

This is an effective use of experts, since customers don't have to share the expert's taste in order to value his input. They can simply use the expert rankings as benchmarks for their own tastes.

Wine.com by eVineyard has Peter Granoff to thank for the taste chart. Peter Granoff, a master sommelier, launched Wine.com with Robert Olson in January 1995. When Wine.com filed for bankruptcy on May 4, 2001, eVineyard, Inc. seized the opportunity to become the largest on-line wine retailer. They acquired some of Wine.com's assets, including the Wine.com and WineShopper.com URLs. Wine.com by eVineyard now offers over 5,000 wines in 27 states, and in 2000 growth in customers and revenues exploded 1,000 percent.

Before he left, Peter Granoff intended to convert Wine.com's taste chart into a search tool. Customers would be able to find wines that are rated high for oak and low for body, for example. They would also learn what wines most closely approximate other wines they have enjoyed. Wine.com by eVineyard has yet to do this, but it will be a wonderful tool when and if they do.

MAKE IT FUN

People enjoy reading stories and looking at pictures; they don't want consumer decisions to feel like work. And stories are the perfect supplement to Wine.com by eVineyard's taste charts. When you click on a wine, a 1999 Valley View Winery Chardonnay for example, you'll find out about the winery, the wine's characteristics, and even what foods to serve with it. In this case, you'll learn that in the 1970s, the Wisnovsky family reestablished Valley View, one of the first wineries in Oregon. The wine itself "showcases ripe pear and peach flavors with rich honey and toasty oak notes." Wine.com by eVineyard tells you that it goes well with cheese ravioli and grilled salmon.

Business Applications

Expert classification (like the wine-tasting chart) is often more useful than expert recommendations. Product expertise can not only be turned into search tools, it can also feed recommendation engines. If I like sweet, complex wines with low acidity, Wine.com could make recommendations to me—not just of other similar wines, but of wines that my nearest neighbors like that may expand my horizons.

Customer reviews are not only informative, they, too, can be thrown into a recommendation engine. Imagine getting reviews only by people who share your taste! In Wine.com's case, that wouldn't be terribly effective because they don't have a huge database of reviews. Not yet anyway. What about your business? Is your database of customer feedback deep enough to support a recommender?

Wine.com by eVineyard really tries to emphasize the tastes of people who are not experts—to a fault in some cases. In the Our

Picks section, employees and customers describe wines they like. These people often explicitly acknowledge in their bios that they're not connoisseurs. That's fine. Unfortunately, these reviewers don't necessarily share the same taste as the customer. If they do, it would be purely by accident. It would be much better if customers were given recommendations by their nearest neighbors. The moral here: *Amateurs are no better than experts at making recommendations—unless they're shown to have the same taste.*

WINE.COM BY eVINEYARD

RECOMMENDER(S): Manual recommender (pick of the week), collaborative filtering (customers who liked X also bought Y), statistical summarization (top sellers).

INPUT(S): Click on a wine, shopping cart.

OUTPUT(S): List of three wines.

LESSON: *With taste-based products, expert recommendations aren't as good as other customers'. Nearest neighbors, though, are best.*

PRICELINE

ON APRIL 6, 1998, Jay Walker had no idea how big the market would be for his brainchild, a name-your-price Internet site called Priceline. He had secured William Shatner as spokesperson and, like many dot-coms of that era, blitzed the media with ads. But when he turned on the servers, he and his colleagues weren't sure what to expect. When the monitor redlined, he suspected a glitch. He decided to turn it off and try it again. When he switched the system back on, it redlined again. He sent someone back to look at the servers. Every single one was busy. Without missing a beat, Walker looked at his co-workers and said, "How many customers did I lose when I turned that switch off?"

Priceline had the benefit of a celebrity spokesperson, Shatner, and their revolutionary model, the first of its kind. Customers made offers for airplane seats, Priceline relayed these offers to the airlines, and within an hour, notified customers if their offer had been accepted. Tickets were nonrefundable.

Priceline began its operations with only two partners: TWA and America West. They showed their results to the other airlines, and soon more were on board. Their name-your-price model was such a success that they expanded into a host of additional markets: new cars, gasoline, rental cars, home mortgages, hotel rooms, and even groceries. Some of this was done through licensed partners, such as WebHouse Club. There was no limit to how high they could go. Couldn't the name-your-price model be used for just about everything?

Deep breath.

At this writing, Priceline's stock is about $2.70, down from a 52-week high of $124.25. It turns out that their reverse-auction model does have its limits. Gas and groceries, for instance. They're no longer offered. Auto insurance, life insurance, wireless, and business-to-business initiatives have also been shelved. Priceline downshifted and the tachometer is no longer screaming in the red zone. They're focusing on their main source of revenue: travel—which is what they do best. Why? Because, according to spokesperson Brian Ek, "Travel products are the most perishable in the world. When that airplane takes off, that empty seat is worth nothing. So consequently, in this business, there is no such thing as a take-it-or-leave-it low price. If you can be flexible, everything is negotiable. And that's really the foundation Priceline is built on."

Despite its struggles, including the resignation of Jay Walker, Priceline appears to be righting the ship. Their 2000 revenues reached $1.24 billion, up 154 percent from the previous year. Maybe more significantly, 56 percent of purchase offers came from repeat customers in the fourth quarter of 2000. With almost 9 million customers and a recent Europe expansion, Priceline seems well positioned to weather the economic downturn many technology-based companies have experienced.

USE EXPERTISE AND RECOMMENDERS TO BUILD CUSTOMER TRUST

At first glance, Priceline's name-your-price model is its most interesting feature. What caught our eye, however, is how Priceline is able to convince customers of its expertise—particularly in regard to hotel rooms. After all, customers agree to nonrefundable reservations without knowing where they're going to be staying. Who would bid for a hotel room without knowing whether they were getting a Four Seasons downtown or a Motel 6 by the airport?

When a Priceline customer selects "hotel rooms," she is quickly presented with a no-nonsense screen that asks for the city, dates, and number of rooms. The screen resembles most on-line reservation screens, which helps customers feel that this is a normal, reliable way to reserve a room. The screen also announces that "All Priceline hotel partners are nationally recognized *name-brand* or *well-known* independent properties." If the customer clicks on either of those links, she'll find that these hotels have asked not to be listed. That's a red flag, obviously, because having a link suggests that you will be given the name of those hotels. But Priceline does its best to position itself around this issue: "Because you can save so much using Priceline, our participating hotels have asked us not to reveal their names." The cool slate-blue screen may calm your nerves. On the right-hand side of the screen, you'll see that they've sold over 4 million hotel nights. That's more reassuring. Their long-standing TV ad campaign, until recently with recognizable pitchman William Shatner, helped build customer confidence. Now that Priceline has established its reputation, it can continue to attract customers without Shatner.

For Priceline's business model to work, customers must first trust the company enough to make a "blind date" reservation, and then have a good enough experience that they return to make future reservations. Priceline could choose from several approaches to building trust in the rating system. First, they could have simply licensed ratings (and branding) from a well-known and trusted hotel-rating guide (like Mobil Travel Guides or AAA). Second, they could list the hotels in each category, so the customer could match her tastes to the hotels without selecting individual ones. Third, they could explain the basis for their ratings with descriptive examples; and fourth, they could provide price figures that reflect the quality of hotels at each rating level.

APPROACH	ADVANTAGES	DISADVANTAGES
1. License other ratings	Existing trust; existing customer base; low effort	Lack of control, trust may not transfer to rest of site/company
2. List hotels	Allows customers to evaluate and calibrate	May jeopardize business model, especially when few participating hotels in an area
3. Explain criteria	Allows customers to envision and select quality level	May set expectations that a specific hotel fails to meet (e.g., bathrobe, mini-bar)
4. Provide price guidance	Allows customers to cross-reference with other experiences or guides; helps guide price selection	May lead to upset customers if they discover discrepancies with hotels they booked

Priceline actually uses only the last two mechanisms. At first glance, it seems that it should be easy to add other trusted rating guides (for example, by allowing a customer to ask for a hotel that is at least Mobil three-star or AAA three-diamond), but doing so might sufficiently dilute Priceline's own image of expertise that it could be counterproductive. Using those brands would also cost them a considerable amount of money. And, by keeping their rating system in-house, Priceline can adjust its ratings more easily based on customer feedback.

PROVIDE DEEP PRODUCT DATA, SO THAT CUSTOMERS
CAN MAKE INFORMED DECISIONS

Priceline classifies hotels on a scale of 1 to 5 stars (including 2½ stars). For each of the categories—economy (1), moderate (2), moderate-plus (2½), upscale (3), deluxe (4), and luxury (5)—Priceline provides explanations of the different hotel ratings and a guide to typical retail prices for hotels in that area. Four stars, for instance, is considered a deluxe hotel with rooms that "often feature upgraded amenities, bathrobes, and in-room safes." Because these hotels usually offer concierge and business services, as well as fitness centers, the average retail price for a Priceline four-star hotel in downtown Minneapolis is $187. Bear in mind that the average retail price varies depending on location, and that some cities don't have five-star, or even four-star hotels—a fact that helps establish Priceline's expertise and credibility.

Priceline's hotel descriptions indicate the quality of the hotel, but what about the location? Most cities are too large for a customer to be equally happy with a hotel in any part of the city. Priceline solves this dilemma by dividing cities into zones. Vancouver, for instance, is divided into six zones: Coquitlam-Burnaby, Delta, Langley, Surrey, Vancouver, and Vancouver International Airport. A map of each zone is available by clicking on the "Details" link.

Priceline's geographical expertise is presented through a subtle, but extremely important, recommender. Without proclaiming its expertise, the site demonstrates that it knows each city and can identify the zones that serve particular needs. In Vancouver, this allows a customer to choose a downtown or airport zone with confidence that the hotels being considered are appropriately close to the desired location.

This design is particularly effective at communicating and allowing customers to evaluate Priceline's expertise. If a customer knows the city, she can quickly tell whether the zones are correct. If she doesn't, she can look at cities she does know to see how well the zones divide those cities. In looking at cities we know well, like Minneapolis and New York, we were convinced.

There are many contrasting hotel-reservation interfaces that attempt to provide geographical information without expertise. Microsoft's travel system (used in Expedia.com, Nwa.com, and Continental.com, among others) presents hotels along with the distance from a landmark such as the airport or downtown. While this information is useful, in many circumstances it betrays a lack of true expertise. Often hotels that are farther away in miles are actually more convenient or even more closely attached to the point of interest. The zone approach requires more work, but it shows increased expertise.

MAKE IT FUN

Princeton did a study on brand awareness and found that the average Priceline customer told eighteen other people about his or her experience. Pass-alongs for movies run about eight on average and restaurants six; and those are some of the highest. With Priceline, you feel like you beat the system, which fuels word of mouth (and mouse). Getting a four-star hotel room for $75—that's fun.

Business Applications

Priceline reminds us of the time when catalogs and mail-order companies regularly offered "grab bag" purchases. So many of them were rip-offs that they eventually fell out of favor. Recently, though, there's been a renaissance. Archie McPhee, a novelty store out of Seattle, sells a Surprise Package for $19.95 and a Jumbo Mystery Box for $39.95. You may get an Amish punching puppet, a pirate lunchbox, and a leopard fez, depending on what they have in stock, but they promise the contents will be three times the value of your purchase. On the other coast (and at the other end of the taste spectrum), Dean & Deluca sells produce grab bags to New York City gourmands. For $78, you can receive eighteen pounds of Fresh Spring Produce—"anything from verdant asparagus to crisp salad greens, fragrant herbs to the sweetest strawberries, enough to fill your fridge for a week. Even we don't know in advance what each basket will bring." Customers, however, trust Dean & Deluca to choose the best of the best.

We envision the grab-bag model incorporating collaborative filtering in the not too distant future, so companies can reward their customers' trust with far more hits than misses. For Dean & Deluca that probably won't make sense because their offerings are tied to whatever fruits and vegetables are in season. But for most retailers, grab bags provide an opportunity to amaze customers by choosing items you know they'll like (using recommender technology).

PRICELINE'S HOTEL MATCHER

RECOMMENDER(S): Manual recommender (using hotel-quality rating system, city zones, and prices) suggests price bids for customers. Proprietary reverse-auction model pushes hotel match to customers after they've committed to a purchase.

INPUT(S): Price, dates, city zone(s), minimum quality level of hotel.

OUTPUT(S): Binding hotel match.

LESSON: *If customers trust your expertise, they will trust your recommendations, and maybe even buy blindly based on them.*

CHOCOLATES ON THE WEB

C HOCOLATES ARE INHERENTLY more difficult to sell on a Web site than in person. Besides being a perishable impulse-driven purchase, the smell of chocolate and the taste of samples are extremely powerful "salespeople."

We looked at two successful chocolate vendors, See's Candies and Godiva, to see how they used product expertise on their Web sites.

See's Candies

See's started in 1921 as a small Los Angeles candy store armed with Mary See's family recipes. Over the past eighty years, the company has grown to over 200 stores, mostly in the western United States. They boast a collection of over 100 different candies and chocolates. The stores pride themselves on always offering a sample and a smile, and on maintaining the small-store feel. As a result, See's has a large and loyal following of chocoholics ranging from people who stop in daily for a single piece (plus a sample) to expatriates who stock up on visits or order by mail.

USE EXPERTISE AND RECOMMENDERS TO BUILD CUSTOMER TRUST

While the Web site is chock-full of company history, it is notably short on service and product expertise. You'll learn, for example, that Charles See, Mary See's son, coined the motto "Quality Without Compromise." What you won't find, however, is a search engine, customer testimonials, top-selling boxes, or much in the way of recommendations.

See's does list seasonal favorites on their home page. The pieces in the Summer Variety, for instance, "may soften a bit, but won't melt." Almond Royale offers a combination of Dutch cocoa, chocolate caramel, and roasted almonds—what they call "an ideal summertime indulgence." Knowing that See's is concerned about chocolates melting in your hands is comforting, but the feeling is short-lived. Despite the seasonal favorites and company history, the Web site doesn't feel like anything more than an on-line catalog.

PROVIDE DEEP PRODUCT DATA, SO THAT CUSTOMERS CAN MAKE INFORMED DECISIONS

On the left-hand side of See's home page, you'll find a list of fifty gift boxes and assortments, some of which lead to a subset of products. Unfortunately, the descriptions are brief, such as "1 lb. Gold

Truffle Box," "1 lb. Black Truffle Box," and "1 lb. Gold Fancy Box." While this might work for a fan devoted enough to know the gift boxes, what about the rest of us?

When you click on the items like the "1 lb. Gold Fancy Box," a small picture of the box of candies pops up with a short description. Often the description doesn't dispel your confusion. In some cases, it may add to it. For example, the "Chocolate & Variety Box" contains "Traditional milk and dark chocolates and a tempting collection of white-coated pieces: Almond Truffle, Kona Mocha, Cashew Brittle, and Divinity Puff." No word on whether there is any coconut or caramel, or even what a Divinity Puff is for the confectionery novice.

Purely in the name of research, one of us tried the company's phone-order line to see whether the service was better. Indeed, it suddenly felt like a knowledgeable small shop again. The operator would arrange a custom box with the items of your choice, answer questions (" Is that hard or soft caramel?"), and even make recommendations. No sample was offered, but the experience was pleasant and the service helpful.

Some of that homey feel has made its way onto the site. When we first visited the site, you couldn't order a custom box. Now you can select from forty-two different candy pieces to create your own mix and even adjust the percentage of each type of candy.

MAKE IT FUN

For nearly thirty years, See's has been part of Warren Buffett's Berkshire Hathaway, Inc. (who bought it from the See family). Buffett is well known for investing in companies with products he understands and for avoiding technology companies. In this case, he's managed to keep the quality of the product and the human-to-human service, but still has a lot to learn about providing service and expertise through the technology of Web-based shops. See's is a company rich with knowledgeable shopkeepers; now it needs an expert virtual shopkeeper on its Web site. Then, and only then, will shopping at See's on-line approximate the fun of visiting their retail stores.

Godiva Chocolatier

Godiva is a premium Belgian chocolatier founded in 1926. It has since expanded to over 200 specialty stores in the United States, over 1,000 retail outlets in stores around the United States, and many more shops around the world. Known for luxury truffles, Godiva lures people to their counters and stores with the smell, look, and taste of fine Belgian chocolate, albeit with kitchens in the States.

Although See's and Godiva have both been atop the chocolate business for years, they differ in many respects, starting with their icons: the bespectacled Mary See and Lady Godiva. As lore has it, Lady Godiva rode naked through Coventry so that an oppressive tax on the townspeople would be reduced. Today, Godiva still displays a flashy side.

The Godiva Web site has a gold color-theme and attempts to portray the luxury of the product. Godiva boasts that they were the "first to create the concept of premium chocolate." In large part, they credit their innovate packaging—including gold ballotins (European-style boxes tied with decorative ribbons)—for their success. That and, of course, their artful chocolates.

USE EXPERTISE TO BUILD CUSTOMER TRUST

On the Godiva home page, your opportunities for shopping are many, but it takes some sleuthing to uncover them, in part because the screen is dominated by huge swaths of their trademark colors: gold and black. By clicking the minuscule Shop Online link, you're presented with six text options: What's New; Summer Collection; Best Sellers; Birthday Celebrations; Classic Chocolates & Truffles; and Biscuits, Coffee and Cocoa. If you follow one of these links, you'll be presented with six elegant gift boxes—mostly unopened—and the option to view additional pages. Once you click on a gift box, then and only then, do you get to the chocolates. It's worth the wait, however. The lavish photographs of white, milk, and dark chocolates rival the many portraits of Lady Godiva herself.

Unlike See's, Godiva's Web site also features a search engine. This comes in handy if you want to find out which products feature caramels (either because you love caramels or because you want to avoid them). It also signals to the customer that Godiva wants to help you find what you're looking for.

If you've scrolled through the many Godiva gift boxes and haven't found the ideal gift and don't necessarily know what to search for with the search engine, Godiva provides a third option—the Gift Advisor. Plug in the recipient (brother, uncle, spouse), the event (anniversary, just because, Valentine's Day), and the price range (under $15, $65 and over, and all $10 increments in between), and—poof—out comes a gift recommendation. Sounds good in theory. In practice, it's bound to raise a few eyebrows. When we entered the same event (birthday) and price range ($15–$24.99), the Gift Advisor came up with four recommendations for fathers; three of those four plus a Heart Assortment, Birthday Ballotin, and Gold Crescent Tin for mothers; and nearly all of them for spouses. Do women like different assortments than men? What sex do they assume "spouse" is, if they assume at all? The Gift Advisor is hardly an exact science, considering that Godiva knows nothing about the gift recipients. As a result, customer trust may suffer.

Although the Gift Advisor recommender misfires, Godiva has the potential to create a powerful recommender. With their My Godiva feature, customers can receive gift reminders and E-mail updates, review their order history, store their payment information and address, and even create an address book for gift recipients. By recording all past purchases, Godiva has all the raw material for collaborative filtering or another sophisticated recommendation engine.

We're fairly certain, however, that Godiva doesn't use this purchase information to make the "May we also suggest . . ." recommendations that appear at the bottom of the screen when you select a box of chocolates. These recommendations do raise awareness of other products, however. For example, a customer looking at the biscuit assortment would discover the availability of biscotti and boxes of individual biscuits (for those who don't like the assortment). Even such a simple recommender mimics salesperson behavior and can preserve a sale; a customer who looks at the collection and thinks "I don't like raspberry" can be directed to chocolate-only biscuits.

PROVIDE DEEP PRODUCT DATA, SO THAT CUSTOMERS CAN MAKE INFORMED DECISIONS

What Godiva does best is deliver product data. Under the link Guide to Godiva, a number of information guides appear. A chocolate guide shows high-resolution pictures and descriptions of every chocolate piece they sell. A link then leads customers to boxes where these chocolates are featured.

With How Godiva Is Made, customers learn about Godiva's two primary techniques: shell molding and enrobing (molding a layer of chocolate around a centerpiece like an almond or cream). Want to know what it's called when chocolate gets warm and forms a dull white color on the surface? Fat bloom. That tidbit, and a lengthier explanation, appears in their FAQ section. For the truly epicurious, refer to Chocolate Trivia and Glossary. You'll learn that Napoleon carried chocolate with him into battle, among other things.

Although Godiva doesn't allow you to make custom chocolate boxes, they do provide a valuable do-it-yourself tool: roughly 200 dessert recipes. It's precisely this kind of "extra" that distinguishes Godiva from See's.

MAKE IT FUN

Godiva could provide technology that would make them stand out not just from chocolate competition, but from Web sites in general. If ever there was a time and place to introduce smell technology, this is it. DigiScents recently folded, but with the right offer, they could be back in business. And more importantly, we could be transported back to the chocolate counter!

Business Applications

Both See's and Godiva could benefit from transferring the expertise found in their stores to their Web sites. Every chocolate-store employee can answer basic questions such as "What do you recommend?" In many cases, the questions lead to a short discovery discussion. "Do you prefer milk chocolate, dark, or a mix?" "Do you like chewy candies?" "Which have you tried so far and liked?" As yet, neither site has gone to these lengths.

Instead, Godiva and See's offer universal recommendations in the form of featured products on the home page. Imagine if they displayed the box you ordered most recently, or a box they think you would like based upon your prior purchases. Only then will these two Web sites begin to compete with their retail counterparts.

As the manufacturer as well as retailer, both chocolatiers have a monopoly on their products, but that doesn't mean they aren't competing. Each Web site competes not only with other brands of chocolate, but also with the risk of customers saying "This is too hard. I'll just wait until I get to the mall" and delaying, or even forgetting about, a purchase. Buying chocolate should be an enjoyable experience, and only by making it enjoyable, satisfying, and unstressful can these companies drive business to their low-overhead Web sites.

On your Web site, are you making universal recommendations? Are you hiding your expertise in hard-to-find places (as Godiva does with its product guide)?

SEE'S

RECOMMENDER(S): None.

RECOMMENDER OPPORTUNITY: See's could recommend individual chocolates and assemble custom boxes based on customers' preferences (indicated by past purchases).

GODIVA

RECOMMENDER(S): Manually edited, product associated (if you buy a biscuit assortment, Godiva may recommend biscotti based on their experts' opinions).

INPUT(S): Current navigation.

OUTPUT(S): List of suggested item(s) that users may click on ("pull").

LESSON: Don't bury your expertise and don't rest on your laurels.

Principle #1: Demonstrate Product Expertise

Quick Tips

- Provide customers with a fast way to find and purchase products. Customers either want loads of detail or virtually none at all (either because they're in a hurry or they already know what they want).
- Every time you interact with your customers, place some recommendations in front of them.
- Recommend only a small number (two or three) of specific products to your customers. Too many and your customers will feel inundated, not courted.
- Include comparisons between products your customers have already purchased and products they are considering.
- Invest in deep information about your products through expert analysis, data-mining tools, customer contributions, and industry resources (Wine.com by eVineyard).
- Give customers information that they can't get elsewhere in the retail world. Make it palatable. Customers prefer stories, images, and bullet points (Wine.com by eVineyard).
- If you use experts, make sure their expertise is translatable

(rating systems), because their tastes aren't the same as "regular people's" (Wine.com by eVineyard).

- Show your expertise through sales figures, deep content, and brands (Priceline's 4 million nights sold).
- Let others speak for you (William Shatner for Priceline, customer reviews at Wine.com by eVineyard).
- Simplify your product offerings (Priceline.com's Hotel Matcher).
- Gain and maintain your customer's trust through customer-friendly offerings (Priceline's detailed hotel rating system and city zone maps).
- Don't fall back on your reputation (Godiva, See's). Push it forward.
- Don't assume that your customers know your products as well as you do. Help them learn while making them feel comfortable (Godiva, See's).

Product knowledge is one of your best assets as a shopkeeper. Use it to make your customers' lives easier: Provide them with just the information they need to make good decisions. If you provide them with too little information, they will not be confident enough in their decisions to buy the things they're hoping to buy. If you provide them with too much, they will take too long to make a decision, which reduces your sales and wastes their time. Most important: Provide effective recommenders that help them quickly find products that fit their needs, and support the recommenders with drill-down links to all of your detailed product knowledge. Customers who want the detailed knowledge can find it and customers who have learned to trust you will be able to make a purchase quickly and efficiently.

Interlude # 1: Mass Customization

Have you purchased a car lately? Good luck trying to get a green Saturn with a manual transmission, powerful engine, and no sun roof. If you want to try to buy a car without a bunch of extra features, you're better off ordering from the factory. Although it might take up to two months to have it delivered (as it did for us), the sheer ability to order from the factory points to a powerful capability of modern manufacturing: the ability to get exactly what you want by ordering it before it is made.

Of course, customization isn't new. We've always been able to buy custom clothes made by a tailor or dressmaker. We've been able to get custom furniture or custom homes. The problem is, you have to pay for it. Through the nose, usually.

The great benefit of mass production is the ability to buy quality merchandise cheaply. Today you can buy very nice ready-to-wear clothes for one-third the price of custom-made. Mass production also supports large warehousing and distribution systems, which allow you to buy not only cheaply, but quickly. These systems serve a dual purpose; they enable factories to even out production of items that are consumed unevenly (storing snow blowers all summer to prepare for the winter rush, for example).

Now, thanks to the science of manufacturing design, customization and mass production have merged. Products with multiple components can be customized into a variety of configurations. Computer-driven assembly lines can work efficiently even when each item is built to different specifications. And the economics of storage and shipping have made it economical, in some circumstances, to produce items as they are ordered and ship them overnight.

What does this mean for the marketer? It means that you may soon have the ability to provide customers with an economically customized product to match their needs better. Sounds great, provided you can determine what they want. In some cases, there will be objective information, such as a customer's measurements for clothing. In other cases, customers may know exactly what they want—a green Saturn with a manual transmission, no sun roof, and a powerful engine. But in many cases, the customer may want or need help in narrowing the options. That's where recommenders come in.

Instead of today's automobile model, where features are bundled for the convenience of inventory (and often to force customers to pay for options they don't want), a recommender for a mass-customized product could understand the manufacturing limitations but otherwise be free to suggest the options that would best meet a customer's needs, or indeed even prompt a customer to buy. One industry where this model is beginning to work is personal computer sales. Assembly of PCs involves many constraints, but manufacturers such as Dell have learned that it is most efficient to allow customers to specify many of the hardware and software options, then to assemble and ship the computer to order. Dell's Web site and catalogs attempt to guide customers through "sensible" combinations of options, usually based on a few basic goals such as price and whether the computer is for gaming or office applications. More sophisticated recommenders could not only present the options, but make suggestions (that a particular user might prefer more memory, or that she might want a more advanced video card, for example). Indeed, customers might be willing to allow the vendor to run a "monitor" on their computer for a week or two prior to purchase to learn about their computing habits and make better recommendations.

2

Be a Customer Agent

They know enough who know how to learn.

—HENRY ADAMS,
THE EDUCATION OF HENRY ADAMS, 1907

The shortest and best way to make your fortune is to let
people see clearly that it is in their interests to promote yours.

—JEAN DE LA BRUYÈRE (1645–1695)

I N *NET WORTH: Shaping Markets When Customers Make the Rules,* John Hagel III and Marc Singer anticipate a future where companies called infomediaries will work solely on behalf of customers to guarantee privacy, get compensated for profiles, obtain discounts, and filter marketing solicitations. They believe customers should be compensated for the value of their profiles. We agree. Infomediaries aren't exactly skyrocketing right now, however. Sites like Mercata, which brought together buying groups to negotiate volume discounts, have folded. Travel agencies, once the bastion of information brokering, are reeling. The human effort needed to be an infomediary is expensive. More significantly, businesses are acting as customer agents themselves, using customer profiles to provide better service.

Partnerships and strategic alliances on the Web have enabled businesses to expand their traditional service. Northwest Airlines is a good example. Northwest arranges hotel and rental-car reservations for its passengers. Northwest gets compensated for referrals and customers get one-stop shopping.

There's an added benefit of multi-service providers: privacy protection. Books like *Database Nation: The Death of Privacy in the 21st Century* by Simson Garfinkel herald the end of privacy as we know it. The business of privacy protection is booming, as evidenced by the number of providers: Anonymizer, Anonymouse, Crowds, and IDZap to name a few. The Commerce Department has created a high-level position to deal with privacy concerns, following the lead of companies such as Microsoft and American Express. Customers want assurances that their profiles won't get into the wrong hands. Multi-service providers limit the number of people who have access to your profiles.

You don't have to be a multi-service provider, however, to be a customer agent. In this chapter, we examine companies that turn customer preferences into purchases. These companies provide extra value, exemplary service, and, in most cases, patented technology for learning from and securing their customers.

Agents

We all know that some agents have a bad reputation. Films like *Jerry Maguire* have portrayed agents as fast-dealing, morally ambiguous characters. And to a certain extent this image has stuck. But the kinds of agents we're talking about are actually powerful advocates for the consumer's needs. They don't sit on the other side of the table from their customers; they sit next to them.

Customer agents listen first, then talk. If you did a survey, most people would say they're good listeners. But good listeners not only listen intently to what the other person is saying, they communicate it back to the speaker through body language (nodding, frowning, tapping their chin), murmurs of approval or disapproval, and questions (for clarification about actions or reactions).

Good agents encourage their clients to open up. So do good companies. They listen to what their customers are saying and reflect it back. In essence, they say, "It sounds like you want . . ." (fill in the blank). They allow customer feedback to guide decisions about their products and services. They ask questions to try to understand the customer better. They even give customers a hand in the process. Clinique, as you'll read in this chapter, uses a skin questionnaire to help customers identify their skin type. Afterward, Clinique is able to make better product recommendations.

Customer Agents

To be a successful customer agent like Clinique, you must do four things:

1. Listen. Learn all you can about your customers. Use this information constructively and persistently. Customers want their needs and problems to be heard. They want companies to take this information and turn it into something useful—a product or service that is personalized for them. They want to be given several options (not too many, otherwise it'll be clear that you didn't listen to them) and they don't want to reenter information every time they visit your site.

2. Anticipate potential pitfalls. Learn where customers fall through the cracks. From its background in catalog sales, Lands' End learned that customers need to be able to picture clothes on themselves, not twiggy models. You'll read more about My Virtual Model in this chapter.

3. Bring customers new business opportunities and insider info. Everyone wants to feel like an insider. Give your customers a glimpse of how your machinery works. Let them know that they're receiving privileged information and offers. The closer you bring them in, the more loyal they'll be. Keep your friends close; keep your customers closer.

4. Get the right products into your customers' hands. Let recommender technology do the work. You take the credit.

Agent for Change

Be an agent for change. Change the dynamic between you and your customers. Don't just present your inventory; allow customers to participate in the exchange. Ask questions. Show them that you're listening. If you treat your customers with respect, you'll get their trust in return.

CLINIQUE

P REMIUM MAKEUP PRODUCTS have long been sold by expert "consultants," mostly in department stores. These experts assess the skin types of the customer and suggest the right products to highlight and flatter the customer (all while offering to demonstrate the products). Clinique is no exception. Founded in 1968, Clinique commands prime real estate in department stores around the country by distinguishing itself in several ways. First, its full name is Clinique Laboratories, Inc., suggesting that their products are made with scientific precision in a sterile environment. The fact that their beauty advisers wear long white coats adds to this effect, as do the names of their products, like Anti-Gravity Firming Lift Cream and Stop Signs Anti-Aging Serum. (Can a love potion be that far behind?)

Beauty is big business—a $40 billion global industry, to be exact—and Estée Lauder Companies, Inc., Clinique's parent company, sells products in over 120 countries. How is it that so many people buy beauty products?

Fear and intimidation tactics work for some companies. Removing fear and intimidation, however, often leads to more sales. Estée Lauder encourages beauty advisers to make their customers feel comfortable with small talk and compliments. They also make the most of every potential sales opportunity. They keep books on clients, so that they can mail birthday reminders, follow up after purchases, and send customers off with written product recommendations even if they don't make a sale.

According to a *Wall Street Journal* article, customers who sit down are 65 percent more likely to buy two or three products, rather than one. So how does Clinique get customers to "sit down" on-line?

Clinique on the Web uses innovative technology to approximate the job of sales consultants—assessing customers' needs, listening to input, and returning with filtered products. No, they don't compliment you on the scarf you're wearing, but they come pretty close.

LISTEN. LEARN ALL YOU CAN ABOUT YOUR CUSTOMERS. USE THIS INFORMATION CONSTRUCTIVELY AND PERSISTENTLY.

Skin Typing, part of a suite of Clinique on-line tools, identifies skin types and tones for both men and women. First you answer a short questionnaire about the color of your eyes, hair, and skin. You're also asked about pore size, the relative oiliness or dryness of your skin, your tendency to break out or suntan or burn, and facial lines. Once you've answered these questions, Clinique invites you to create a permanent profile, so that all future product presentations are tailored to your skin type. Both Clinique and their customers benefit from this permanent file: Customers don't have to reenter their skin-type information every time they visit the site, and Clinique sells more because their recommendations match their customers' skin traits.

Based upon skin type and tone, Foundation Finder places women in one of ten categories, so that Clinique can recommend appropriate foundations. The Foundation Finder begins by asking you to choose your level of coverage: sheer, moderate, or full. Then Clinique recommends matching products and colors. If your skin type is IV, skin tone is olive to dark, and you prefer sheer coverage,

Clinique recommends Almost Makeup SPF 15 in the color Deep. You have the option of seeing all color options for this product if you're so inclined.

The fact that Foundation Finder builds upon information entered in Skin Typing is evidence that Clinique is listening to its customers—and providing rewards for that effort in the way of personalized products.

ANTICIPATE POTENTIAL PITFALLS

The Looks Maker is designed to cross-sell to customers who already have a favorite product or two. In response to the lipstick or eye shadow you already use, the Looks Maker suggests additional products that might help you "complete the look" in either a casual or a dramatic fashion. Just out of curiosity, we tried to order the lipstick Deep End, which it recommended, but on the next screen we were advised that that product had been discontinued. Not much point in recommending items on back order, out of stock, or discontinued. Clinique's recommender system should have a rule in place for these contingencies.

BRING CUSTOMERS NEW BUSINESS OPPORTUNITIES AND INSIDER INFO

For men, Clinique offers shaving and sports tips. What could Clinique tell men that they don't already know? Well, did you know that right-handed men tend to shave their left sideburn shorter or that you should apply shaving creams and oils against the grain, but always shave with the grain? Naturally, most of Clinique's tips nudge you toward their products, like M Lotion, which helps replenish lost moisture after exercising.

GET THE RIGHT PRODUCTS INTO YOUR CUSTOMERS' HANDS

Clinique lives up to its scientific image. The Web site itself feels as clean and white as an operating room. Like doctors, Clinique is not afraid to ask you about oily skin or your pore size. In some ways, the

Web makes it easier for them to ask these questions. And, in return for your honest answers, you receive products that are designed for you. Clinique knows that many of their customers don't simply want to search for a product and have it shipped, but want the experience of exploring colors, products, and looks that will help them feel and look their best. Skin Typing, Foundation Finder, and the Looks Maker enable Clinique to narrow the product field to a manageable number for each customer.

Business Applications

Clinique follows the rules of good agenting. They provide you with insider information (all but bringing you into the lab with them), apprise you of new products, and anticipate potential pitfalls (recommending products to you that don't match your skin type). Their site isn't cluttered and offers several options in terms of negotiating the site (fast paths, new user paths, and search options). And they ask questions that everyone can answer.

Most importantly, Clinique puts customers' input to good use. Too many businesses fail to realize that with customer knowledge comes an implied responsibility: to use this knowledge to create personalized products and remember it for all future transactions. Pharmacies are expected to remember your allergies whenever they fill new prescriptions and verify that these prescriptions won't conflict with others you're taking. You must take the same responsibility to serve your customers' best interests.

There's a reason why cosmetics counters get the prime real estate in malls: They know how to sell.

CLINIQUE

RECOMMENDER(S): Looks Maker (manually edited, product associated), Skin Typing and Foundation Finder (segmentation through questionnaire).

INPUT(S): Looks Maker (products you want matched), Skin Typing and Foundation Finder (answers to questions about your skin and preferred level of foundation coverage).

OUTPUT(S): Looks Maker (explicit set of product suggestions), Skin Typing and Foundation Finder (products that match your skin type). Persistent use of Skin Typing as you go forward.

LESSON: *Ask, learn, remember, and use.*

LANDS' END

BACK IN 1991, Lands' End's president Richard Anderson coined the term *direct merchant*. *Mail order* didn't do justice to the company, he felt. Since collaborative filtering offers a return to the customer-savvy merchant and a departure from one-size-fits-all marketing, it bears repeating Anderson's rationale:

A marketer deals with many; a merchant deals with one.
A marketer moves from the mind; a merchant moves from the heart.
A marketer is logical; a merchant is perceptive.
A marketer does business across the world; a merchant does business across the counter.
And finally, a marketer bets his all on the System; a merchant bets his all on His Store.

Largely due to this philosophy, Lands' End has been recognized as an extremely customer-friendly operation. They stand by their products and service. In fact, customers can return any of their products at any time. All Lands' End products are "Guaranteed. Period."

Lands' End has proven itself as a high-quality, reasonably priced direct merchant. But how does that translate on-line?

Well, first of all, Lands' End customers are twice as likely as the rest of the population to have on-line access. That doesn't hurt. They also have a relatively high median income ($60,000 per household). Neither of these factors would matter, however, if Landsend.com didn't distinguish itself with technology-supported, customer-centered clothes marketing. Lands' End's outstanding in-novations make shopping on-line far more fun than ordering over the phone. Customers must agree, because sales for Landsend.com more than doubled in the past year—from $61 million to $138 million.

LISTEN. LEARN ALL YOU CAN ABOUT YOUR CUSTOMERS. USE THIS
INFORMATION CONSTRUCTIVELY AND PERSISTENTLY.

My Personal Shopper is a personal assistant that recommends clothing based on four types of preference data. After identifying whether they're shopping for work or leisure, customers are asked to express preferences among six pairs of outfits—shown in a suc-cession of "A or B" choices, like choosing between lenses in an eye exam. Then customers are asked about fabric, color, and cut prefer-ences (no purple, no cashmere, etc.). At this point, the system makes quick recommendations, but customers can refine the rec-ommendations by specifying the type of clothing and occasion for which they are shopping. Behind the scenes, we assume the site analyzes the customer's purchases, along with marketer-specific categorizations and other sales data, to create personalized and situation-specific recommendations.

Customers use My Personal Shopper in a manner similar to the way they would consult an in-store personal shopper. The assis-tance provided can help them navigate through an overwhelming selection of products to find a few to consider buying. At the same time, customers who are concerned about their own ability to judge whether clothing is appropriate for a particular occasion (work ca-sual or leisure "dressy," for instance) can buy with greater confi-dence, thanks to the recommendation of an "expert." Lands' End benefits both from serving customers who might otherwise become frustrated and leave, and from suggestive selling (which includes cross-sales). As a customer shops at Lands' End more frequently, the personal shopper gets better, learning more about the customer's preferences and creating a barrier for competitors seeking to lure away the customer. With further refinement, personal-shopper software could also be used to contact customers when new products, or newly discounted products, of particular interest become available.

ANTICIPATE POTENTIAL PITFALLS

Want help with purchasing decisions? Confused about the features of a certain product? With Lands' End Live, customers can speak with a representative over the phone or by live text chat as they peruse the on-line catalog.

Customer-service representatives can be helpful, but sometimes customers prefer the advice of a friend or loved one. Landsend.com accommodates these customers with their Shop with a Friend feature. Although only one person can make the purchase, two people can browse together and add items to one shopping bag. Landsend.com offers a chat feature with this service and protects dual users with passwords.

Finding interesting products is only half the hurdle for on-line, or even catalog, clothing sales. All too often, the clothes that look great in the photo look awful on our all-too-imperfect bodies. While some catalog retailers, including Lands' End, make a point of hiring models with bodies actually found in nature, those bodies still aren't necessarily found in our homes. We may be taller or shorter, slimmer or wider, and generally just built differently from the model. A result of the mismatch between photo and reality is a high rate of clothing returns.

My Virtual Model allows Lands' End customers to see clothes on a model built to their body shape. Customers can create a model by answering a set of questions (about hair color, eye shape, skin tone, silhouette, height, weight, and even hairstyle), or by having their body scanned at a touring Lands' End body-scanning truck. Once the model is built, customers can update it at their leisure.

The model is used both to show clothes and to provide style advice personalized for the customer's body. Customers can view clothes not only from the front, but also from the often-less-flattering side and rear views, and they can get advice such as the advice Joe received, including: "Stick to fabrics that are light to medium weight and quite supple" and "Avoid horizontal stripes and large pattern prints."

My Virtual Model is embedded in a shopping system that recommends and helps users keep track of outfits of interest. By putting whole outfits together, this system both shows customers how clothing will look in context and encourages purchasing complete outfits, rather than just individual pieces. Until using the system, it never would have occurred to Joe to buy casual shoes from Lands' End along with shirts and pants. It must have a similar effect on other customers, because customers who use My Virtual Model have a conversion rate that is 26 percent higher than customers who don't.

BRING CUSTOMERS NEW BUSINESS OPPORTUNITIES AND INSIDER INFO

At Lands' End, you dictate the pace and direction of your shopping experience. If you want to put up your feet for a while, they invite you into their library, where you can read about anything from fabrics to the history of the "woodie" station wagon. The site also includes a detailed history of their founding, principles of doing business, supplier relationships, and a photo of their founder, Gary Comer. Clearly, they have nothing to hide.

GET THE RIGHT PRODUCTS INTO YOUR CUSTOMERS' HANDS

Taken together, Lands' End Live, Shop with a Friend, My Personal Shopper, and My Virtual Model place Lands' End at the forefront of personalized on-line clothing sales. These tools can help often-apprehensive on-line clothing shoppers navigate an overwhelming set of alternatives and then buy with confidence.

Business Applications

We could talk all day about how Lands' End succeeds as a customer agent, but we'll keep it to five distinct points:

1. The Lands' End features we've discussed don't travel with customers to other stores, creating a barrier against the competition. And because it's actually fun to log personal information into Lands' End creative features, customers are put in the mood to shop.

2. For some kinds of products (bathing suits, for instance), you not only have to know about your customers' concerns, but *customers have to know* that you know. Features like My Virtual Model convince customers that you know what it's like to be them.

3. Rather than asking customers text-based questions, consider using visual images the way Lands' End does. Evaluating two sets of outfits allows customers to relax. There's no wrong answer. With pair-based decisions (similar to what you get in an eye exam), customers don't even have to understand their own preferences; they just go with their gut reactions. And by presenting outfits rather than individual products, you give customers an opportunity to see products working together in harmony. They may decide to purchase an entire outfit, not just a stand-alone item.

4. While it's been lauded for its ability to move overstocked goods, Lands' End may soon be known for much more due to their slogan "Don't worry about what's best for the company. Worry about what's best for the customer." Lands' End and QuickDog.com, the company behind the personal-shopper software tools, are actively marketing their Personal Shopper system to a variety of on-line retailers. At about $500,000 per license as of this writing, it may be a steal. Note to yourself: The technology you design to serve customers may create a new niche business.

5. Creating revolutionary technology is almost a must in this day and age, and integrating this technology is the next frontier. We can imagine a Lands' End site in the future where, once you've created a virtual model, all the clothes you see (including the outfits shown in the Personal Shopper evaluations) are displayed on your model. Lands' End could also integrate its body-type recommendations into the clothes presented for you after you've gone through the Personal Shopper evaluations. Even a site as imaginative as Lands' End has room for improvement.

LANDS' END

RECOMMENDER(S): My Personal Shopper (manually edited, product associated), My Virtual Model (3-D graphics mixed with segmentation—based on weight, height, and other features).

INPUT(S): My Personal Shopper (work or leisure, pair-wise outfit decisions, and fabric, color, and styling preferences), My Virtual Model (scanned or entered body shape).

OUTPUT(S): My Personal Shopper (set of recommended items, depending on what area customer searches in—shorts, shoes, etc.), My Virtual Model (ability to view clothes on your body type and receive general recommendations for your body type as well as full outfits).

LESSON: *If customers invest personal information, you get a lasting competitive edge.*

MITCHELL'S CALENDAR APPRENTICE

T OM MITCHELL, a professor at Carnegie Mellon University and author of *Machine Learning*, demonstrated a glimpse of the future with his Calendar Apprentice (CAP), a non-commercial application. CAP is a personal scheduling agent with expertise in learning how individual users manage their calendars.

In our final chapter, "The Future of Collaborative Filtering and Recommender Systems," we'll talk about how intelligent agents are being developed to simulate customer behavior (and fill in data gaps, so that collaborative filtering can perform even better). For our purposes here, it's important to note that intelligent agents are also being deployed in products. From CAP, we hope you can imagine ways intelligent agents might improve your products.

LISTEN. LEARN ALL YOU CAN ABOUT YOUR CUSTOMERS. USE THIS INFORMATION CONSTRUCTIVELY AND PERSISTENTLY.

Internally, CAP has extensive hand-coded knowledge about the *attributes* of meetings. It knows, for example, that the time, duration, attendees, and the type of a meeting may matter. In a university setting, for example, it can distinguish among students, faculty, department heads, deans, and external visitors. It knows a little bit about locations. But when it starts, it knows nothing at all about the preferences of its users. All it knows is how to learn.

A CAP user trains the system in the way he might train a human assistant. At first, an assistant knows very little and watches the boss perform tasks. As each example is observed, the assistant begins to infer rules. If a meeting is requested by Sue and the boss schedules a thirty-minute meeting in his office, the assistant may assume that future meetings with Sue will also be thirty minutes and in the boss's office. Of course, such early assumptions are likely to be wrong. As more examples occur, however, the assistant can see when earlier generalizations are wrong and develop rules that are more sophisticated. Eventually, the boss trusts his assistant and allows him not only to suggest actions, but even to act on his behalf. At this point, the assistant moves from training (and therefore extra work for the boss) to carrying out work (and therefore being helpful).

CAP works the same way. As new meetings arise, CAP uses its prior knowledge to suggest default durations, locations, and other scheduling details. When CAP is right, it saves its "boss" the effort of manual scheduling. When CAP is wrong, the boss can take advantage of a "teaching opportunity" to correct its mistakes. Over time, CAP learns enough that the boss can trust it to respond to meeting requests, or at least a subset of them, without waiting for human assistance.

ANTICIPATE POTENTIAL PITFALLS

Life is chaos. Only organization gives you a sense of control over a hectic schedule. The problem is that organizers often create more work than they alleviate.

Mitchell used the CAP system as his sole calendar tool for sixteen months (as did some colleagues). It learned rules with a simple "if . . . then" form, and tested these rules against recent examples. For example, it learned that:

> If   Position of attendees is Grad Student, and
>   Single-attendee is Yes, and
>   Sponsor of attendees is Mitchell,
> Then   Duration is sixty minutes

In simple English, Mitchell's one-on-one meetings with his own grad students are usually an hour. (This rule turned out to be true about 60 percent of the time, and would be superseded by more specific rules.)

Unlike most organizers, CAP didn't create more work. It worked harder as time passed and its confidence grew.

Business Applications

CAP illustrates two very important concepts. First, it shows how progressive learning develops good customer agents. Whether a system is recommending bistros, books, or bed linens, it needs to start by taking time to learn the preferences of the individual customer it is trying to serve. Today's recommender systems often do this by presenting customers with options (and eliciting feedback, sometimes in the form of explicit ratings). Other times they have historical customer-preference data. When a long-term relationship is developed, they may adopt the CAP model of simply learning from interaction when it naturally occurs. The more confidence a customer demonstrates in a recommender, the more the recommender should act on that customer's behalf.

Furthermore, CAP shows how an agent can provide progressive value to a customer, building up customer loyalty and creating barriers against competition (like Lands' End). Just as Mitchell would be loath to start training a new calendar assistant after investing sixteen months in CAP, customers who build learning and trusting relationships with agents are unlikely to start over with a new agent. While this principle is generally well recognized in conventional business, it is often overlooked among today's on-line merchants.

MITCHELL

RECOMMENDER(S): Machine learning technology (also knows attributes of interest—i.e., whether meeting is with students, deans, or professors).

INPUT(S): Meeting data and feedback on its recommendations.

OUTPUT(S): Suggestions based on "if . . . then" scheduling rules and level of confidence demonstrated by user.

LESSON: *Start recommending immediately, but allow customers to display confidence in your recommendations before making assumptions on their behalf.*

TiVo

WHAT IF YOU could pause live TV? What if you didn't have to set a timer or use videotape? What if you could create your own TV schedule and play just the shows you wanted to watch when you wanted to watch them? The Archie Bunkers of the world would rejoice, of course. Even the "Kill your television" people might come around.

If you own a TV and watch any station other than PBS, you know about TiVo, a digital video recorder, which uses a hard disk to mimic the functions of a VCR. Unlike a VCR, though, TiVo will automatically record programs featuring your favorite actors, directors, keywords, or categories with its Wish List function. You can't see programs in advance of their normal broadcast times, but you can program TiVo so that it skips reruns, displays only channels you like, and saves programs indefinitely.

TiVo uses a modem to download a play list of all the shows that will play over the next week and lets the user select among those shows. If the user watches only one hour of television a day, TiVo can make sure that that hour is the best television available from twenty-four hours of broadcast over hundreds of channels. TiVo's on-screen menu is easy to use and, with its many additional features, habit forming. With TiVo, a parent can begin recording a one-hour show at 8 P.M., go tuck the children into bed, and come down at 8:20 to begin watching the show. If the watcher doesn't mind fast-forwarding through commercials, she is likely to be done watching the show at 9 P.M., when it would ordinarily finish!

LISTEN. LEARN ALL YOU CAN ABOUT YOUR CUSTOMERS. USE THIS
INFORMATION CONSTRUCTIVELY AND PERSISTENTLY.

Like the other sites we've discussed in this chapter, TiVo employs a recommender system designed to observe and learn from its users—but with this, TiVo fails impressively.

TiVo collects data from every user about which shows she watches, and which ones she rates on a seven-point scale (three thumbs down, to neutral, to three thumbs up). Based on these ratings, TiVo records other shows that it thinks the user will like. Since TiVo knows so much about what the user has been selecting, you would think it would be able to do a great job. It doesn't. TiVo seems to use simple demographics. Apparently, people who watch soccer are mostly Gen X-ers who also like extreme sports. John's family often watches soccer with his eleven-year-old daughter. We are not interested at all in skateboarding, jumping off mountains, or any of the other sports that TiVo keeps recording for us, no matter how many thumbs-down we press. We also love old Cary Grant movies, but that doesn't mean we love *all* old movies.

ANTICIPATE POTENTIAL PITFALLS

One of the golden rules about being a customer agent is that you narrow down the field of products for your customers. Recording every old movie that plays over the course of a week isn't impressive; it just creates extra work for the customer. Recommendations need to come at a finer level of granularity. In other words, TiVo's recommender should better discern subtle taste shadings. And, over time, its recommendations should change. TiVo's magazine is called *TiVolution*. Unfortunately, there's precious little evolution with the recommendation feature, even with all the information the thumbs-up-and-down system provides.

BRING CUSTOMERS NEW BUSINESS OPPORTUNITIES AND INSIDER INFO

TiVo misses the opportunity to create a life-changing service. Not only could it replace the VCR, it could even replace the whole notion of broadcasting. Right now broadcasters are under the tyranny of the clock; the exact time they choose to broadcast a show often determines its popularity. There is also considerable pressure for prime-time shows to appeal to the greatest number of people possible. This begets a least-common-denominator problem: Interesting or creative shows that might find a small but very loyal fan base never get made at all. Since TiVo would free the broadcaster from the tyranny of the clock, these small-market shows could be broadcast when there are relatively few viewers (4 A.M., for instance). The fans of the shows would use TiVo to record them whenever they were broadcast, and then watch them at their convenience.

TiVo could also circumvent the bandwidth problem. Television is broadcast over a big chunk of the radio-frequency spectrum on the airwaves, but there simply isn't enough room for everyone to receive his or her own personal television broadcast between eight and ten on Monday night. With TiVo, we could use all twenty-four hours and shift show times without worrying about the effect that might have on an audience.

Business Applications

Clearly TiVo is not without virtues or promise. According to TiVo's Web site, 96 percent of users would recommend TiVo to their friends and family. We do too, provided we don't have to watch any more motor cross.

Once you've got egg on your face, it's hard to get it off. TiVo promises to be a time-saving device. In a lot of ways, it is. But because it uses technology that doesn't listen to customer reactions, TiVo's recommender actually wastes its customers' time. For many customers, that's worse than wasting money.

TiVo

RECOMMENDER(S): Proprietary, but seems like segmentation (we suspect TiVo places you in a demographic category based on shows you rate highly, then recommends programs targeted at that particular audience).

INPUT(S): Ratings (thumbs up and down), shows you watch (they *may* use this), and what you do with the shows they recommend (apparently not used).

OUTPUT(S): Automatically recorded programs and list of recommended programs (suggestions).

LESSON: *Your job doesn't end when you recommend products. Study what customers do with your recommendations so that you can improve your service.*

Principle #2: Be a Customer Agent

Quick Tips

- Don't just listen to your customers. Reflect back what they're saying. Ask questions that respond to their preferences and personalize the products you select for them. (See also our discussion of Ask Ida in "Principle #3: Maintain Excellent Service Across Touchpoints," in the Best Buy profile.)

- Follow up with customers like Clinique does. Make sure that your service worked for them. If it didn't, don't give up hope. As Harry Beckwith, author of *Selling the Invisible*, says, "To err is an opportunity."

- Keep your friends close; keep your customers closer. Bring them insider information (Clinique's Skin Typing).

- If you don't know much about your customers' preferences, you can always ask. Clinique encourages customers to enter their favorite product, and Clinique will recommend products to go with it (Clinique's Looks Maker).

- Never recommend products that are out of stock (Clinique).

- Take time to learn the individual preferences of your customers. Notice changes in the service options they choose. Allow them the opportunity to manage their own preferences, like Lands' End does with My Virtual Model. Or, if a pattern emerges, ask them if it's okay to update their profile.

- Pair-based decisions are an easy way for customers to reveal their preferences. And, if matching sets are presented, it may lead to sales of more than one product (Lands' End).

- Offer an experience customers won't get anywhere else— Clinique's Foundation Finder and Looks Maker, Lands' End's My Personal Shopper and My Virtual Model, and TiVo's ability to pause live TV.

- Creating proprietary technology that fills a niche can lead to a lucrative secondary market: those interested in your software (Lands' End).
- Let them see who you are. Businesses are impersonal. Agents have a face, like Lands' End's founder Gary Comer.
- Agents can provide progressive value to a customer, building up customer loyalty and creating barriers against competition (Mitchell's Calendar Apprentice).
- The promise of superior technology (TiVo) can be a double-edged sword. If you don't deliver on even one element of that promise, the whole house of cards can come down. TiVo has some of the biggest enthusiasts on the market today, but their recommender undermines that enthusiasm.

Be an agent for change. Don't sit on the other side of the table from your customers. Pull up a chair next to them and take the time to learn about who they are, so that you can represent them better. Offer your customers personalized products and services to show them that they've made the right choice. In the whorl of Internet noise and activity, your site should be a safe and welcome enclave. A place where "everybody knows your name."

Interlude #2: Permission Marketing

Coined by Seth Godin, "permission marketing" describes the circumstances under which customers consent to receive marketing material. Permission marketing is the opposite of traditional broadcast marketing in which the marketer makes it hard for the customer to avoid getting a one-size-fits-all message pitched at him. In permission marketing, the customer identifies which offers she is interested in and which she is not. In most cases, the marketer then asks the customer how she would like the messages to be delivered—by E-mail, phone, the Web, paper mail—and delivers just the offers the customer wants in the manner she prefers.

At CDNOW, for instance, customers can sign up for periodic E-mails. These E-mails announce new releases by their favorite artists, special discounts on CDs they may have been considering, and information on new artists who are similar to artists they have enjoyed in the past. Customers benefit because they don't have to scour music reviews or music stores to learn about CDs they might like. CDNOW benefits by creating customer loyalty and increasing the likelihood of purchases and return visits.

Permission marketing treads a fine line between being a helpful service and an annoyance. Often, the marketer will be tempted to send the customer more information than he requested, to increase the value of the customer to the business. If this information violates the explicit and implicit permission granted by the customer, the customer may retract his permission. For example, Yahoo! was recently bashed in the popular press for changing their policies and signing up customers for mailing lists they had already chosen not to receive. Once the customer has denied you permission to contact him, it is too late to ask! Yahoo! is learning this the hard way— many customers are leaving. Customers may also balk if the offers come too fast and furiously. The art of permission marketing resides in the ability to present material to the customer at a reasonable pace and degree.

One way to ensure that customers don't become annoyed is to provide incentives in return for their permission to receive marketing materials. MyPoints.com matches marketing efforts with the declared interests of its members (sports, family and home, travel, and other categories). Then, by visiting Web sites, taking surveys, reading and responding to E-mails, and trying out services, members earn purchasing points—at no cost. Members can redeem these points at Blockbuster Video, JCPenney, Red Lobster, and many more participating businesses.

Collaborative filtering can also work as an incentive in permission marketing. After all, collaborative filtering allows marketers to present personalized offers (not just based on a few declared interests, as MyPoints does, but on complete purchase histories, and other information), which customers appreciate far more than general promotions. Customers are more likely to stick around if the permission-marketing system presents offers that interest them. Collaborative filtering helps considerably in this regard.

In sum, collaborative filtering and permission marketing share a symbiotic relationship. With collaborative filtering, marketers often want to explain how and why they use personal customer information. Permission marketing techniques—letting customers dictate what information they reveal, how they prefer to receive material, and how often—help put customers at ease and make the benefits of collaborative filtering more apparent. Permission marketers, on the other hand, benefit from using collaborative filtering to generate personalized messages and recommendations for individual customers.

Maintain Excellent Service Across Touchpoints

3

> Love is not measured by how many times you touch each
> other but by how many times you reach each other.
>
> —CATHY MORANCY

IBM RAN AN AD a while back where a woman walks into a light store, hoping to pick up the light she ordered on-line. Two clerks tell her that the Web site and the store site don't use the same ordering system. Naturally, the customer bristles. "I came in here 'cause I thought I might—"

"Find the same things that were on the Web site?" one of the clerk interrupts.

Because every line rhymes with "light," this ad probably irritated you as much as it did us. But that was the point of the ad: vicarious frustration. The clerks smile and applaud themselves with lines like "Excellent insight, Dwight," as the customer finally gives up.

Is it unreasonable for customers to expect the same products on-line that they find in retail stores, and vice versa? Should they be able to order on-line and pick up at the nearest store location? Should pricing be consistent

across all fronts? What about service? Should you respond to customer E-mails the way you would phone calls? Will you be able to
phase out call-center operators? How do different data-processing
systems affect collaborative filtering and personalized content?

Many, if not most, bricks-and-mortar companies consider their
on-line business a separate entity. Technically, a lot of them are.
Best Buy notifies customers that their site "is, in effect, a national
store for Best Buy" and advises them to expect some price discrep-
ancies. There are the Web people and the retail people, and distinguishing between them makes sense for a number of reasons: taxes,
inventory, accountability, software incompatibility, cost of systems
integration.

Your customers don't care.

No matter where your customers are or how they try to reach
you, they demand the same high level of service. If your name appears in one venue, customers are going to assume the same level
of service in another. When they're mistreated, they won't begrudge
one arm of your service, they'll begrudge the whole thing.

If you tell customers something once, through any one touchpoint, they expect you to know it everywhere. Think how frustrating it would be if you called your doctor to say you felt sick. The
doctor asked what the problem was, you explained in detail, and
she said to come into the office. When you arrived, however, she
acted as though she'd never spoken with you: "Why are you here?
What seems to be the problem?" How much would you trust that
doctor? How long before you found another one?

Discounts

Companies can alienate customers with offers that apply only
on the Web, by phone, or at retail stores when there isn't communication across touchpoints. At a Days Inn in Mankato, Minnesota, recently, we learned that their rock-bottom rate was available
only on-line or via their 800 number. In calling the 800 number,
we found out that they were sold out of rock-bottom rate rooms.

The Mankato Days Inn reservation desk didn't know this; only the 800 number operator did. Nobody came out a winner.

Most customers understand the incentives to use Web sites: They're easier for companies to service and staff, cheaper to maintain, and they are an opportunity to show customers new products and deep content. Customers are willing to pay extra for the convenience and immediacy of buying a tennis racket at a retail store, rather than waiting for it to ship. Be careful not to abuse their goodwill, however, by discounting at a substantially higher rate in any one touchpoint. If the difference is more than 10 percent, customers may resent the purchase and, by association, you. Think hotel minibars. How do you feel when you spend five dollars on a can of Coke?

Recommendations

Pricing and discounts aren't the only areas of concern when operating multiple customer touchpoints. Recommendations can be complicated, too. If you're an airline, you can't pitch a summer vacation package in good conscience when other passengers are waiting in long lines at the check-in counter, so it makes sound business sense to offer Web discounts where customers can be tempted by offers at their leisure. Less harried retail environments, on the other hand, can provide valuable face time with sales staff and exposure to new products. Williams-Sonoma mall employees can suggest Frontera grilling sauces to someone who's purchased a barbecue grilling gift set. Recommendations work in all venues, depending on your staff, products, time frame, and pitch. From the companies we examine in this chapter, you'll get some idea what is most appropriate for yours.

What really distinguishes first-tier companies from second-tier ones is whether their recommendations spring from all of a customer's purchases, or just purchases in one venue. As we've stated before, the more customer data you have, the better your recommendations. After all, you can not only zero in on who your customers' nearest neighbors are, but you can avoid making the same recommendation twice, or, even worse, recommending an item the customer has already purchased through one of your other touchpoints.

Plus, building a learning, recognizing relationship across all touchpoints creates better competitive barriers. With stock brokerages, for example, if you make a call to Charles Schwab, you want the representative to know what your last transaction was, whether it was done over the phone, on the Web, or through a broker. If there is a smooth transfer of information across touchpoints, you'll be less likely to take your business elsewhere.

We realize that updating and coordinating over multiple interfaces may not be cost-efficient in the short term for some companies. Just consistency across Internet sites can be a challenge. Some companies maintain over 100 different sites. Here in Minnesota, Medica is one of them, but they're in the process of consolidating their sites and installing common platforms. Smart move. If you buck the trend and decide to tread water, others will be swimming upstream, catching customers. The sound you hear off in the distance? It's a waterfall.

Time Travel

Fifty years ago, people might have anticipated hovercrafts or jetpacks in the new millennium. Instead, we've got scooters and SUVs. The *Jetsons'* way of life is still far off. The modes of travel haven't changed radically; it's what we do when we travel that's changed.

With the Internet, Palm Pilots, pagers, cell phones, and about a million other devices, workers are now on call twenty-four hours a day, seven days a week. The car is for talking on the phone, planes are for catching up on paperwork and reading, and trains are for checking E-mail. People check messages when they're having a kidney stone out and taking painkillers. Work happens.

Shopping happens too. Gone are the days of catatonia-inducing download waits, thanks in part to faster processors, DSL, and broadband cable. As a result, people aren't surfing the Web like they used to. They're no longer content to spend an hour on one site. They're doing reconnaissance missions. They want to shop when the spirit hits them. They may be stuck in traffic, at the airport, watching a football game at home—you name it.

You can make yourself accessible to these techno-junkies or suffer the consequences. The more communication devices we create, the more we have to hide behind. Over 6 billion E-mails are sent *daily*. E-mail is informal, less secure than snail mail, and non-binding (in most circumstances, anyway)—in other words, perfect for hiding behind. But customers log tardy and impersonal responses in their memory and your reputation will be sure to suffer. Are you hiding from your customers behind your E-mail interface?

Convoluted phone mazes and lengthy wait times send an equally bad message to customers. Do you use push-button technology to make it hard for customers to reach you? Or do you use phone technology to serve them better? Can your customers get special offers over the phone? How long does it take them typically to get to the right person, or the right information? We waited twenty minutes on AOL's billing department 800 number the other day, and then another twenty minutes to reach a technology consultant. Don't make your customers buy a speakerphone just so that they don't get ear burn. It's not fair to your customers, or to your customer-service reps.

Product Placement

In *Why We Buy*, Paco Underhill stresses four points repeatedly:

1. The more contact with employees, the more customers buy.
2. The longer customers stay, the more they buy.

3. The easier products are to reach, the more customers buy.
4. The easier products are to carry, the more customers buy.

Product placement is a science. Grocery stores place sugar cereals and candy on low shelves so children can reach them. In studying customer behavior, Underhill found that it takes about ten steps for customers to get oriented in stores. That's where high-margin items and shopping baskets should be. Products for the elderly shouldn't be stored on bottom shelves, where they have to bend over. Best-selling products should be in the middle of the aisle; products you want to plug should be placed just to the right of them. Underhill's book is full of helpful tips like these.

Retail businesses go to a lot of trouble to get products into customers' hands. Every sales counter in America now has point-of-purchase displays. Every aisle has endcaps. Before customers can buy products, they must see them. So why is it that bricks-and-mortar companies seem averse to doing business across channels? The whole reason behind having an Internet presence is to increase sales and exposure to their products. Why can't customers pick up or return something they bought on-line at a retail outlet? Any store visit provides a valuable sales and marketing opportunity. Customers may purchase something else or see a product that they later buy.

We've mentioned some of the reasons why businesses keep their Internet operations separate (taxes, inventory, accountability, software incompatibility, cost of systems integration), but there's another: They want to reap the benefits of do-it-yourself Internet shopping without paying for customer support. Ideally, they want to phase out all contact with their customers. They don't want to pay for 1-800 calls or phone operators. They don't want to pay for sales reps to answer E-mail. They're enthralled with the idea of letting customers do all the work.

These businesses would do well to remember Underhill's tip: *The more contact with employees, the more customers buy.* Underhill calls it the "interception rate." For retail stores, if the interception rate is 25 percent or less, it's "dangerously low." Customers know when they're being blown off in all media, however. Phone mazes that prevent you from hearing a human voice are a pretty good indication of a company that doesn't care. The same goes for Web sites that create link circles, where customers think they'll be able to get a customer-service number or help function, only to wind up back on the home page. If businesses made a practice of trying to buy on their own sites, you get the feeling help would be on the way. Make sure your Web managers buy products from your store—and that they go through the regular customer-service process when they encounter difficulties.

Here, then, are the rules for maintaining excellent service across touchpoints:

1. *The more contact with customers, the more they buy.* Don't shy away from your customers. Good shopkeepers welcome contact, no matter how it comes. The very least you can do is provide store locators on your Web sites and phone numbers where actual people will pick up. Use technology to increase contact, not decrease it. Automation can reduce costs, but it's not worth it if your customers have a harder time finding what they want.

2.) *Maintaining excellent service doesn't mean equal service. Use the advantages of each touchpoint.* Companies that have had success in one venue often look to duplicate it on the Internet. Some of them don't succeed, however, because they don't alter their customer interfaces to fit the medium. The Zagat Guide, which we profile in this chapter, falls under this category. On the Web, companies need to take advantage of content, custom order, and recommender capabilities.

3.) *Recognize customers and recommend across touchpoints.* Recommendations aren't just for the Web. They happen everywhere you do business. In the future, customers are going to be able to carry their preferences and purchase histories with them (with smart-card technology), but in the meantime you need to integrate customer information across all touchpoint fronts. The more data, the better your recommendations. And the better your ability to serve and retain customers. With the number of interfaces customers now use, they want some assurances that they're dealing with the same business they trust.

Pressure Points

The Japanese word *shiatsu* means "finger pressure": *shi*—"finger," *atsu*—"pressure." Practitioners believe that our energy, or *ki,* travels through meridians around the body, which correspond to our internal organs and health (both mental and physical). There are approximately 365 pressure points located along these meridians. In shiatsu, finger pressure is applied so that blocked energy can be released and flow more freely. This concept of pressure points originated with the Chinese, who believed that no problem could be treated in isolation. Tension in the back and neck, for example, might only be a symptom of the real cause.

Your business may have more touchpoints than you realize— advertisements (TV, radio, Internet, print), products, mailings, catalogs, business cards, phone operators, employees, and branch offices, just to name a few. There may not be 365, but you need to address them all. Otherwise, your energy (and your customers) will get blocked. Remember, the source of your problem may not be where the symptoms arise. Sluggish sales on the Web may be a result of phone operators failing to refer customers rather than poorly chosen featured products.

Good Ki

In this chapter, we examine companies that are negotiating touch-point hurdles. Two of them are bricks-and-mortar stalwarts (Barnes & Noble and Best Buy), one is primarily phone- and Internet-based (Ticketmaster), one is print-based (Zagat's), and one has access to a retail presence only through its parent company (Reel.com, via Hollywood Video). Through their examples, you'll learn how to maintain a consistent level of service across channels. *Excellent service,* we should probably add, since maintaining mediocre service across channels won't get you a kiss on the cheek, let alone good *ki.*

BARNES & NOBLE

WHEN WE STARTED this book, Barnes & Noble was going to serve as one of our best examples of how *not* to integrate touchpoints. Here was the top-selling bookstore chain with over 550 retail stores battling against Amazon.com for market share in on-line book sales and failing to capitalize on its major bricks-and-mortar advantage. When we visited Barnesandnoble.com in mid-2000, the site advertised a wide variety of delivery options, including next-day delivery and even same-day delivery in New York City. But there was no way to order a book on-line and pick it up at your local Barnes & Noble retail store.

Barnes & Noble's retail and on-line operations, despite sharing a name, kept each other at arm's length. This decision wasn't arbitrary; operating separate businesses allowed the on-line store to avoid having a "business presence" in most states, and thereby avoided the obligation to collect sales taxes in those states. However, in its attempt to save customers a few percent in sales tax, Barnes & Noble overlooked the dramatic opportunity to deliver books to their customers more rapidly and efficiently (and therefore more cheaply). At the same time, it missed the substantial opportunity to bring customers into the store, possibly selling more books.

In October 2000, Barnes & Noble announced a more closely integrated business presence between the retail stores and the Web. In this new model, customers can return or pick up books purchased on-line at their local store, join Readers' Advantage (a frequent-customer program that applies to both on-line and in-store purchases), and place in-store orders at Internet service counters.

THE MORE CONTACT WITH CUSTOMERS, THE MORE THEY BUY

Barnes & Noble revolutionized the book business with superstores. Now Barnes & Noble offers the kind of service that small independent booksellers used to: community events, book discussions, and increased customer-and-employee interaction.

At the new Internet service counters, Barnes & Noble employees can search on-line inventory and place orders. "We know that multi-channel customers spend more, and we see our new Internet service counters as keys to increasing sales in both the retail and on-line channels," said Steve Riggio, vice chairman of Barnes & Noble, Inc. and Barnesandnoble.com. Some customers may prefer self-service kiosks like they have at Eddie Bauer, Best Buy, and Lands' End, but Barnes & Noble values customer contact. If a book is out of stock or a customer is having a hard time finding a title, Barnes & Noble staff can take that opportunity to make recommendations.

The Internet service counters have some limitations, however. John recently went into Barnes & Noble to buy a Dungeons and Dragons book for his son's birthday. The salesperson hadn't heard of D&D, so she wasn't able to make a good recommendation. As a result, John drove to a local D&D specialty store and purchased a book there—a scary experience he would have preferred to avoid. If Barnes & Noble had a recommender (using purchase histories), John wouldn't have taken his business elsewhere.

Like most bricks-and-mortar companies, Barnesandnoble.com offers a retail store locator, using ZIP codes. When you type in your ZIP code, you not only get a map, mileage, address, phone number, and directions to nearest locations, you also get a listing of upcoming events and readings. By clicking on the author or event or book title, you can learn more about the work being read. Barnes & Noble clearly isn't trying to hide their retail stores from you. The message is loud and clear: Contact us any way you want. We're easy to find.

MAINTAINING EXCELLENT SERVICE DOESN'T MEAN
EQUAL SERVICE: USE THE ADVANTAGES OF EACH TOUCHPOINT

In the first quarter of 2000, Barnes & Noble opened a free on-line university, the first of its kind. The courses range from "Understanding Poetry" to "All Aboard: The Railroad in American History." To date, over 250,000 people have enrolled in classes, lots of them repeat students. Barnes & Noble University isn't an accredited program, but the message boards where professors give assignments and students converse have led to gatherings off-line (attending Shakespeare tragedies, for example). Despite its being a free university, students aren't the only ones who prosper. In essence, Barnes & Noble professors recommend books to would-be students. And, naturally, students will likely purchase the course books through Barnesandnoble.com.

Barnes & Noble Digital allows customers to publish their own books through a partnership with iUniverse. They also reissue out-of-print books as print-on-demand titles from their Memphis facility, paperbacks that are virtually indistinguishable from the originals. In 1993, John gave his copy of *Saint Mary Blue* to a student who was struggling with chemical dependency. He couldn't find a new copy to buy, since it was out of print. He even wrote to Barry Longyear, the author, to find a way to get a copy. No luck. Now he can buy a new copy from Barnes & Noble, even though the original is still officially out of print.

Although eBook sales have yet to take off, Barnes & Noble wasn't content just to peddle them. They decided to publish them, too (to the consternation of a number of publishers, we should probably add). It's probably too early to tell whether that will prove lucrative over the long haul, but Barnes & Noble has tried to spur sales by offering free Microsoft Reader downloads and even free digital classics like *The Scarlet Letter* and *Frankenstein*.

Barnes & Noble takes advantage of its on-line touchpoint in a way that adds value to its main source of business—its bricks-and-mortar stores. Since eBooks haven't taken off, Barnes & Noble doesn't have to take up costly shelf space in their retail stores, and yet they've positioned themselves in the event that they do become more popular. The costs of promoting them on-line are negligible. And Barnes & Noble University not only builds brand loyalty, it replaces employee/customer interaction with customer/customer interaction—at considerably less cost. Don't be surprised if you see university programs crop up elsewhere on the Web.

RECOGNIZE CUSTOMERS AND RECOMMEND ACROSS TOUCHPOINTS

Barnes & Noble increases stickiness at the same time that it facilitates movement. With the Readers' Advantage program, customers receive 5 percent off on-line purchases and 10 percent off in-store purchases. The $25 registration fee not only provides Barnes & Noble with an additional source of revenue, but also encourages customers to buy more. After all, customers will have to spend at least $250 to recoup their registration fee.

On the recommendation front, Barnes & Noble could do more, though. When you go to check out, Barnesandnoble.com tells you what other customers purchased based on the items in your shopping basket. These recommendations don't take into account your own purchase history, so that feature could be improved. With the information garnered by the Readers' Advantage program (which tracks on-line and retail sales) and their huge customer list, Barnes & Noble could recommend with incredible accuracy if they used collaborative filtering. Your nearest neighbors would be almost guaranteed to share your taste. We imagine a time where you could swipe your Readers' Advantage card in the store and get recommendations, or get recommendations on-line based upon in-store purchases.

Barnesandnoble.com does do a good job of recommending tie-in products (sound tracks, for instance). They also send out twenty-one E-mail newsletters, monthly or quarterly, to customers who sign up for them. The newsletter topics range from bargain books to the latest Christian releases to science fiction, fantasy, and horror. Unlike the music clubs we discuss in "Principle 4: Box Products,

Not People," Barnesandnoble.com allows you to sign up for as many as you'd like. The danger here, however, is inundating customers with E-mails if they have far-ranging tastes. The problem is that the E-mails are *selected personally,* but *prepared for a mass audience.* It would cost them very little more to prepare one monthly E-mail for each customer that lists only the titles that individual customer would be most interested in—across *all* genres. The E-mail could be even more persuasive if the recommendations used collaborative filtering to find items the customer didn't even know she would be interested in.

Business Applications

Barnes & Noble illustrates a number of takeaway principles:

1. Use on-line touchpoints to introduce products that might not warrant shelf space—eBooks, for instance.
2. Frequent flyer/buyer programs allow you to track all of a customer's purchases. Since customers often show one personality at work (buying work-related books, for instance) and another at home (buying gifts and/or personal products), buyer programs that travel across touchpoints can lead to recommendations that reach the whole customer (both work and home personalities).
3. If you have a strong bricks-and-mortar presence, encourage on-line customers to take advantage of it. In Barnes & Noble's case, on-line customers may feel more loyal to Barnes & Noble's retail outlets (and Barnes & Noble in general) if they are encouraged to attend readings by their favorite authors. Resist the urge to save a couple of percentage points by keeping your touchpoints separate. Separate touchpoints will separate you from your customers.

BARNES & NOBLE

RECOMMENDER(S): Collaborative filtering (doesn't use customers' own purchase histories, however).

INPUT(S): Shopping-basket items.

OUTPUT(S): Suggestions from customers who have bought one or more of the items in the basket.

LESSON: *Know your customers across touchpoints, so you can recommend more effectively.*

BEST BUY

H EADQUARTERED HERE in Minnesota, Best Buy probably isn't a company you would peg to be in the on-line vanguard. Maybe it's because we Minnesotans are a reserved, frugal lot. If you've seen the movie *Fargo,* you know that Minnesotans enjoy the simple pleasures: a hot fire, a cup of hot chocolate, a warm blanket, and a good hot dish—basically anything that will keep us from freezing to death.

With nine-month-long winters, you have to keep moving. Best Buy does. In fiscal year 2001, they opened sixty-two new stores, acquired Musicland, and launched BestBuy.com. With so much going on, it's no wonder they're adding inventory to the on-line site in phases. As of this writing, customers can find consumer electronic products, music CDs, and DVD movies on the Web. The rest will come later.

THE MORE CONTACT WITH CUSTOMERS, THE MORE THEY BUY

BestBuy.com's Intelligent Sourcing inventory management system ensures the availability and deliverability of every warehouse product no matter how the order comes in (on-line, through the catalog, or through 400-plus retail stores). Their twenty-four-hour Customer Care boasts a "1 touch to a live voice" feature for Web customers when they dial 888-BestBuy. And Clarify eFrontOffice ensures that Best Buy's Customer Care representatives receive up-to-date customer information, including preference, service, and order histories.

As we mentioned earlier, Best Buy considers BestBuy.com to be its own individual store, so prices may vary a little between it and retail outlets, but by allowing pickups and returns at retail stores from Web orders, Best Buy meets two key customer needs: convenience and cost savings. First, Best Buy waives shipping charges for store pick-ups. Second, by allowing customers to pick up or return the item at a retail store, they don't have to wait for a delivery and perhaps receive the dreaded "Sorry we missed you" slip from UPS.

Web and retail integration also provides two opportunities for increased sales. Web buyers may be more willing to order merchandise about which they are unsure. After all, they can return it at their local store, and even look it over at the store *before* deciding whether to take it home. At the same time, people who order products on-line and choose store pickup may discover other products in the store that they would otherwise not have ordered (since they didn't see or choose them on-line).

MAINTAINING EXCELLENT SERVICE DOESN'T MEAN EQUAL SERVICE: USE THE ADVANTAGES OF EACH TOUCHPOINT

BestBuy.com allows you to enlarge images of products and view them from multiple angles. In addition, Best Buy's on-line Shopping Assistant will sort products for you by brand or price (most expensive first, of course). Lots of sites do that, but Best Buy allows you to compare features of each product head to head, in considerable depth. If you're interested in a clock radio, for instance, the Shopping Assistant first asks you four questions: "Do you want a clock radio with a built-in CD player? Would you like dual alarms? Will you mount your clock radio underneath a counter or cupboard? Do you have a brand preference?" Based upon your preferences, Best Buy lists the products alphabetically. When you click the Compare box for each product you're interested in, Best Buy returns with their features. With the clock radios we chose, Best Buy compared twenty-one separate features, including weather alert, battery backup, and TV band.

All the product information Best Buy provides serves two purposes. One, it helps customers make informed purchasing decisions. Two, customers may be persuaded to buy more expensive products when they learn the added features they'll receive. Customers may decide they really would prefer a clock radio with a CD player and a TV band.

RECOGNIZE CUSTOMERS AND RECOMMEND ACROSS TOUCHPOINTS

In 2000, Best Buy took an equity investment in Etown (featuring the virtual saleswoman Ask Ida) and now that site is inactive, although traces of it remain in Best Buy's Shopping Assistant. We miss Ask Ida's ability to ask customer-oriented questions and make unbiased recommendations, however. Best Buy, because it must maintain relationships with its vendors, amasses lots of product data, but it doesn't rank them based on what's best for your expressed preferences. As a resource, the Shopping Assistant works well. As a recommender, it could stand some improvement.

We checked out Active Buyer's Guide (ABG), one of the leading product-comparison sites, just for comparison. For digital cameras, ABG asks you which of nine features you're interested in (optical zoom, plays MP3's, diopter adjustment, flash type, etc.), then asks you the maximum price you're willing to spend and what brands you find most desirable. Then ABG poses a series of trade-off questions. Would you prefer Digital Camera A (with 10X optical zoom and two-second delay between shots), or Digital Camera B (with 5X optical zoom and one-second delay between shots)? These trade-off questions recall Lands' Ends pair-based clothing decisions and work well at narrowing down suitable products. Unfortunately, ABG's Adaptive Recommendation Technology doesn't listen quite as well as Ida used to. Even though we expressed an interest in 10X optical zoom during the trade-off questions, the cameras that were recommended to us didn't even have 5X optical zoom! Also, if you tell ABG that product brand is least important to you, it still asks you on the following screen which brands you find most desirable. ABG claims to be working solely for the customer, but there seems to be an underlying imperative to find out what customers think of certain brands. If brands are extremely important to customers, then in all likelihood they would shop at those sites, not a product-comparison site. Of more importance to customers, we believe, is product reliability, for instance.

Back before Etown shut its doors, we researched digital cameras with Ask Ida. Ida's first question was "How do you plan on using the images you'll shoot with your digital camera?" The customer checked all that applied from among: Web pages, E-mail, or making prints. Ida next asked about the customer's experience with cameras, and then the desired price range. After only three questions, Ida made her initial recommendations. The customer could still select from a set of additional questions to answer at the bottom of the screen, however. Because the customer was put in charge of the dialogue, Ida felt more like a real salesperson. And since the questions often related to the customer's intended uses for the camera rather than evaluations of complicated features like diaptor adjustment, the process was less intimidating and more elucidating. Below its recommendations, Ida also listed less suitable products, and even unsuitable ones (based upon the customer's preferences). These helped show how search restrictions affected Ida's recommendations. Ida was working for the customer, matching the customer's needs with products that fit those needs. Other recommenders often feel like they're working for the manufacturers, because they ask all sorts of confusing questions about product details that most customers don't understand.

Who do your recommenders work for? If they work for your customers, they work for you.

Business Applications

Product-comparison sites have been purchased by larger entities at an alarming rate. Who can blame Best Buy for wanting the power of Ask Ida all to itself? Amazon bought Junglee to get at their virtual database technology, Jango was purchased by Excite for use with Excite's affiliated sites, and Deja.com had its customer reviews purchased by Half.com (who, in turn, is owned by eBay). Unfortunately, companies like Best Buy confront two disadvantages in building comparison engines within a single Web site. First, individual companies typically have a smaller catalog than sites like Etown (Ask Ida). Second, customers will wonder whether the recommendations are serving them or the Web sites.

The answer isn't necessarily to extend product comparisons to products you don't sell. Or to buy the next Ask Ida. The answer is to interact with your customers. Ask questions that focus on them, not the products. What do they want to use the product for? Then allow customers to modify their answers by choosing more questions. Pair-wise decisions and/or trade-off ratings (like ABG's) work well, provided the final recommendations incorporate that feedback in a noticeable way. Finally, though, it comes down to whether you approach product searches from the customer's point of view or your own. They notice, and they care.

As you build product comparisons and recommenders on your own site, think about what you're doing to make sure customers trust your recommendations. You get to give bad advice only once!

BEST BUY

RECOMMENDER(S): Shopping Assistant (searchable database).

INPUT(S): Answers to questions about product interests.

OUTPUT(S): Sortable list of recommended products.

LESSON: *When doing product comparisons, ask questions that fully consider the customer's point of view. They should be questions that everyone can answer.*

TICKETMASTER

W ANT TICKETS TO Janet Jackson? The Boston Pops? Yankees spring-training games? Ticketmaster's ticket distribution network is so entrenched that only a few brave venues and performers are willing and able to forgo their powerful, if expensive, sales support. In 2000 alone, Ticketmaster sold more than 83 million tickets.

With a near-monopoly on off-site ticket sales for most events, Ticketmaster might seem to be the least likely company to focus on providing better on-line customer service. After all, they've killed off the competition. Ticketmaster, however, was quick to realize the cost-saving power of the Web. Every ticket sale that can be handled on-line reduces the need for ticket agents staffing sales desks and phone lines.

THE MORE CONTACT WITH CUSTOMERS, THE MORE THEY BUY

Ticketmaster began selling tickets on the Web in November 1996. They maintain 3,800 retail Ticket Center outlets. And a lot of people probably know Ticketmaster's phone number by heart. Ticketmaster is everywhere. If you want to buy tickets, there's almost nowhere else to go. So now, Ticketmaster comes to you.

Ticketmaster owns CitySearch (e.g., twincities.citysearch.com), and the "buy ticket" links from CitySearch go directly into Ticketmaster. In June 2001, Ticketmaster announced that its event-ticketing services would be made available to AOL and CompuServe's 31 million members through "AOL Box Office by Ticketmaster." But that's not all. Ticketmaster increases its contact with customers through performance venues (5,000 use Ticketmaster's services in the United States), content sites, and E-tailers such as ArtistDirect.com—a music site with substantial information, CD sales, fan merchandise, and music downloads. A direct deep link takes you from Ticketmaster listings to the ArtistDirect page, and searching through concert listings on ArtistDirect provides an opportunity to buy the tickets through Ticketmaster.

MAINTAINING EXCELLENT SERVICE DOESN'T MEAN EQUAL SERVICE: USE THE ADVANTAGES OF EACH TOUCHPOINT

Ticketmaster has done a wonderful job extending their presence to the Web. Customers can browse and search by state, venue, type of event, or ticket alert (for soon-to-go-on-sale tickets). Once the customer finds an event of interest, Ticketmaster is unsurpassed in providing fan-friendly and knowledgeable selections for a ticket search. For an ice-hockey game, for example, in addition to picking seats by price and level, customers can select whether they want to be on the half of the ice where the home team or the visitor shoots twice.

Once you select the type and number of tickets, the system gives you a set of the best available seats matching those criteria and it holds them for up to five minutes while you decide whether to purchase them. During this time, you can look at the seating map for the arena (with separate maps for different types of events at multi-purpose venues), just as you would in person at a Ticketmaster outlet. Indeed, for informed buying, Ticketmaster.com is at least as good as in-person sales and better than telephone sales. And if you're not convinced, Ticketmaster.com provides convenient access to the nearest retail outlets in your area and local phone exchanges.

Things do break down a little during a sales crunch. Major events, like a Billy Joel/Elton John concert tour, can sell out in mere minutes. Over time, sophisticated techniques have evolved to handle the crunch for in-person and telephone sales. In-person centers will often provide claim numbers to people in line, and then rapidly buy as many good tickets as possible, offering them to people in the order they arrived (and also allowing them to shop or otherwise entertain themselves for the hour or two it takes to sort out the mess). Telephone sales use sophisticated "traffic management" techniques, developed by phone companies to handle the flood of calls to radio contests, that generate locally produced busy signals to avoid clogging the network.

The Web as a whole, and Ticketmaster's Web site in particular, have difficulty shedding overloads. Ticketmaster's Web servers, while continually improving, have had times when high traffic slowed them down unbearably (even to the point where buying the ticket in five minutes was iffy, let alone looking at the seat map). Undoubtedly, these problems will continue to shrink as the scale of Web services improves and as the Internet starts to support high-reliability service.

It would be easy to blame Ticketmaster for busy signals and overloaded servers, but the nature of their business handcuffs them. Ticketmaster can only assure customers that no preference is given to any one avenue, which they do. All ticket purchases come from one shared pool of tickets. Perhaps the clearest indication of the fairness and effectiveness of their Web site is the number of users. In the first quarter of 2001, their Web site accounted for 29.5 percent of all ticket sales ($49.5 million)—an increase of over 70 percent from the year prior. Not bad, considering that there are seventy-nine retail outlets in Minnesota alone.

Soon Ticketmaster customers will be able to print their own tickets, eliminating another touchpoint hurdle. In the past, purchasing tickets over the Web or phone meant that you had to take the extra step of picking them up at Will Call windows if there wasn't time for the tickets to be sent to you. Now, using Print My Own (PMO), customers can print tickets at home with a special bar code that allows one customer admission.

RECOGNIZE CUSTOMERS AND RECOMMEND ACROSS TOUCHPOINTS

Surprisingly, Ticketmaster doesn't use a recommender system to recommend events. One of the reasons we chose to examine Ticketmaster was because of the screaming potential for collaborative filtering.

As the largest single provider of sports, music, arts, and family-event tickets, Ticketmaster has a veritable treasure chest of customer information. Ticketmaster could not only send E-mails announcing local concert dates of musicians you've seen in the past, it could recommend concerts based on the ticket purchases of your nearest neighbors. Those neighbors could be amazingly help-ful, since Ticketmaster extends into so many different venues. Not only could the site recommend tickets to a visiting David Hockney exhibit, but it could use knowledge from City Search customer rat-ings to suggest a restaurant you'd like nearby for lunch. And since Ticketmaster knows all about inventory, they can reward their best customers with cheap tickets that would otherwise be unsold (see "Interlude #7: Viral Marketing").

As it stands, the only recommendation Ticketmaster makes is implicit. Based upon the price range and type of seat you request, Ticketmaster recommends a seat for you. In some ways, this experi-ence is comparable to the way Priceline recommends hotels.

Business Applications

The takeaways for Ticketmaster are threefold:

1. Your contact with customers can spread to other sites, not just through advertising, but by direct deep links.
2. You may be recommending to customers without their knowledge. Like Priceline's Hotel Matcher, Ticketmaster recommends seats to customers who may not be aware how much Ticketmaster knows about venues.
3. It's cheaper to sell on the Web. By providing quality service across touchpoints, Ticketmaster has managed to build a substantial on-line ticketing business—one with very low per-transaction costs (yet one earning high per-transaction fees).

TICKETMASTER

RECOMMENDER(S): Proprietary seat-ranking system (based on knowledge of venues).

INPUT(S): Price, date, artist, and seat preferences.

OUTPUT(S): Best available seats for the price, venue maps, and views from specific seats (in some instances).

LESSON: *If customers trust your recommendations, you can serve them quickly and cheaply. You might also bring them back more often if you extend your recommendations to products they might never have considered (such as the David Hockney exhibit).*

ZAGAT GUIDES

O NE OF OUR FAVORITE recommender systems is also one of the most trusted names in restaurant reviews: the Zagat Guide. These guides, available both on-line at Zagat.com and in print, evaluate restaurants in major cities around the United States and selected cities worldwide. But, unlike Michelin Guides, Mobil, and other expert evaluations, the Zagat score and critique is based entirely on the opinions of Zagat Guide readers.

Zagat Guides started in 1979 with a New York City restaurant guide edited by Nina and Tim Zagat. They had been surveying their friends about restaurants (in a city where there are so many that you could choose a different one three times a day for the rest of your life), and their compilation of honest reviews from "ordinary people" became widely popular and has since expanded into forty-five regional guides as well as guides to hotels, resorts, and spas. The formula is simple. Restaurant-goers rate restaurants on 0-to-3 scales for food, décor, and service; their average scores are then multiplied by ten, resulting in a 0-to-30 scale. They also estimate the cost and may add comments. The guide then averages the numeric ratings and editors assemble short reviews from the submitted comments. The guide even indicates whether a particular restaurant has consistent or highly varying ratings (good to know if a place is a "love it or hate it" experience).

The result: massive coverage of restaurants in many major areas (as well as top restaurants nationwide, even in uncovered areas). Readers were enticed to review restaurants with the promise of getting a free guide, and today many carefully craft pithy reviews in the hopes of being quoted. Best of all, the tastes represented are tastes of ordinary people, not "stuffy food critics." It seems like the perfect example of community filtering.

Well, almost. Fifteen years ago, New Yorkers were in love with the guide. Today, we hear critiques as often as compliments. Too many mediocre restaurants get good ratings because only the people who like them bother to rate them. Many people say that they trust ratings of 26 or higher (out of 30), but are skeptical about the lower ones, because there are too many raters with "bad taste." What's happening? As the community broadens, it is becoming more diverse. Suddenly, people who enjoy $100-a-person French dining are being averaged with people who enjoy $1.00-a-person french fries. Especially for accessibly priced restaurants, the reviews are becoming more diverse, but also more positive.

A local example illustrates this problem. The review for a local Mediterranean restaurant, La Belle Vie, shows good scores (26 for food, 25 and 23 for décor and service). But the text reveals a split:

> While some speak only of "great promise" and opine it "could be outstanding," converts are convinced it's already a "very special" "escape" that's well "worth the drive."

Which is it? The answer, perhaps, lies in the question of who holds what opinion. Customers can't help but wonder, Am I like the naysayers or the converts?

THE MORE CONTACT WITH CUSTOMERS, THE MORE THEY BUY

In Zagat's case, contact with customers isn't the problem. If anything, they have *too much* contact with customers under their current business model, for reasons we described above. The problem is that all the divergent voices have diluted the final product.

MAINTAINING EXCELLENT SERVICE DOESN'T MEAN EQUAL SERVICE: USE THE ADVANTAGES OF EACH TOUCHPOINT

In many ways Zagat's is much better on-line than in print. Having a search facility and the ability to sort by different features makes it possible, for example, to list the Japanese restaurants in Vancouver by quality of food, or the top restaurants in New York by neighborhood. The ability to have frequent updates is also nice. But there is still something key lacking.

"My Zagat's" doesn't exist yet, but it seems like such a good idea that it has to happen sooner or later. Instead of (or in addition to) averages and edited reviews, we'd like to receive a personal score for each restaurant, based on the people whose taste in other restaurants most closely matches ours. We'd also like to be able to see their reviews, perhaps in their entirety. In a print guide this was impossible. But on the Web it is not only possible, but in some ways easier than editing "common" reviews. Besides, if we were members of My Zagat's, we'd suddenly have more than altruistic reasons for reviewing restaurants. The more restaurants we rated (especially those we dislike), the better the system would be at finding restaurant soul mates. Add personalization and we have a new incentive not only to be honest, but to be thorough. And one day, My Zagat's could add a feature to find a restaurant *and people to eat there with.* (Dating services already do this, but how about compatible meals for couples?) Watch for My Zagat's, an idea too tasty to pass up.

RECOGNIZE CUSTOMERS AND RECOMMEND ACROSS TOUCHPOINTS

Zagat's delivers its recommendations seamlessly across touchpoints—on-line and in print. The problem is that they're both universal recommendations, not personal ones. And, as such, the only recognition Zagat's affords customers is free copies of the print edition for written reviews. Zagat's could create a hierarchy of on-line critics—based upon how many restaurants they review and/or how frequently those reviews are read and appreciated by others.

We not only envision My Zagat's in the near future, we expect that Zagat's will find a place in wireless technology. After all, people most often need restaurant recommendations when they're in the car or on the street. Wireless technology would provide people not only with good recommendations, but also with recommendations for restaurants that are nearby.

Business Applications

In print, universal recommendations may be necessary. The problem is that they result in average tastes—and no one is exactly average. Whenever possible, we lobby against universal recommendations, as you'll see in the next chapter, "Box Products, Not People." On-line, the hurdles to personalization are much lower, so universal recommendations are easier to avoid.

Personalizing your Web site might inspire improvements to your products, not just your service. With the improvements in publishing technology (recall Barnes & Noble's Print on Demand feature), a My Zagat's print edition may not be too far off.

Is there a way for you to create a My Zagat's?

ZAGAT GUIDES

RECOMMENDER(S): Statistical summary.

INPUT(S): Numerical ratings (0–3) volunteered through mail and E-mail.

OUTPUT(S): Numerical scores (average price, food, décor, and service).

LESSON: *Avoid universal recommenders, especially on-line.*

REEL.COM

I N OUR "INTRODUCTION," we talked about MovieLens, the video recommender site we created at the University of Minnesota. We never intended for MovieLens to be a commercial site; we simply used it as a testing ground for collaborative filtering. Reel.com, on the other hand, was selected by *Yahoo Internet Life* magazine as the best place to buy videos in both 1998 and 1999. Along with the Internet Movie Data Base (imdb.com), Reel.com is still a favorite haunt for movie buffs looking for reviews, screen credits, and the latest interviews. Both sites, however, are now run by two far larger entities: Amazon (imdb.com) and Hollywood Entertainment Corporation (Reel.com).

The dot-com bloodletting of 2000–2001 left few unscathed. Quality-content sites became prime pickings for bricks-and-mortar heavyweights. Reel.com is not noteworthy on that account. What makes Reel.com interesting is that Hollywood Entertainment Corporation now routes Reel.com customers to a third party, Buy.com, to purchase videos.

Sites relaying customers to large, secure, reputable merchants like Buy.com have become increasingly common. The danger, however, is losing valuable opportunities to generate recommendations across touchpoints. And losing brand power. In 1998 and 1999, Reel.com was voted one of the top ten E-commerce brands by Opinion Research International. Now, though, it sits under the shadows of two heavyweights. Hollywood Video is the world's second-largest video chain, with more than 1,818 stores in 48 states (average of one new store a day), and Buy.com has 3.5 million customers and received the 2001 World Class Award for Best E-Commerce Site in the July 2001 issue of *PC World* Magazine.

THE MORE CONTACT WITH CUSTOMERS, THE MORE THEY BUY

It certainly doesn't hurt that both Buy.com and Hollywood Video have prominent links to Reel.com. Hollywood Video has a link to Reel.com on its home page, along with direct access to Reel.com's movie-search and movie-match features. On the Buy.com Video page, there is a link under the title "Go Hollywood" to Reel.com.

Whether Reel.com sells more is another story. Unlike Best Buy, whom we examined earlier in this chapter, Reel.com's customers can't order videos on-line and have them delivered to a nearby Hollywood Video, nor can they return on-line purchases to the physical store. Reel.com customers aren't given a single compelling reason to visit Hollywood Video stores, and Hollywood Video customers don't get incentives to use Reel.com, which might bring them back sooner. Judging from the staff's reluctance to answer our calls and E-mails, we suspect that Reel.com is not long for this world.

MAINTAINING EXCELLENT SERVICE DOESN'T MEAN EQUAL SERVICE: USE THE ADVANTAGES OF EACH TOUCHPOINT

Reel.com has a lot of fun features. Movie Anatomy rates movies across a ten-point scale in sixteen categories: sex, violence, profanity, drugs/alcohol, family appeal, Hollywood style, action, humor, romance, suspense, drama depth, character development, offbeat energy, cinematography, sound track, and special effects. Very impressive. Parents probably benefit the most from this offering, because they can determine whether a certain movie is appropriate for their kids, but knowing a movie has a lot of "offbeat energy" might be reason enough for someone else to rent it.

With some more recent movies, you can play trailers using Real Player or Windows Media Player. The site also offers timely interviews and articles, festival info, awards information, a free newsletter, and more.

On the other hand, Reel.com essentially disappears outside the Internet. We know of no advertising or access through Hollywood Video's retail stores. This is highly unfortunate. If Hollywood Video had on-line kiosks that allowed us to use features like Movie Anatomy, we might never leave the store empty-handed. By comparison, the display boxes on Hollywood Video shelves often don't tell you much.

RECOGNIZE CUSTOMERS AND RECOMMEND ACROSS TOUCHPOINTS

On its Rental Guide page, Reel.com displays the "Top 10 Hollywood Video" rentals on VHS, on DVD, and for kids. In addition, three or four separate links take you to the Hollywood Video site where you get information about their new release guarantees, exclusive offers (like buy two VHS movies, get one free), new release dates, gift certificates, and the like. The Hollywood Video site comes up in a new window, reinforcing the sense of separation from Reel.com.

Third-party merchants, like Buy.com, don't always allow the referring site the opportunity to make point-of-sale recommendations. Reel.com circumvents this problem by making recommendations a large part of their operation. On the left-hand side of the screen, where most sites have a search feature, Reel.com offers Find It! (a standard search engine) and Match It! (a recommender). When the customer enters a movie title using the Match It! feature, Reel.com provides two sets of recommendations: Close Movie Matches and Creative Movie Matches.

Nowhere does Reel.com indicate the precise differences between Close Movie Matches and Creative Movie Matches, but the matches in general are supposed to elicit "similar films that cover the same subject, appeal to the same audience, or provide a similar moviegoing experience." A little vague for our liking. However, the results are quite good—better than their editors' pick feature, anyway. If you plug in *Top Gun,* for instance, the Close Movie Matches are *Days of Thunder* and *An Officer and a Gentleman.* For these recommendations, Reel.com provides one line of explanation. *Days of Thunder* is "another mainstream, popular Cruise vehicle, with fast-paced auto race setting."

Close Movie Matches often feature the same directors and/or actors in the movie you're trying to match. Creative Movie Matches, from what we can gather, may not be as likely to please. For *Top Gun,* the Creative Movie Matches listed are *Air America, Firefox,* and *Iron Eagle*—all flying movies. *Iron Eagle* is described as a "More gung-ho air force action/thriller from jingoistic '80s." Between the two sets of recommendations (Creative Movie Matches and Close Movie Matches), Reel.com covers their bases—romance, flying, Tom Cruise—but there's no guarantee that viewers will like all or even most of them.

Although Reel.com doesn't divulge how they arrive at their

movie matches, we assume their editors make the pairings. Imagine the effort that took. Not only did they create movie matches with every single movie, but they wrote a line to describe how the movies differ. In other words, every time *Days of Thunder* comes up as a recommendation, the description line must change ever so slightly so that it reflects its relation to the movie being matched. Collaborative filtering , in our experience, predicts better and is *far* less labor intensive. Collaborative filtering also doesn't ignore your reactions to movies you've already seen, the way Reel.com does.

Although it operates only one touchpoint, Netflix.com makes far superior recommendations to Reel.com's (by using collaborative filtering and customer ratings) *and* they mail movies to you! If you're interested in on-line rentals, we highly recommend Netflix.com.

Recently, Reel.com switched from selling through Buy.com to 800.com and then Amazon.com. The transparency and ease of changing these partnerships highlights how shallow the alliances are. We are eagerly watching the tie-in with Amazon to find out whether Reel.com builds a deeper relationship, and to see whether and how they integrate their separate profiles and recommenders.

Business Applications

1. Just providing links to affiliated sites isn't enough. Stitch them together with recommendations. Hollywood Video, for instance, could let you rate movies you've rented from them. That data could then be integrated into Reel.com's recommenders. The transaction site, Buy.com, could be stitched into the equation too. Provided other participating vendors were willing, Buy.com could make recommendations across company lines. If someone bought a Canon printer, a recommendation might pop up for one of Reel.com's movies, based upon Buy.com's knowledge of the customer. Every contact opportunity with a customer is a potential for recommendations.

2. Manual recommendations can be a lot of work. There's

almost no reason to edit recommendations manually to the degree that Reel.com does. First of all, writing a sentence of description for every possible recommendation scenario amounts to writing *Moby Dick* several times over (depending on the depth of your inventory). Secondly, experts aren't the best evaluators of an individual customer's taste; his nearest neighbors are.

REEL.COM'S MATCH IT!

RECOMMENDER(S): Manually edited, product associated.

INPUT(S): Movie title.

OUTPUT(S): Films with similar subject, audience, and/or actors (including one-line explanations and predictions).

LESSON: *Three is a crowd, unless recommenders work seamlessly across businesses.*

Principle #3: Maintain Excellent Service Across Touchpoints

Quick Tips

- The more contact with employees, the more customers buy. What's *your* interception rate?
- If you mistreat customers, they won't begrudge one arm of your service; they'll begrudge the whole thing (the original Barnes & Noble approach).
- Consider promoting products on-line that you can't afford to keep on retail shelves (Barnes & Noble's eBooks and print-on-demand service).
- Frequent buyer programs and discount cards can be used to create a recommender database (Barnes & Noble's Readers' Advantage).
- Don't let tax rules dictate your business decisions (i.e., creating a separate Internet business). Being a single

business may cut shipping and inventory costs, in addition to providing better service to customers (Barnes & Noble).

- Allowing customers to pick up and return Web purchases at retail stores is not only good business, it often generates business. Think about how much you spend on advertising, trying to get people into your stores. Plus, the convenience of returning items will encourage customers to purchase more on the Web (Barnes & Noble, Best Buy).
- In-store Web kiosks allow customers to get detailed information on products, view products not on display, and place orders (Best Buy).
- Providing detailed product comparisons will help customers make good decisions—and keep them loyal to you (Best Buy).
- Pair-wise decisions and/or trade-off ratings work well, provided that the final recommendations incorporate that feedback in a noticeable way (Best Buy).
- Maintaining excellent service across touchpoints doesn't necessarily mean maintaining equal service. On the Web, offer innovative, customer-friendly technology (Ticketmaster's Print My Own tickets, Best Buy's Shopping Assistant, Barnes & Noble University).
- Multiple touchpoints can be a fresh start. Ticketmaster, once infamous for busy signals, is now much more accessible.
- Excellence across all touchpoints generates good word of mouth and builds trust between you and your customers (Ticketmaster).
- A site that gets tons of feedback but only makes universal recommendations can lose its effectiveness (Zagat's).
- Using a third-party purchasing site (Buy.com for Reel.com) often leaves a bad impression. It feels like a bait and switch. Even if you don't lose sales, you may lose the opportunity to make personalized recommendations at the time of sale.

It's one thing to induce customers to use your Web site, and it's another to irritate them by not answering the 800 number. Be accessible. Court your customers. Let customers approach you in the way that they're most comfortable. Put out the welcome mat. Know their names, account numbers, last transactions, mailing addresses, and other preferences. It's no longer acceptable to blame problems on servers being down or phone operators who didn't make a report of previous transactions.

Maintaining excellent touchpoint service starts with having store locators on the Web, but it goes much farther. Like shiatsu, there's a philosophy behind it: caring for the *whole* customer.

Interlude #3: Bricks and Mortar

Many of the most compelling examples of recommenders are drawn from Web-based businesses. In part, this is because Web-based businesses have had greater pressure to innovate and to grow quickly, but in part it is because the Web itself makes it easier to customize your storefront for each customer.

Bricks-and-mortar businesses, even those with no electronic presence at all, can still make effective use of recommenders. There are three keys to developing a successful bricks-and-mortar recommender application: (1) identifying customers; (2) learning customer preferences; and (3) finding an appropriate place to make the recommendation. Let's look at how a video-rental store, a supermarket, and a cookware store can employ recommender systems.

A video-rental store has a built-in advantage for recommending: Customers are forced to identify themselves in order to rent movies. With customer consent, it would also be easy to get customer-preference data; indeed, customers could be given bar-code stickers with which to rate movies as they return them. Even easier would be for customers to set a slider on the video box to reflect how much they liked the film (currently, clerks must review each returned video to check it in and determine whether it is rewound). All that remains is making the suggestion—a key opportunity, given research that shows that many video-rental customers leave stores without ever finding a film to rent. There are many opportunities here. Customers could swipe their card at a kiosk to get suggestions (and search the database of available films), employees could have access to a recommender to help guide customers, or both.

Supermarkets have also learned to identify their customers. Many provide "couponless coupon cards" that customers swipe or scan to get credit for purchases and obtain discounts. Increasingly, supermarkets also recognize customers through coded coupons sent by mail. With high-volume purchasing, supermarkets most commonly use implicit measures of interest—if a customer buys an item, or buys it repeatedly, then she must like that item. So how do they take advantage of this knowledge? To date, supermarkets have mostly focused on coupon-printing machines at the checkout stand. These coupons are designed both to induce new purchases and to bring the customer back to this supermarket again soon. Other alternatives include a promotion-printer at the start of a customer's shopping, or a regular personalized newsletter sent to the customer's home as a reminder to pick this supermarket for his shopping.

What about a larger-purchase environment such as a cookware store? Stores like Williams-Sonoma train their employees in suggestive selling techniques; they know to recommend bread mix or a cookbook to people who buy bread machines. And the salespeople and marketing professionals can lend their expertise when customers are in a quandary. What they often lack, however, is the knowledge of customer-purchase history. A customer who comes in today for a sauté pan may have bought a bread-maker last month, and may be a cookbook collector. These stores have two big challenges: customers are unlikely to identify themselves before checking out (at which point they may do so through a "membership card" or credit card), and the checkout lane is often a bottleneck, making it an unattractive place to start a lengthy sales discussion. For such an environment, marketer-assisted recommenders may be most effective. A marketer can identify a small number of products that the store wants to promote; these products can be kept in large quantities near the checkout stand. The recommender system can be integrated into the cash register. As soon as it knows who the customer is, it can quickly offer the most appropriate item from that set, if there is one. In this case, the salesperson works together with a marketer and the recommender system to provide recommendations for cross-sales.

The physical store has an advantage because the customers are a more captive audience than at a Web store. Use that advantage to offer better service to customers who visit you.

Box Products, Not People

Caged birds accept each other but flight is what they long for.

—TENNESSEE WILLIAMS, *CAMINO REAL* (1953)

A CCORDING TO A Gallup poll, 60 percent of Americans find premarital sex morally acceptable compared with only 21 percent in 1960. Women over fifty are only 35 percent satisfied with "how things are going in the U.S."; households with an income over $75,000, on the other hand, are 62 percent satisfied. According to Misterpoll.com, 73 percent of respondents believe that aliens exist. We've become a polling culture. Thanks to better demographic information than ever, we can discern not only trends as they evolve, but also how certain blocks of people feel.

The urge to poll and classify is intoxicating. Advertisers want to know where potential customers are. Politicians want to know how their constituents feel about specific issues. Entertainment and news outlets want to engage their subscribers. In a country of over 250 million people, we want to know how other Americans feel about all sorts of things. We want to know where we stand.

The consequence, however, is that we're lumped into cells, not a melting pot. We're black inner-city youth, upper-class middle-aged WASP, conservative southern landowner, working poor, etc. These boundaries are increasingly difficult to extricate ourselves from, no matter how much we protest.

Back before cable, we watched network TV. If we didn't like the program, well, we could go outside. Now we have over 200 stations. As consumers, we can watch *The News Hour with Jim Lehrer* and then MTV. We can climb outside our boxes by watching programs that may not be intended for our particular demographic. Television stations, show producers, and advertisers, however, are still forced to target groups of people. These groups of people are much narrower than they used to be, hence the term *narrowcasting*. But due to the restrictions of the medium, television advertisers can't get their messages to all the right people. Even in our forties, we might want to watch MTV, but chances are we won't want to buy Oxy pads. The more stations there are, the more advertisers can narrowcast, but some messages will undoubtedly misfire. The same holds true for billboard and radio ads (Web-based radio is a different story, as you'll see in our Launch profile later in this chapter).

Pitches Are Products

We've talked about how recommenders can be personalized. Ads can too, because pitches are products in their own right.

In the past, when only network TV existed, marketers trotted out the same ads for everyone: Palmolive, Maxwell House, and the like. Now, in the era of narrowcasting, marketers generate different pitches for the same product depending on the venue and the audience. Miller Lite's "less filling" ads might play on fitness programs, while "tastes great" ads could conceivably air on the Food Channel (although our bet would be on *The Man Show* or ESPN). Television and radio still have some inherent limitations, though. Television and radio marketers can appeal to smaller segments than they used to, but they can't personalize pitches for individuals. Unfortunately, this has led marketers to assume that the same holds true in other media.

In print, on the phone, and especially over the Internet, marketers can and should target individuals, not groups, through collaborative filtering and other recommender technology. These media aren't bound by the restrictions of television and radio. They can liberate their customers by appealing to their unique sensibilities. They can go the extra mile.

Print

Catalog companies like J. Crew send out different catalogs to different customers based upon demographic information. Not bad. But, as we mentioned in Interlude #3, grocery stores now print coupons at the register based on items you just purchased and your entire purchasing history as documented through buyer-card programs. Sure, they still have circulars aimed at a much wider audience for items they want to move, but the coupons you receive at the register are ones you're more likely to use because you've shown an interest in those products. These coupons will also introduce you to new brands and products you might not have considered.

Phone

Remember the story of GUS from our "Introduction"? Phone operators can produce amazing results with collaborative filtering. Even cold-calling phone solicitors could take a few tips. Too often, we get the telltale "click, click" before the solicitor picks up and by then we're eager to hang up. Phone solicitors would improve not only by eliminating the irritating delay (and the "click, click"), but also by customizing pitches based on demonstrated customer preferences. If they're calling someone they've sold to before, they should suggest items that person is likely to want, based on purchase history. If they don't have purchase histories at their disposal, they should ask questions that elicit preferences. "Do you prefer miles or low interest with your credit card?" "Would you like an hour of free calling every month, or five cents a minute, with your long distance?" In "Principle 2: Be a Customer Agent," we showed how helpful preferential questions can be. Lands' End used them in their My Model feature, as did Clinique with Looks Finder and Skin Typer, as did Ask Ida before her demise. The result is that users feel that they're being listened to and products are being customized for them.

Internet

On the Internet, DoubleClick and Angara demonstrate how the right ads can be placed in front of just the right audience using sophisticated data-collection strategies—without even having to ask questions of the customer. We examine both companies in this chapter. Customer preferences can be gleaned in new and exciting ways, page views can be customized easily, and customers don't have to be lumped into simple demographics. On the Internet, there's no excuse for not personalizing.

Demographic Downfalls

The problem is, simple demographics don't begin to tell the story of individuals. People who like chess can also like football and chili contests. People cross taste lines all the time if they're permitted to. That's what makes people interesting: their quirks, their inexplicable tendencies to hate peanuts but love Reese's peanut-butter cups. Think about how much more people would step outside their demographic groups if they were not only permitted to, but *encouraged* to.

The vestiges of mass marketing still hound us, however. Businesses insist on feeding the same products and ads to people who share the same age, race, gender, and class. Their defenses run the gamut:

1. Profiling according to age, race, gender, and class is better than recommending the same thing to everyone.
2. More often than not, people *do* fit into the boxes we create.
3. It's cheaper and easier for us to keep doing what we're doing.

These defenses are all legitimate, but ultimately inadequate— at least in media where the opportunity to personalize exists. Plus, the results are demoralizing. Demographics can be self-fulfilling prophesies. If it's drilled into us that because we're young, white, middle-class girls we should drink Pepsi and like Britney Spears, we probably will. But it doesn't mean, in a world where we weren't pigeonholed, that we wouldn't buy something else.

Imagine that because you're white, seventy-five years old, and a middle-class woman, you got to see only *Matlock, The Golden Girls,* and *Murder, She Wrote.* Or a twenty-five-year-old upper-class black man who got only *Cosby* reruns. Racial profiling and profiling your customers both spring from the same lazy, prejudiced philosophy.

Box Products, Not People

We're past the mass-marketing era, but its vestiges still hound us. Here's how you can succeed with one-to-one marketing, revamped to include the power of today's recommenders:

1. Treat customers as individuals, not demographics. It's often impractical to create new content for every individual, and maybe impossible due to the nature of your business, but you can still treat customers as individuals. Let their preferences, not stereotypes, dictate which products and messages you present to them.

2. Individuals evolve. So should personalization. If you put a customer in a box that doesn't fit him, let him out. Personalization isn't a one-time event. Angara uses a control group to determine whether their personalization techniques are working. If they're not, the system adapts, not the customer.

3. *Provide real-time updates.* Change as you learn about your customers. They might have to start out in a box because you don't know them well enough, but let them out once you realize what they're *really* like.

Due Diligence

Don't get us wrong: Demographics help. They increase the likelihood of delivering products and services to people who will most appreciate them. But you can do better than using only demographics. In this chapter, we examine companies that *do* do better. They resist the urge to rely strictly on demographics and traditional profiling—processes that can alienate customers if they're placed in a box that doesn't fit them.

The companies in this chapter use recommenders like collaborative filtering to collect data, reach customers, and automate the process of selecting products for individuals. DoubleClick and Angara are at the cutting edge of on-line data collection and advertising. The Children's Place uses Net Perceptions products to customize outbound E-mail campaigns. And product-of-the-month clubs like BMG and Columbia House—well, we tell them how they could improve.

DOUBLECLICK

I F YOU'VE BEEN on the Web, you've probably been shown personalized ads courtesy of DoubleClick. Over 50 percent of Fortune 100 companies use their service, and more than 11,000 networked Web sites display their ads. Not surprisingly, DoubleClick is the largest ad network on the Internet.

The average click-through rate for banner ads is low (0.8 for every 100 ads shown), and conversion rates are even lower (only 1.7 percent of those who click through purchase an item). Companies might have a sense about where their customers go on the Web. Timberland customers, for instance, probably visit Outsidemag.com or Gorp.com. Nokia customers might visit Redherring.com or Wired.com. But where else should they spend money to display ads? How do they ensure that their ads reach not only their customers, but the best prospective customers?

As an ad network, DoubleClick drums up client companies who want to advertise their products and services. Then DoubleClick "recommends" customers who will be the most likely to act upon the ad. DoubleClick might also choose which of a client's ads to show to a customer (Pepsi's Bob Dole ad or its Britney Spears ad, for example). The client companies pay DoubleClick a certain amount of money every time their ad is shown on any site in the network. DoubleClick, in turn, compensates the display sites. The ad rate depends, too, on how much information about their clients the display sites furnish.

Ad-inventory management is a complicated business. If you don't have enough people from an appropriate demographic to show a Rolex ad, for instance, you have to fill in with other ads and hope that later you'll be able to make it up with Rolex ads. Here, too, ad networks are at an advantage. With the amount of traffic DoubleClick's network receives, it is more likely than a single ad server to match advertisers' interests with customer profiles.

TREAT CUSTOMERS AS INDIVIDUALS, NOT DEMOGRAPHICS

Because of its network approach, DoubleClick has a great deal of customer information at its disposal. DoubleClick knows what information you've requested through searches, your movement through affiliated sites, marketing E-mails you've opened, and anything you've entered in registration forms. With thousands of sites contributing this information, DoubleClick can make better-informed decisions about ad placement than an ad server on a single site. For instance, Charlie might visit Porsche.com, read an article about the American Le Mans Series, then decide to go to

Fishmarket.com (a made-up site). At Fishmarket.com, Charlie would be shown ads for very expensive fish, which it presumes he enjoys and can afford due to his expensive car tastes. Depending on his previously demonstrated interests, he might even be shown an ad for a very particular kind of fish, like swordfish. He might also be shown an ad for an expensive car at the fish site.

INDIVIDUALS EVOLVE, AND SO SHOULD PERSONALIZATION

It may be that Charlie was doing research about Porsches for work and the best he can afford is a '92 Chevette. With enough exposure to Charlie, DoubleClick will pick up on this. First of all, he likely won't be responding to the ads DoubleClick sends his way. Secondly, DoubleClick's network will gather more extensive information about his interests.

PROVIDE REAL-TIME UPDATES

DoubleClick presents its ads in real time. As people like Charlie move throughout the Web, DoubleClick displays ads that will capitalize on their latest interests.

Business Applications

In a sense, DoubleClick facilitates the "selling" of information about customers from one site to another. The fact that Charlie read information about Porches was passed along to Fishmarket.com without his permission. If Charlie so chooses, he can opt out of DoubleClick's information-gathering procedures (on their Web site), but the default network system records his every movement (provided he visits network sites).

Despite providing an opt-out clause, DoubleClick was sued for running an information-gathering network without customers' knowledge and consent. In April 2001, a United States district court judge ruled that DoubleClick didn't violate the Electronic Communications Privacy Act, the Computer Fraud and Abuse Act, or the Wiretap Act. Had the judge not decided that customer information is owned jointly by Web sites and customers, the ruling might have gone the other way.

As of January 2002, DoubleClick had decided that maintaining their network wasn't worth the expense or the potential resentment from customers. They provide personalized ads within individual sites now, not among a larger networked collection of sites.

Whether you operate a network or an individual Web site, it's important that you take a hard look at your opt-in/opt-out procedures. While there's seemingly a big divide between giving customers the opportunity to opt-in versus a default program that assumes the customer's consent, it's often more complicated than that. Customers are less likely to resent an opt-out option if it is clearly visible, and not something they have to search long and hard for.

DOUBLECLICK

RECOMMENDER(S): Proprietary algorithm (displays ads to most likely purchasers, controls volume and frequency of ads, adheres to restrictions of display sites, and works within yield-management promises to advertisers).

INPUT(S): All implicit—sites you've visited and actions you've taken (searches, followed links, purchases) are gleaned through cookies and GIF tags.

OUTPUT(S): Personalized selection of ads.

LESSON: *Networks allow for better personalization and inventory management. They also raise challenging privacy issues that have to be addressed on a case-by-case basis.*

ANGARA

DOUBLECLICK CAN TARGET the right ads to customers who have visited any sites in their network. Is it possible, though, to present customized products and services to people who've never been to your site before? Yes. Angara's Marketing Optimization Platform does just that. It records over 800 separate customer attributes and tracks them for over 100 million Internet browsers. With this information, Angara can help companies recognize visitors the very first time they come to their Web sites, even if they're traveling anonymously (using an identification scrambler).

Most companies know how to get visitors to their sites through advertising and other promotions, but visits rarely turn into purchases (less than 5 percent of the time). Angara makes it much more likely that visitors will stick around long enough to become customers. Then, once customers have purchased a few items, collaborative filtering and other recommender technology can increase the likelihood of sales.

When customers visit members of Angara's consortium, cookies are placed on their computers. Angara reads this information and relays that user's profile to other Web sites in a fraction of a second, so that customized information can appear for first-time users. Angara delivers its solution through an application service provider (ASP) that takes only a few days to set up and requires no software or integration with legacy systems, since the software is run on Angara's site. Another product, the Angara Reporter, provides insights into how sites should customize E-mail and direct marketing, and display content based upon reactions of users.

Angara operates much like DoubleClick's network model. Members of Angara's consortium collect information about their visitors and then Angara makes it available to other users. Like DoubleClick, Angara gets to keep all of the data, increasing the value of the network to their customers in the future. Over the long term, Angara has the potential to possess information on every visitor to the Internet, and to have that information in a form that would be very expensive to duplicate. This gives Angara a long-term competitive advantage. Further, Angara sells its service on a rental basis, so it gets a steady stream of income from its customers.

TREAT CUSTOMERS AS INDIVIDUALS, NOT DEMOGRAPHICS

Based upon a customer's demographic, behavioral, and geographic attributes and previously visited Internet sites, Angara places him into one of several segments. When that customer arrives at Brooks Brothers or Fingerhut (some of Angara's more prominent clients), he is whisked to the home page designated for members of his segment. Brooks Brothers, for instance, uses four separate home pages in response to Angara's segments. Because Angara studies so many customer attributes (800 in all), the segments they create can be customized to each company. They evolve out of unique patterns of behavior that Angara observes at each site.

INDIVIDUALS EVOLVE, AND SO SHOULD PERSONALIZATION

Angara uses a controlled experiment to determine whether customers are receiving the right content or products. For every three customers in a given segment, Angara places one in a control group, which receives a site's default content. If the three segmented customers aren't purchasing more than the customer in the control group, then Angara may suspect that something's wrong. Either the segment as a whole is receiving the wrong content, or maybe one or more customers should be placed in a better-fitting segment. Angara automatically rectifies these situations.

PROVIDE REAL-TIME UPDATES

Angara continuously manipulates content and segments for better performance. Its algorithms are designed to do this automatically.

Privacy

As was the case with DoubleClick, Angara must address privacy concerns head-on. In their privacy policy they announce: "We do not use personally identifiable information—name, address, phone number, E-mail address or credit card information—from consumers in the reporting and targeting services that make up the Angara Converter." Personally identifiable data may be accumulated by Angara's partners or by individual Web sites, but Angara prohibits them from linking this information with data collected by the Angara Converter. Angara also offers and honors an opt-out cookie for customers who don't want to receive personalized content.

Because Angara knows and learns so much about 100 million Internet users, it's in a position where it could probably provide sites with customized prices (i.e., this person can afford to pay two dollars more). Amazon's experience provides a cautionary tale in this regard. Amazon learned that it could offer discounts, but it couldn't change the base price of products without angering its customers. When Amazon secretly changed prices different customers saw for the same items, the customers quickly found out through discussion and chat groups—and demanded that Amazon change its practices. We don't believe Angara engages in this practice. We simply want to remind you that customers will find out if you abuse the power these new information-gathering tools create, and they may choose not to do business with you.

Business Applications

Angara helps its customers make instant recommendations. Its success depends largely on its ability to gather information on customers quickly. While you may not be able to do it in a fraction of a second, as Angara does, position yourself so that you can find out as much information about your first-time customers as possible. Toy stores might ask, "How old is your child?" Cut to the chase. And if one of your initial recommendations misfires, reload quickly.

ANGARA

RECOMMENDER(S): Segmentation-based ASP recommender based on a huge database of demographic information for use by other sites.

INPUT(S): Sites you've visited and actions you've taken (searches, followed links, purchases), gleaned through cookies and GIF tags.

OUTPUT(S): Precise demographics for Web customers, even anonymous ones and first-time site users.

LESSON: *Turn first-time visitors into buyers. Start recommending right away.*

THE CHILDREN'S PLACE

THE CHILDREN'S PLACE is a specialty retailer of apparel and accessories for children from newborn to twelve years old. They maintain 547 stores in 47 states, and about 100 of those stores opened in the past year alone. With many more store openings planned, The Children's Place is well on the way to its goal of operating over 1,000 stores in the United States.

In May 2000, The Children's Place sought out Net Perceptions for a targeted E-mail campaign. They wanted some assurance that their customers would not only open the E-mails, but would make purchases. The click-through rate for E-mail campaigns is notoriously low. A study conducted by Forrester Research determined that the average click-through rate for E-mail campaigns based on in-house customer lists is a mere 10 percent. The conversion rate of click-through customers was even more depressing (only 2.5 percent), resulting in an overall success rate of 0.25 percent of recommendation E-mails converted into purchases.

Here in Minnesota, "spam" is a spicy pork product first, and unwanted E-mail second. Getting your customers to open your E-mails can't be any harder than hawking Spam. Provided you maintain histories of past customer purchases or other interest barometers (such as wish lists or followed links), there are several approaches to using a recommendation engine with E-mail campaigns:

1. Have the recommendation engine recommend which items should be suggested to a fixed set of people.
2. Have the recommendation engine recommend a set of people to send a fixed item to.
3. Have the recommendation engine recommend both people and items simultaneously.

The "normal" use of recommendation engines is to recommend items to people based on past purchase history. The Children's Place chose option 2 because they had a set of five products they wanted to sell. To accomplish this, our colleagues at Net Perceptions couldn't use the traditional collaborative-filtering algorithm. The interface demanded that they be able to give it products, and get the most likely purchasers in return. Logic suggested that they could just operate collaborative filtering in reverse, but in trials that proved cumbersome and faulty. They had to create an entirely new algorithm.

Their efforts were rewarded by some fairly impressive results. With the new algorithm, 19.1 percent of the E-mail recipients clicked on the link provided to view the product, and 14.3 percent of them purchased the product. The overall purchase rate was 2.73 percent—almost 11 times the industry average! That only begins to tell the story. Successful recommendations led to considerably larger shopping baskets at The Children's Place.

"These are spectacular results," said Debra Brummer, director of E-commerce for Childrensplace.com. "Not only was our overall sales rate three times our expected goal, but the average basket size of the orders placed was 114.5 percent of our normal order. We learned from our test that Net Perceptions not only helped us boost sales of the five selected items, but also prompted sales of related items not part of the study."

Not long after, Brummer came to work with us at Net Perceptions.

TREAT CUSTOMERS AS INDIVIDUALS, NOT DEMOGRAPHICS

E-mail campaigns have grown in popularity because they're cheap to produce. Compared with direct mail, which can cost between $1 and $2 per piece, E-mail often ranges between 1 cent and 25 cents. But just because it's cheap doesn't mean that the same E-mail should be unloaded on your whole customer base. Customers learn very quickly whether or not your E-mails are worth opening—often after only one E-mail. They may ask to be taken off your list, and it's hard to bring back those customers once they've been alienated.

Target individuals like The Children's Place did and you'll be pleasantly surprised. If you find success with E-mail campaigns, be careful not to get over-eager, though. CDNOW discovered that switching from biweekly E-mails to weekly E-mails increased sales. Twice a week, however, proved to be too much.

INDIVIDUALS EVOLVE, AND SO SHOULD PERSONALIZATION

Recommenders have to adapt to the changes of your customers. The Children's Place sells a lot of items for kids, whose needs and wants change at a rate much faster than most adults. Recommendations to seven-year-old Johnny will be grossly out-of-date a few years later. His sizes will be different, as will his tastes. Recommenders must factor age into the equation, and prioritize most recent taste preferences, so that recommendations aren't ignored—or, worse, insulting.

Business Applications

The moral: If it's what your customer wants, it's not spam. Instead of sending a universal offer "Socks for sale," send E-mails to customers based on buying histories (their own and their taste neighbors'). Avoid the junk-mail feel. Many E-mail promotions look personalized, based on the greeting or title. Take the next step by personally selecting content (text or items) to match your customers' interests.

THE CHILDREN'S PLACE

RECOMMENDER(S): Collaborative filtering.

INPUT(S): Customer purchases.

OUTPUT(S): Targeted E-mail to customers (for five featured items).

LESSON: *If it's what your customer wants, it's not spam.*

LAUNCH

D O YOU EVER GET tired of switching from radio station to radio station trying to find music you like? Even when you find a station playing a favorite song, chances are the song's already half over. Soon enough, you're off shopping for another station. Sometimes it feels like you're switching from ad to ad, not song to song.

Launch has revolutionized radio. With their innovative model, you don't have a reason to switch stations. Launch plays only what you want to hear. Launch even tells you why it picked each song for you. The station sits innocuously on your computer screen, allowing you to provide feedback or respond to advertising at your leisure—without interrupting the music.

So how is it that Launch plays what you want to hear? Well, first of all, Launch users can select music according to eighteen genres (folk, electronica, Latin, and reggae are some of the categories). Within these genres, Launch offers nearly seventy sub-genres (Latin jazz, trip hop, and spoken word, for example). Users can rate all of these different types of music on a 100-point scale, and Launch then incorporates these ratings into each individual user's play list.

What's most amazing about Launch, though, is that as Launch begins to stream music, users can rate individual pieces of music, artists, and albums. Over time, Launch tunes the music it selects for each user according to their ratings. The result is just like having a radio station that plays exactly the music you want—with no awful DJ chatter!

Launch has encountered some speed bumps along the way. In the past year, they had to settle a copyright-infringement case with Universal Music Group, paying for past performances and entering into a new licensing agreement. The rights to some of the songs in their digital library are still under negotiation (only about half of Launch's 173,000 songs are available for personal Launchcast stations). Launch's customers also can't pick out exactly the songs they want to hear, due to industry regulations. Like traditional radio stations, Launch must follow the usual rules about selecting music to satisfy their contractual obligations to the holders of the music copyrights. For instance, Launch can play only three selections from a single CD within a three-hour period. However, the Launch DJ is not constrained by having a large, diverse market to serve. Rather, the Launch DJ is focused entirely on serving this one user as well as it can.

With Launch, users have a number of listening options. In addition to their own Launchcast stations, users can listen to "fan stations"—stations established around a particular artist, like the Rolling Stones. On the Rolling Stones' fan station, for instance, listeners will be treated not only to songs by Mick Jagger and company, but also by other artists that Rolling Stones' fans enjoy, like Cream and Dusty Springfield.

Okay, so Launch has a lot of great features, but how does it make money? Launch makes its money through advertising on the site, and by offering to sell music and related products (like T-shirts). Launch chooses which products to offer by selecting products that are related to the music that is playing. Since users like the music, they are likely to be tempted by the products. Products featuring the Grateful Dead are offered when a Grateful Dead song is playing. In many cases, users don't even feel like they're being advertised to: It's just convenient that when a song you really like is playing, you are offered the chance to buy the CD. It helps immensely that these ads don't interrupt the music.

Recently Launch became part of Yahoo! Launch provides users

one more reason to stay at Yahoo!, increasing the value of the portal and the opportunity for advertising and direct sales.

TREAT CUSTOMERS AS INDIVIDUALS, NOT DEMOGRAPHICS

Launch takes what has historically been a broadcast medium and converts it into a personal medium. Each person hears exactly what she wants to hear. Play lists on radio have historically been targeted to capture a particular demographic and the music played to be acceptable to everyone in that demographic. Music that was on the edge of a demographic group's interests seldom, if ever, got played. Also, if a listener's tastes run outside of a particular genre, she had to switch stations.

Now, the possibility emerges of play lists that are targeted to an audience of one, and of advertising to that same audience of one. This wouldn't have been possible in the pre-Internet era for at least two reasons. One, there simply isn't enough bandwidth to send a special radio signal over the airwaves to everyone. Two, even if we could build radio stations like that, we don't have enough DJs to design play lists for every individual separately. Now we have the ability to use computer programs to create automatic play lists based on individual interests (that run *across* genres)—and the Internet to deliver it right to us no matter where we are.

INDIVIDUALS EVOLVE, AND SO SHOULD PERSONALIZATION

The preferences of Launch users help to establish recommendations for the fan stations. In addition, each individual Launch user becomes a DJ. Wouldn't it be nice to be able to listen to other DJs? Well, you can. Launch lets you listen in on other users' stations—featured DJs (who have rated over 2,000 songs and are given "addict" status), popular DJs, and recommended DJs (based on similarities with your preferences), in addition to friends' or family members' stations. These DJs expose you to music you might not otherwise think to request from Launch and that Launch might not recommend because of your genre and subgenre ratings.

PROVIDE REAL-TIME UPDATES

By listening to its users, Launch becomes an expert in their tastes in music. The user is happy to share information with Launch because the more information she shares, the better the job Launch does of selecting music to play. In fact, users love the opportunity to share their opinions with Launch. When a song they hate comes on, they quickly press the X on the Launch screen, which immediately stops the song and guarantees that the song will never be played for them again. If it's the artist they hate, they rate the artist low so that that artist will seldom if ever be played for them. Conversely, when music they like comes on, they rate it high so that they are likely to get a lot of that type of music.

Can you imagine how satisfying it is to press a button that banishes a hated song from ever being played on your radio station again? Now that's real-time personalization.

Business Applications

At music stores, customers often don't have the opportunity to listen to new CDs before they buy them. Their primary exposure to new CDs is likely through radio or the store's sound system. As a result, customers might not know or remember the name of the artist or song they hope to buy. They may buy the wrong album by mistake. Or they might not want to bother the person at the counter to find out what's playing on the store's speakers. Worse, they may never hear music they would really enjoy (due to traditional radio's tendency to overplay a small selection of popular artists). By allowing customers to buy music as they're listening to it, Launch increases the likelihood that they'll be satisfied. They have the band, album, and song name right in front of them. The sheer convenience of the transaction leads to more sales. The moral: *Recommenders will not only help increase the exposure of customers to your products, but they might also lead to more convenient purchasing.*

Learning your customers' individual preferences will allow you to target ads more precisely. Not only are Launch's ads directed to the customers most likely to appreciate them, but they're done in a way that isn't as intrusive as traditional radio ads (annoying pitches that prevent you from hearing music).

By satisfying all of their customers' music interests, Launch solves their industry's main business model problem: customers leaving when a song they don't like comes on. If you can present products to your customers that they like *all* the time, they won't leave. Consider, too, ways customers can prevent seeing products they have no interest in.

LAUNCH

RECOMMENDER(S): People-people matching (we think) with filtering to fit your rules (how much you like country music, no Mariah Carey) and theirs (can't play three selections from the same CD in a three-hour period).

INPUT(S): Ratings of songs, artists, albums, and other users.

OUTPUT(S): Music chosen for you with prediction and explanation ("Fans of Miles Davis recommend . . .").

LESSON: *Treating people as individuals can create radically new business opportunities. Also, super-targeted ads aren't annoying if the customer has rated that product highly— they're a beneficial service you provide.*

PRODUCT-OF-THE-MONTH CLUBS

W E HAVE ALL BEEN deluged by offers to "get 12 for a dollar!" All we have to do is "buy 3 more in the next 3 years!" Music clubs, book clubs, and a whole range of product-of-the-month clubs entice us with these or comparable promotional offers. Then comes the landslide of mailings: monthly buyer guides that include a "selection of the month" that will be sent automatically unless you explicitly decline it with a return postcard. In theory, these selections of the month are fantastic choices that you'll be thrilled to own. In practice, they're a pain in the ass.

We took three of the biggest product-of-the-month clubs (Columbia House, BMG, and Book of the Month Club) and examined their shipping practices, pricing strategies, and levels of personalization.

Shipping

Amazingly, BMG and Book of the Month Club (BOMC) still employ the automatic-shipment model. While built on the idea that automatic shipments force customers to make active decisions each month or buy by default (both of which increase revenue), customers loathe the model, in part because they often forget to send in the postcard and then have the inconvenience and expense of returning unwanted merchandise. BMG and BOMC credit you for the expense of returning the selection of the month, provided you do so within ten days, but the hassle is considerable nonetheless—fretting over the ten-day period, going to the post office to mail packages, and waiting to see if your account is, in fact, credited. No wonder customer attrition is high.

Thankfully, Columbia House offers an alternative. Customers simply have to purchase five regular-priced CDs over a two-year period. They don't automatically get sent CDs and they don't have to fill out postcards. Thank you! Finally, someone listened to the moans of all the little people!

Pricing

In terms of pricing, BMG, BOMC, and Columbia House all share the same model: providing a big up-front hook, followed by higher-than-discount-retail prices on the commitment-fulfilling purchases (once shipping and handling fees are included). BMG offers 12 CDs for the price of 1, BOMC offers 5 books for $1, and Columbia House offers 12 CDs for $11.88. The challenge of having higher-than-retail prices leads these and other product-of-the-month companies to offer a number of incentives, including discounted CDs and books that do not count toward the obligation and earned discount purchases with every full-price purchase.

Personalization

BMG offers only fourteen music genres for members to choose from, and they don't use any recommender technology in their on-line search function. Remember, too, that they automatically mail the selection of the month unless you tell them not to via postcard or E-mail. The likely result: You frequently receive products in the mail that you didn't ask for and don't like. Too bad.

BOMC approaches personalization from a different angle. They don't make personalized recommendations, but they do use cookies to customize their Web site based upon what books members put in their shopping baskets. That's a good thing because the site itself isn't the easiest to navigate. You can't search for a specific author or title without using an alphabet link. In other words, if you're looking for books by Don DeLillo, you have to scroll through all authors beginning with the letter D, and perhaps even hit links for subsequent D pages. Ordinarily, you might try to call or E-mail a customer-service rep for help if you couldn't find what you're look-ing for. Try again. Unless you're a member, BOMC doesn't grant access to the customer-service E-mail address and you have to look very hard to find a phone number. Hint: It isn't listed under the "How do I contact Customer Service?" FAQ (frequently asked questions).

With personalization, Columbia House is the closest to getting a gold star. On the Web, they recommend artists based upon your searches. If you enter David Bowie, for instance, Columbia House recommends thirty-one other bands—from ABC to Todd Rund-gren. Thirty-one bands is *way* too many, but at least they're throw-ing their hat in the recommender ring.

Off-line, Columbia House's personalization model is tradi-tional, coarse-grained segmentation. Members self-classify into one of seventeen genres of music (three more than BMG), which Columbia House calls "the music I like most." Selections of the month and the entire monthly catalog are customized for that genre. As a result, customers with tastes that nicely align with the provided genres may find a good set of music. Others with more eclectic tastes (someone who likes ballads, whether country, folk, rock, or otherwise, for example) are forced to place themselves in a category that doesn't fully represent their interests. Granted, members can always order CDs outside their preferred genre, but Columbia House's marketing efforts won't recognize these "out of the box" forays.

TREAT CUSTOMERS AS INDIVIDUALS, NOT DEMOGRAPHICS

Product-of-the-month clubs do so little to recognize individuals it's frightening. We should point out, however, that segmentation does allow product-of-the-month clubs to negotiate substantial volume deals on a particular item (which the Book of the Month club is famous for) and minimize the effort required to present related interviews and reviews. The great deals are the Faustian bargain that leads to ignoring the customer: Personalization would cost more. In some cases, technology is reducing the pain of this arrangement. The product-of-the-month club can press its own CDs or print its own books, and can make money on runs of hundreds instead of tens of thousands. Further, recommenders can now recommend people who are the best ones to receive a particular product from a small set of possible products (see "The Children's Place" in this chapter).

INDIVIDUALS EVOLVE, AND SO SHOULD PERSONALIZATION

Can product-of-the-month clubs profitably increase their level of personalization? We think so. Using collaborative filtering, they could avoid the loss of sales when the customer already owns the selection of the month and increase the success rate of customers liking and buying the promoted CD or book. This information could be gleaned from an implicit or explicit rating system, which these companies have yet to deploy. Columbia House, BMG, and BOMC all have tremendous customer information at their disposal; as a result, they would have absolutely no difficulty in finding nearest neighbors for their customers. Their recommendations would be spot-on. The selection of the month would be based on member taste, not rigid categories. At the very least, their catalogs could be made more modular without severely compromising efficiency, so a customer might get a selection of pages (country and gospel, for instance), rather than single-genre fare. We see personalization-of-the-month clubs on the horizon, but right now it's just a mirage.

PROVIDE REAL-TIME UPDATES

Product-of-the-month clubs are interested only in updating your bill. Well, that's not entirely fair. They do a decent job of updating information about their artists. They also do a good job of recommending primarily new items, so you're unlikely to have them yet. But there's no real way they can update your profile because they use such broad segmentation to begin with.

Business Applications

Marketers must choose the nature and level of personalization appropriate to their competitive position, customers, and industry. The product-of-the-month club pricing model attracts customers seeking a big discount up front, and hopes to keep them excited with a combination of appealing catalogs and promotional offers. Book and music retail stores, on the other hand, often receive customers who aren't willing to commit to a series of purchases and prefer the convenience and immediacy of a physical store.

Even if your business model appears to be set in stone, there may be ways to add personalization. For product-of-the-month clubs, customers might be willing to accept a monthly product shipped automatically if the product was generated through an effective recommender like collaborative filtering (remember the Dean & Deluca grab bags we mentioned at the end of our Priceline profile in "Principle #1: Demonstrate Product Expertise"). At the very least, personalization would create a competitive barrier. There are a lot of people willing to jump ship from the clubs we mention here when they see a better ship leaving port. Maybe the business-model problem wasn't the automatic shipments and postcard responses; maybe the problem was poor matching of customers to products!

PRODUCT-OF-THE-MONTH CLUBS

RECOMMENDER(S): Manually edited.

INPUT(S): Genres (for music clubs).

OUTPUT(S): One primary recommendation for genre listeners (or one primary recommendation for the whole club, in the case of BOMC).

LESSON: *Giving everybody the same product is like giving everybody oatmeal.*

Principle #4: Box Products, Not People

Quick Tips

- Demographics can be self-fulfilling prophesies.
- The more information you collect, the harder it is for competitors to steal your customers and the greater the value of your service (DoubleClick and Angara).
- Networks allow for better personalization and inventory management (DoubleClick and Angara).
- There's a fine line between recognizing your customers ("Hello, John") and being overly aggressive ("I know what you did last summer"). Allow your customers to opt out of data collection (DoubleClick and Angara).
- Angara can help Web sites recognize individuals who've never even been to their sites before. Can you recognize these potential customers?
- Install a control group so that you can identify customers who have been placed in the wrong demographic (Angara).

- Recommendation engines can plug in products, get people, and clear inventory (The Children's Place).
- Personalized recommendations not only increase conversion rates, they often vastly increase total sales (The Children's Place).
- If it's what your customer wants, it's not spam. The Children's Place increased their conversion rate (over eleven times the industry average) *and* average basket-size orders.
- Allow customers to control how much of the unknown they're exposed to. With Launch.com, you can dictate how much new music gets played.
- Customers love the "Never again" option. Allowing customers to rate items they like works well. Too few businesses allow customers to rate items they don't like. Take a tip from Launch.com here.
- If you can present your customers with products they like *all* the time, they won't leave (Launch).
- Recommenders will not only help increase the exposure of customers to your products, but they might also lead to more convenient purchasing (Launch).
- Advertising doesn't have to be intrusive. If you provide an enjoyable experience, allowing customers to sample your products, they will appreciate the opportunity to buy these or related products (Launch).
- Segmenting customers has its liabilities (product-of-the-month clubs)—do you listen to just one genre of music?
- Even if your business relies upon bulk volume purchases, you can still personalize your offerings (product-of-the-month clubs). Don't be a slave to your business model.
- Allow customers to self-select into more than one genre or product category (product-of-the-month clubs).

At the beginning of this chapter, we quoted Tennessee Williams: "Caged birds accept each other but flight is what they long for." Your customers long for flight. They don't want to be placed into cells where they don't belong.

If you've been a member of a product-of-the-month club, recall how irritating it is to have to send in postcards and return products that were sent automatically. That's the feeling customers have when they're fed advertising and products they're not interested in.

Learn about your customers, personalize well, and you'll become a desired destination, not a cage.

Interlude #4: Bringing Customers Back

With few exceptions, businesses depend on repeat customers for the majority of their revenues. They want customers back in the place, virtual or physical, where shopping happens. How can businesses bring back customers who've lapsed? How can they increase the frequency with which a customer visits them?

Amazon.com invests heavily in bringing customers back, since they know that customers won't just stumble across their shop in a mall. They offer a wide selection of newsletters, on topics ranging from children's books to cooking to toys for grown-ups. Customers subscribe to newsletters that interest them (an example of permission marketing); and if a book or product does interest them, one click takes them to that product on Amazon's Web site, where Amazon hopes they will not only buy it but also browse for other products. A more personal, and for us more effective, feature is Amazon Eyes. Joe stumbled across this feature when looking for books by Tracy Kidder, one of his favorite authors. Amazon asked if he wanted to be notified when new books matched his current search. He agreed, and now he gets notified any time a new Tracy Kidder book is released. While more than half of his notices are releases of new editions (large print, on tape, et cetera), every two years or so he hears about the next Tracy Kidder book. One click later, he's on Amazon and ready to buy.

Both editors' newsletters and Eyes are good examples of bringing customers back, but each could be better if they incorporated the recommender technology Amazon already has. How about a "newsletter for me" that selects from across Amazon's bounty of newsletters to pick the set of books, toys, and other products I'd most likely like? Or a "far-sighted" version of Eyes that would find "close matches" as well, helping Joe get through the two-year drought between Tracy Kidder books (and perhaps helping him find the "next Tracy Kidder").

Bringing customers back has three key elements: finding an enticing item, making it easy to follow the item into the "store," and making sure the store has other enticing items nearby to attract additional sales. Amazon does well on all three, but the company could do better by personalizing its offerings with a recommender.

Watch What I Do

No one means all he says, and yet very few say all they mean,
for words are slippery and thought is viscous.

—HENRY BROOKS ADAMS (1838–1918)

The most important thing in communication is to
hear what isn't being said.

—PETER DRUCKER

ACTIONS SPEAK LOUDER than words. People ask "What have you *done* for me lately?" not "What have you *said* for me lately?" Actions are hard data. And data is what makes recommender engines like collaborative filtering churn.

In this chapter we'll teach you how to interpret the actions of your customers so that you can make accurate recommendations. It's often more difficult than it might seem. First of all, actions come in many different forms: written communication, purchases, page visits, items placed in a shopping cart, and more. Second, customers have multiple personalities. At work they may purchase accounting books. At home they may buy science fiction.

How do you know which purchases to base your recommendations on? The trickiest actions to interpret, however, may come from customers or competitors who are trying to undermine your efforts for self-serving purposes.

When making recommendations, it's important to remember three things:

1. Actions speak louder than words.
2. Determine actions by context.
3. Respond to customers' reactions to your recommendations.

1. Actions speak louder than words. Do you always say what you're really thinking? If you did, you'd wind up with the bruises and casts that Jim Carrey gets in *Liar, Liar,* where his son's birthday wish condemned him to a life of brutal honesty.

Don't expect your customers to be honest with you—verbally. Most people, especially those of us in the Midwest, tell people what they want to hear: "Sure, I liked your velour teddy-bear tea caddies." "No, the bacon-wrapped carrots look good. I'm just not hungry." In conversation with your customers, you just can't count on honesty. Their motives may range from not wanting to insult you to not wanting to look stupid to wanting to get a free sample. It takes effort to complain, and sometimes people just don't want to commit to that effort unless there's clearly something in it for them. Sometimes, too, customers just don't know what they want.

If you ask someone in the grocery store which soft drink they like better, Pepsi or Coke, they may try to imagine your stake in the issue and respond accordingly. They might try to beat the system, in other words. But customers aren't likely to buy products they don't want just to manipulate a recommender system. As they're purchasing items, they're not thinking "If I buy this, what am I going to be recommended in the future?"

In many cases, you're better off studying customer actions rather than verbal input. Written comments, purchases, page views, and items placed in shopping baskets are usually quite accurate indicators of a customer's interests. They're not infallible, but they are far better than verbal commitments because they reflect time, energy, and money spent by your customers.

2. *Determine actions by context.* Seeing through misleading or contradictory information is no easy task. DoubleClick and Angara know where people go on the Web, but they don't always know *why* they go there. Just because I click on a sweater at Nordstrom doesn't necessarily mean I'm interested in it. In fact, I could choose to see a larger image of it because I think it's hideous.

Over time, customers' preferences rise to the surface. Sophisticated recommenders may take preemptive measures, however, so that the data pool isn't skewed. They may weed out aberrations. Sometimes they will allow customers themselves the opportunity to correct mistaken assumptions, especially in the case of gift purchases. If the customer enters a different delivery address other than the one they've stored in their profile, for instance, recommenders may ask the customer if that item is a gift, or simply ignore that purchase when making recommendations.

Two sites that we profile in this chapter, Google and PHOAKS, use even more sophisticated measures to detect red herrings—and they do it without burdening customers with extra work. Their success lies in their ability to determine honest actions using automatic algorithms. PHOAKS screens out thinly veiled advertisements from its newsgroup messages and Google ranks the importance of all the sites on the Web in order to generate better-quality search results. From their examples, you may get some ideas about how you can control both your data pool and the recommendations you give your customers.

3. *Respond to customers' reactions to your recommendations.* Companies often forget that their responsibilities continue after they've made a recommendation. As a result, they miss a terrific opportunity to learn whether their recommendations have succeeded.

Waiters are trained to check back on tables a few minutes after they've delivered the food in case customers need ketchup or silverware. Good businesses do the same.

BizTravel was a Web-based travel agency for business travelers that kept an extensive list of travel preferences for users. BizTravel watched what customers did, but it did painfully little about it. For example, if your profile indicated that you liked a window seat yet for twenty flights in a row you changed the request to an aisle seat, the next time you booked a flight you were still set for window. This level of monitoring is not hard to carry out (both travel agents and airlines now offer to update your profile when something you request doesn't match it), but BizTravel didn't make this effort. Today they're out of business.

In this chapter we examine companies that use the actions of their customers to create more valuable services. They don't take people at their word. They take action.

PHOAKS

P HOAKS (www.phoaks.com) stands for "People Helping One Another Know Stuff." The system, developed by Loren Terveen and Will Hill at AT&T Research, helps visitors identify useful sites in Usenet News. Usenet News is an Internet-based discussion forum with tens of thousands of "newsgroups," which discuss topics ranging from quantum physics to *Buffy the Vampire Slayer*.

Let's say you want to find helpful sites on windsurfing. From the PHOAKS directory, following the recreation heading (*rec@*), you'll find windsurfing listed among fifty or so other activities and hobbies. By clicking the windsurfing link, you'll be presented with the windsurfing sites that visitors have found most helpful.

So how does PHOAKS collect this information? They could ask Usenet visitors to rate sites. Or they could have an editorial staff evaluate all the sites in certain domains, like progressive activism and survivalism (two topics listed in PHOAKS's directory). But that would cost a lot of money and take an excruciatingly long time. By the time these editors posted their results, the sites might be out of date or better sites might have cropped up.

ACTIONS SPEAK LOUDER THAN WORDS

Instead of asking visitors how they liked certain sites, PHOAKS examines what they do. Namely, what they post in their newsgroup messages. Amazingly, these messages are all processed automatically—through a statistical summarization recommender. So roughly 4,000 new opinions are added daily without having to hire a slew of editors.

But how does PHOAKS know whether these newsgroup messages are legitimate? And how do they rank the opinions?

DETERMINE ACTIONS BY CONTEXT

First, PHOAKS scans all newsgroup messages, looking for Web page URLs. Then PHOAKS employs a substantial number of endorsement-recognizing filters. For example, URLs that appear in a message's "signature" or that point to a page on the message-sender's own site are not considered endorsements, since they are too likely to be either identification or self-serving. Likewise, PHOAKS filters out .announce, .answers, .jobs, or .binaries groups since they don't provide helpful opinions. PHOAKS also checks to make sure the URL isn't mentioned in a negative context (e.g., "Never go to http://www.badsite.com") and that it isn't left over in the text of a message being replied to.

Once all of the endorsements are collected, PHOAKS ranks sites based on the number of endorsements from distinct individuals. The sites are then presented on a page that shows both the number and the date of endorsements. Curious PHOAKS users can even click through to see a copy of the endorsement to try to understand why users liked the site. (Zagat on the Web, which we profiled in "Principle #3: Maintain Excellent Service Across Touchpoints," would benefit greatly from this ability.)

RESPOND TO CUSTOMERS' REACTIONS TO YOUR RECOMMENDATIONS

Visitors can E-mail thefolks@phoaks.com with their reactions to the PHOAKS site recommendations or respond to the PHOAKS survey (with lots of space for written comments) through the Pheedback link. Since the site recommendations aren't generated by PHOAKS personnel, however, visitors probably learn more from reading users' messages that mentioned the Web sites.

Business Applications

By watching what people do, PHOAKS solves two problems. First, they reduce the effort of gathering ratings to zero. People naturally mention Web sites in their messages. Second, they increase the honesty of the system. By tying recommendations to actions taken in a visible community, they make it much less likely that users will try to cheat the system (by recommending bad sites, for example). Since each user's vote counts only once, a single recommendation is unlikely to make much of a difference. And a string of messages from heretofore unknown users (particularly with similar E-mail services) would look suspicious and probably lead people to doubt the veracity of the recommendations.

PHOAKS illustrates how idle on-line chatter can become valuable. The folks at PHOAKS didn't have to reinvent the wheel. They used a pre-established Web community and built their service around it. Are there fan clubs, book clubs, and other sources that might form a basis for recommendations for you? By examining their natural interaction, you might also be able to gather data for collaborative filtering.

PHOAKS

RECOMMENDER(S): Statistical summarization over self-defined community.

INPUT(S): Text articles.

OUTPUT(S): Ranked listing of recommended sites by number of recommendations, dates, and text messages (can be pulled by users).

LESSON: *Look for pre-established communities that might form a basis for recommendations.*

GOOGLE

F OUNDED IN 1998 by Larry Page and Sergey Brin, Google has become one of the most popular search engines, handling more than 120 million searches a day. With thousands of networked PCs, Google speeds search results back to users in a fraction of a second. Pretty impressive considering Google boasts an index of 1.6 billion URLs.

Google prides itself on its bare-bones home page: lots of white space and a simple search box. Don't be fooled into thinking that there's not much going on beneath the surface, however. With their Advanced Search options, users can search according to language, date, and part of the page where the word (title, URL, etc.) appears. Google also enables users to search strictly for images and filter out adult material if they're so inclined. Under the Preferences link, Google offers a machine-technology translation device that will convert Italian, French, Spanish, German, or Portuguese pages into English. So if your high school Spanish is a bit rusty, not to worry. Google even keeps copies of the pages it indexes so users can retrieve the contents even if the site is temporarily (or permanently) off-line.

All of these features are customer friendly, but what makes Google special is their PageRank system. Like many search engines, Google ranks pages using keywords. You type in keywords and Google returns the pages that contain these keywords, ranked in order from the best match down. What distinguishes Google from the rest, though, is that they also rank pages according to how important they are within the Web. Of course, importance on the

Web is difficult to define, and it's even more difficult to compute across all the billions of Web pages available today.

ACTIONS SPEAK LOUDER THAN WORDS

Google uses a very clever approximating technique to estimate importance: The more sites that link to your page, the more important you are. In addition, Google counts links to your page that come from other pages that are themselves highly rated. So if Bill Gates chooses to link his page to yours, that's taken as a very strong indication of the importance of your page. If your credit's good with Bill, it's good with us. The end result of these credit checks is that overall search quality improves. You don't get middle-school science projects ranked highly when you search for "atomic particles." Instead, you're more apt to see something from the Fermilab.

Google doesn't respond to their customers' actions as much as they respond to the actions of the Web-authoring public at large. By analyzing link structures, Google vastly improves its page recommendations to users. In effect, they combine actions (links) with words (keywords entered by the user).

DETERMINE ACTIONS BY CONTEXT

The preferences and search options we described above allow users to dictate the parameters of their search. In very subtle ways, though, Google intercedes on the user's behalf. If users enter a street address and a city or ZIP code, for instance, Google places a street map at the top of its page rankings. Likewise, if a user enters a stock-ticker symbol, Google returns with a stock quote, assuming that is what the customer is looking for. Google even corrects spelling and doesn't let capitalization throw it off course.

RESPOND TO CUSTOMERS' REACTIONS TO YOUR RECOMMENDATIONS

In many ways, PageRank evolved out of the shortcomings of pure keyword text analysis. Web pages can manipulate simple keyword searches, so the recommendations that users receive aren't always very helpful. You wind up with too many middle-school reports or thinly veiled advertisements.

Google's approach is still subject to certain types of attack. For instance, a user who wants his page to appear artificially important can create a whole bunch of other pages and link them to his page. Google uses algorithms that try to prevent this sort of ballot-box stuffing. The specific algorithms change as users find ever more sophisticated ways of trying to trick Google. Co-citations are hard for Google to stop, however. For instance, our research Web site gets frequent E-mails from other movie sites saying they've linked to us and asking us to link back to them.

Could Google return more personalized searches? We can imagine a search engine that not only weighed the importance of Web pages in its algorithm, but also weighed pages preferred by the individual user. If a user liked ESPN, for instance, the pages linked to ESPN would become higher-weighted. In addition, Google could use collaborative filtering to upgrade (or downgrade) pages based on the opinions of others.

Business Applications

The barriers to publication are gone, resulting in an abundance of content on the Web. The problem is finding high-quality content. From Google, it's clear that accessing this content takes a higher level of problem-solving initiative than simple text analysis. Google uses community actions to determine a quality hierarchy, and then incorporates the results into their searches.

Here, then, are a few things to consider:

1. How do customers find you on the Web? How well linked are you?
2. Does your search engine return the products the customer is looking for? Does it anticipate the customer's desires— the way Google does with stock symbols, street addresses, and other "clues"?
3. Have you taken steps to avoid being manipulated?

GOOGLE

RECOMMENDER(S): Statistical summary of ratings (importance of a site determined by number and quality of links).

INPUT(S): Links between Web sites.

OUTPUT(S): Ranking of sites generated through keyword searches.

LESSON: *Take steps to avoid being manipulated.*

AMAZON.COM

A MAZON.COM is a remarkable success story—an on-line bookseller that has not only survived but thrived in competition with its brick-and-mortar adversaries. Book buyers are accustomed to flipping through books before buying; they are used to large stores with an excellent selection of books, all carefully arranged to call their attention to popular ones. How Amazon has succeeded in this environment is a story reported in many fine books and articles. In essence, they capitalized on the declining service in many bookstores by providing easy-to-use interfaces for browsing and searching; extensive information about the books they carry; and community features such as book reviews and author chats. It also helps that they carry virtually every book that can be sold.

Another hallmark of Amazon is their extensive use of recommender systems, which learn from both customer actions and explicit customer ratings. From the home page forward, Amazon customizes the books and other products it suggests based on each customer's profile. Amazon recommends books (overall and within departments), authors, music, films, artists, directors, and other products and talent. Amazon also offers a wealth of features to help customers build and maintain their profiles. In this section, we focus particularly on those profile maintenance tools, as they show that Amazon has learned an important lesson about watching what their customers do.

ACTIONS SPEAK LOUDER THAN WORDS

How does Amazon learn which books, music, videos, and other products its customers prefer? Do they simply ask customers to rate them? At first they did, but for several years they've known that customers don't generally rate enough items to build good profiles. So now Amazon combines purchase data with explicit ratings. When Joe looked at his Amazon profile, he found that only about 20 percent of the items were there because he rated them; the other 80 percent were items he'd bought, some of which he subsequently also rated. In this case, actions (purchases) speak louder than words (ratings) because there is no immediate reward for rating items. The reward for buying, however, is a package arriving on your doorstep a few days later.

DETERMINE ACTIONS BY CONTEXT

We've often heard people complain that "Amazon's recommendations aren't very good." A friend of ours was recommended *Final Exit: The Practicalities of Self-Deliverance and Assisted Suicide for the Dying* while shopping for William Styron's *Darkness Visible*—a book about coping with depression. While neither of us has been encouraged to commit suicide, we too have experienced rather poor recommendations (alongside excellent ones).

In the past, without access to the internals of Amazon's system, we had to do our best to reverse-engineer the cause of odd recommendations. For the most part, we sensed the problems arose due to context. Joe noticed that he was receiving odd (and low-quality) recommendations for movies and music. When he looked at his profile, he saw only books (he hasn't ordered other products from Amazon). Apparently his book tastes are not good predictors of his music or movie tastes, even though they lead to good recommendations of other books. This isn't surprising. If you find a hundred people who share your taste in books, what percentage will also share your taste in music? Will it even be better than chance?

Amazon has no mechanism for recognizing the different roles that the same customer may play in making different purchases from their site. John plays three very different roles: as a professor, he buys mostly technical, computer science books; as a father, he buys mostly children's books; and as a gift-giver, he buys whatever seems best for the recipient. Notice the problem. If you try to mix all three of these together, you get an odd mishmash: Is John an eclectic computer prodigy who is otherwise still a child? Or a child-at-heart computer professional? And what of those gift books, some of which he'd never want to read himself? Clearly, Amazon could benefit from some explicit, and implicit, role identification. John should be able to note "this is a gift" and have the purchase excluded from his profile. Perhaps he should be encouraged to identify a couple of roles, so his children's book tastes don't lead him to see *Windows XP for Teenagers* when he's looking for technical books.

Thankfully, Amazon has recently added a new feature called "Why was I recommended this?" If a customer is curious about the recommendation process, Amazon tells her which other items in her profile were most influential in the recommendation. This can help in several ways. If Joe, for instance, sees that a book was recommended because of the Tracy Kidder books he likes, he may be more willing to take a chance on it. If John sees that he's being recommended a business book based on the books he bought for his children, he will realize that the match may not be so good. If Joe gets music recommendations based on the books he's bought, he may decide he needs to rate more music to get better recommendations.

RESPOND TO CUSTOMERS' REACTIONS TO YOUR RECOMMENDATIONS

While Amazon occasionally strikes out when carrying their recommendations too far afield or when ignoring the purchase context, they do an excellent job of helping their customers get back "on base." The recommendation center provides feedback on just what is the customer's profile (how many items, and how many of these are explicitly rated) and has a big link to follow to "improve your recommendations." This link leads to an interface that allows you to examine your profile, add or change ratings for items in it, delete items from it (gifts, for instance), and rate additional books. And the customer presumably has an incentive to cooperate here, since they've already expressed an interest in improving their recommendations. Other parts of Amazon's interface have easy rating opportunities as well. Customers can rate any product (though often it seems to take too many clicks to do so) and can, of course, buy it as well (the reaction Amazon would most like!).

Business Applications

Throughout their store, Amazon watches what people do. The next step, perhaps, would be to incorporate more tentative feedback. Which books do people spend time reading samples from? Which suggestions sent by e-mail led customers to follow links back to the store? We expect that Amazon is already collecting this data, if they follow their past patterns, and will improve their targeting of recommendations and the customer's experience. After all, nobody browses through *Books in Print* to buy a book; with so many choices, people need help—they need recommendations.

AMAZON

RECOMMENDER(S): Too many to list. On our last visit, we counted 23 separate recommenders.

INPUT(S): Current navigation, history of purchases, and explicit ratings.

OUTPUT(S): Product recommendations.

LESSON: *A bad recommendation is a learning opportunity.*

MY YAHOO!

GOOGLE'S SEARCH PERFORMANCE is unparalleled, but it doesn't offer the personalized features that the heavyweight portals do. Yahoo, Excite, MSN, Netscape Netcenter, and AOL keep piling up user options. At My Yahoo!, users can select a variety of different channels for each page: headlines, weather, stocks, TV listings, personal calendar, E-mail, horoscope, and much more. Within many of these channels, the user can further customize the content, selecting the sources and topics of headlines, the region for weather and news, favorite teams for sports, and which local cinema listings to display. My Yahoo!'s options extend to the display of the page itself. Users can choose the background colors and themes, change the layout from two columns to three, and arrange the items on their page in the order they want them to appear from top to bottom.

By allowing users to check E-mail, pay bills, listen to Internet radio stations, purchase anything from CDs to jewelry, and read articles from *E! Online News* to the *New York Times,* portals like My Yahoo! take care of virtually all your needs. Why would you need to go anywhere else?

ACTIONS SPEAK LOUDER THAN WORDS

At My Yahoo!, users select all their preferences. They choose which sports scores to display, what news articles from which news organizations, even what comics. So what's the point in making recommendations to these users? This is the trap that My Yahoo! falls into.

There are several reasons why recommenders should be used, even when customers select their own preferences. For one, recommendations can be used to notify users when new material is made available. My Yahoo! has a New on My Yahoo! section displayed on the front page of its portal, but these are generic recommendations. There's no "my" feel at all, since the recommendations are made to everyone. Joe subscribed to all of the Minnesota professional sports channels (football, baseball, and basketball) long ago. When the Minnesota Wild (a new hockey team) started, My Yahoo! had a new channel for the team and the ability to display its games in its scoreboard. It never even mentioned it. Joe also subscribed to the only local news channel for Minneapolis/St. Paul. Recently, he noticed that the site had added a new, second source for local news. Did My Yahoo! ever let him know? No.

Recommendations can also help customers understand their interests better. Just because a My Yahoo! user doesn't choose to display Ellen Goodman's columns doesn't mean he wouldn't like them. He might not have ever read her work. Either by directly asking users or by inference from the channels selected, My Yahoo! could recommend new channels.

RESPOND TO CUSTOMERS' REACTIONS TO YOUR RECOMMENDATIONS

Whether it realizes it or not, My Yahoo! recommends articles to its users. Unfortunately, it doesn't properly analyze and respond to the actions users take with these articles. At the least it would be useful to have an option that removes articles you've already read, not only from the category where you read it, but also from all of the other categories where the same article may appear (this is common when subscribing to, for example, US News and "Top Stories," which overlap heavily). Even better would be replacing the already-read article with another article to read, so there is always new content, even when you've read the "top three" stories in an area. You can always get back to articles you've read by clicking on the header. But how about going all the way to real personalization? Why not take the next step and learn from the articles the user chooses to read? If the user selects a variety of articles on a topic, the system could recommend additional articles, or even a channel on that topic. If the user never reads any of the auto-racing articles in sports, maybe the system should offer to filter them out. My Yahoo! could also learn to interpret actions (through, for example, tracking links followed) in context (perhaps morning, afternoon, and evening) so that it could recognize and react to different patterns of usage, even for a single user. My Yahoo!, and all the portal sites, have access to vast stores of information about their member interests. They can (and often do) use this information to target advertising more accurately. Isn't it time for them to apply the same information to better personalize the portal itself?

Business Applications

Because My Yahoo! doesn't learn from individual users' preferences and actions, users don't get the benefit of timely recommendations. And My Yahoo! doesn't benefit from the extra advertising they would receive from users' missed page views. Worse, dissatisfied users might leave for another portal, not realizing that the content they want is actually available (such as Minnesota Wild scores).

Customers do want offers delivered to them—if the offers reflect their demonstrated interests. They don't want to have to update their preference options weekly just to see if there's something they might be missing. They might as well change portals or companies.

A business that learns its customers' preferences at the outset but doesn't bother to incorporate subsequent interactions doesn't maintain its level of service. It gets progressively worse. Recommendations need to improve over time. Even if your customers don't know about collaborative filtering, they can sense whether or not you're watching what they do.

Learn from your customers' actions. Recommend new products that they'll be interested in as they come out. And don't be afraid to recommend additional products as you learn more about your customers' tastes.

MY YAHOO!

RECOMMENDER(S): None. My Yahoo! simply turns home-page preferences into a customized newspaper.

RECOMMENDER OPPORTUNITY: My Yahoo! could convert users' explicit preferences and the actions they take with their customized newspaper into recommendations for new features and/or articles.

LESSON: *Personalizing in a dynamic environment requires dynamic updating.*

Principle #5: Watch What I Do

Quick Tips

- Look for pre-established communities that might form a basis for recommendations (PHOAKS).
- Cheat-proof your ratings system. Google uses the number of links, not keywords, and links from high-ranking sites to rank pages. PHOAKS filters out signatures.
- Generating ratings for customers can be effortless. They can be done automatically by analyzing keywords or links (PHOAKS, Google).
- Explain your data-collection methods (PHOAKS, Google).
- Allow access to the source of recommendations so visitors can judge for themselves whether the reviewer should be trusted (PHOAKS).
- Anticipate your customers' intentions. Google displays maps when a user searches for a city.
- Correct your customers' mistakes. Google works around misspellings and capitalization inconsistencies.
- Combine ratings with purchases data (Amazon).
- Tastes don't always run across product divisions. People who share musical tastes may not share the same literary sensibilities (Amazon).
- Allow customers access to *full* profiles, so that they can understand how recommendations are made. Then make it easy for them to improve their recommendations (Amazon).

- Explain recommendations to customers (Amazon).
- Don't require customers to update their profiles continuously, but help them do so when they wish (My Yahoo!).
- Too many portals and E-commerce sites allow customers to select personalized content but then fail to follow up. Don't wait for customers to realize what's missing or broken. By then they may have left your service. Personalizing in a dynamic environment requires dynamic updating (My Yahoo!).

When it comes to recommending, don't take your customers' word for what they like. Take their actions. Then watch to see if your customers really do appreciate your recommendations. The recommendation process doesn't end, at least not as long as you create new products and services. It's an action/reaction cycle: Recommend; watch; recommend; watch; recommend. The more you watch, the better your recommendations become.

Interlude #5: Privacy

When Lorrie Faith Cranor, Joseph Reagle, and Mark S. Ackerman surveyed Web users to learn how they felt about privacy, they discovered that many users are aware that data is being collected about them. Many users are okay with this, provided the data is not personally identifiable. Different types of personally identifiable data are viewed as more invasive: giving an E-mail address, for instance, is less invasive than giving a phone number. The key to users' comfort, though, is what will be done with the data. Most users are comfortable giving information to a business in order to receive better, more personalized service. However, users almost universally dislike giving away information that might be passed along to other businesses to send them unsolicited offers.

If you want to reap the benefits of collaborative filtering, you must address privacy issues head-on. First, you must make sure to receive appropriate permission from your customers. In many parts of the world it is sufficient just to offer an option for customers to "opt out" if they do not want you to keep data about them, but in an increasing number of places you must explicitly ask permission before requesting, using, or keeping any data about visitors to your site. Complicating matters even more, your practices may need to take into account where the data is stored, where the customer lives, and where the interaction center is located.

For concerns specific to your business, you'll need to speak with legal professionals, but in general, we advocate the following philosophy: Communicate to your customers what data you collect, why you collect it, and what you will do with it. Be responsible with their data. Don't do anything with your customers' information that you would be embarrassed about if they knew you were doing it. If you want trust, you must be trustworthy.

Emerging technology may make this balancing act easier. The Platform for Privacy Preferences Project (P3P) is designed to be integrated into browsers to let users easily manage relationships with multiple Web sites and identify what types of information they are willing to share with each site. When a user arrives at a Web site, the site queries the browser to ask what information the user is willing to share. P3P negotiates with the site according to its privacy policy, and shares with it only information the user is comfortable sharing at that level of privacy. For instance, a trusted site that promises never to send unsolicited marketing material and never to sell its data to a third party may get personal information about what kind of music the user likes so it can create a more personalized experience for the user. On the other hand, an untrusted site that does sell data to third parties might receive no information— and might even have its cookies blocked when it asks the browser to store them. P3P is in its infancy, so it is too early to tell how well it will do in practice, but the technology is a step forward for user management of privacy.

As a society, we are just beginning to craft new understandings of privacy that fit the electronic age. Technology has created new privacy challenges by making easy what was once impossible. Now, new technology is emerging that may help us regain control of privacy in the digital age. The successful retailer will watch closely the emerging privacy initiatives, and work to make sure that customers always know their privacy is respected and protected.

Revolutionize Knowledge Management

> You never know till you try to reach them how accessible men are; but you must approach each man by the right door.
>
> —HENRY WARD BEECHER (1813–1887)

ET'S SAY YOU'RE a heart-valve manufacturer and you've got a seal problem with your current proto-type. You want to try to find a solution, and try to find an expert. Would you realize that the expert you want works in submarine technology? How long will it take you to find that person?

What if you manufacture roadside flares and your flares are burning too quickly? Would you think to call a tobacco consultant who works with a coated cardboard substrate that could solve your "slow burn" problems?

Intota, a division of Sopheon, solved both of these problems. Intota's Internet service supplies companies with the experts and expertise they need in over 33,000 specific areas of science, business, and technology. Intota solves problems quickly—often within hours. If you need esoteric knowledge, Intota's a good place to go, since they have a huge database of experts in just about every imaginable field—and they guarantee your satisfaction. You simply type keywords into their search engine and up pop expert bios and the opportunity to reach these experts by phone or E-mail.

Often times, though, the knowledge or expertise you need is housed within your own company. The problem is that the right person to contact is sometimes as hard to find as a "slow burn" expert or a submarine technician. If your company consists of only ten employees, you're in luck. Or if you play racquetball with someone in the potato-chip division, she might be able to direct you to the person you should talk to. If you work in a large global corporation, though, and can't depend on serendipity to deliver experts to you, you're out of luck. You might end up paying an outside expert, or an expert-locating service like Intota, to find information you already have at your disposal. That can be as frustrating as it is costly.

Thankfully, the end is in sight. Now employees in your company can use collaborative filtering to find each other and the information they need. No more duplication of effort and expense. No more aggravating hours on the phone following dead-end leads. No more out-of-date databases.

For most of this book, we've talked about how recommenders can be used to provide personalized products and services to your customers. Well, it only stands to reason that you can use recommenders in your own workplace. Turn the recommenders inward and find out what you're missing: personalized E-mail, a dynamic database, and expertise on demand.

In this chapter we show how Tacit mines E-mail to uncover knowledge communities. Procter & Gamble demonstrates how collaborative filtering can help employees discover documents and experts using public-work products. ReferralWeb reveals the personal connections employees might use in order to reach an expert. And MITRE studies the actions of every employee to establish personalized training programs.

All four of the systems we profile in this chapter adhere to the following maxims:

1. Information pathways and employment hierarchies are different.
2. Identify expertise and employee relationships using work by-products.
3. Knowledge is a product.

1. Information pathways and employment hierarchies are different. The people with the knowledge you need may be anywhere in the corporation. If Greg needs to contact Laura about the dishwashing-detergent line, he simply calls her up, right? In reality, it's often not that easy. Laura may have been reassigned to a different department. Greg may have to settle for a new hire who isn't up to speed on the competition. Or he may call Laura's superior, who doesn't want to admit that Laura knows more than he does. Greg may never reach Laura. Following the employment chain, up and down, until you find the information you need can be exasperating or, worse, completely unproductive.

If information is distributed only according to employment hierarchies, business grinds to a standstill. Just as every department may have someone who needs to know about personnel policies, so might many departments have people who need to know about the company's Asia efforts, even when these people all report to different managers and vice presidents. If information is disseminated only from the top down, it never reaches the right people in time.

Information is created and discovered by each and every employee, and only a small fraction of that information rises to the top of an employment hierarchy. Information doesn't like to move vertically. It doesn't really like to move laterally, either. It likes to sit and gather dust. Occasionally it moves around, but the direction it flows in is often unpredictable.

2. Identify expertise and employee relationships using work by-products. People don't like to enter or update profile information. Period. It's work that always gets pushed to the back burner. As a result, conventional databases are often out of date and incomplete. This leads to more procrastination on the part of employees in entering documents or profile information. Why be vigilant when the rewards are so meager?

The systems we examine in this chapter study the work that employees produce so that employees don't have to register and update their interests explicitly. It's a seemingly small change, but databases are revitalized in the process. All of a sudden, Greg finds Laura. Not tomorrow, not next week—now. She's recommended to him because their common interests have been identified automatically.

Customers' interests are identified by their activity on Web pages, their purchases, and their reactions to recommendations. Employees' interests are identified by their written work, time spent on certain documents, and the people they've worked with, among other ways.

The results are astounding. Not only do your employees find the people and expertise they need, they also establish relationships that will help set the groundwork for future collaborations.

3. *Knowledge is a product.* Knowledge comes in a variety of forms: training programs, expert identification, document retrieval, and many others. If it's not personalized, however, your employees may not want it. Think about how you feel when you get yet another all-employee memo discussing matters that have nothing to do with you. Unpersonalized knowledge may not be worth your employees' time and effort. In some cases, they might as well just work to discover the knowledge they need for themselves. The result: You end up paying for the same work to be done twice, if not many more times.

Naturally, privacy concerns are raised any time personal information is collected. Your employees deserve assurances that the information they're contributing will be used *for* them, not *against* them. Knowledge-management systems (with and without the use of recommenders) need to be explicit about the information they collect and the ways it will be employed. In this chapter, we'll show you how to negotiate these delicate issues.

TACIT.COM

O N THEIR WEB SITE, Tacit cites a study of global companies that revealed that 88 percent of employees didn't feel they had access to lessons learned by their co-workers. Seventy percent of those polled felt that company knowledge wasn't reused. By 2003, Tacit estimates that the average annual cost for re-creation of work will reach $5,850 per employee.

By incorporating all published and unpublished documents that a company creates into its knowledge-management system, Tacit aims to reduce this amount of rework (and the resulting cost to companies). What makes Tacit particularly notable, and controversial, however, is their decision to mine employees' personal E-mail exchanges.

IDENTIFY EXPERTISE AND EMPLOYEE RELATIONSHIPS USING WORK BY-PRODUCTS

No CEO is going to spend hours preparing a profile of his interests, much less updating it every month or so. Knowledge systems that assume that each user is going to create and manage his or her own profile often fail because users don't take the time to keep the profile up to date. Over time, the relevance of discovered information deteriorates as people's interests change.

Tacit solves these problems by automatically discovering the profiles of users based on their behavior. Users just keep reading, writing, and sending their E-mail messages as they ordinarily would. Meanwhile, Tacit captures two types of knowledge: *explicit knowledge* (knowledge that has been written down, captured, and stored in the knowledge-management repository) and *tacit knowledge* (knowledge that is in people's brains but not in the knowledge-management system).

The repeated use of words and phrases in your outbound E-mail becomes an implicit profile of your interests. With Tacit, any time anyone else in your company sends a message marked for public use, it is matched against your profile to see if it's something you might be interested in. If so, it is automatically routed to you—even if you weren't on the original list for the message. The senders of E-mail don't have to think about who might find individual messages valuable; they just need to send messages, and the messages will automatically go to the people who most need to see them.

But what about privacy? What if I send an E-mail to the CEO criticizing my boss? Does my boss see it? I'm sure she's interested! Suddenly, communicating across the employment hierarchy doesn't sound so great.

Users cannot be tricked into using a system that violates their privacy because they will avoid using the system completely, or find other ways to subvert it. Tacit must have strong privacy protections to make sure users are protected. Hence, KnowledgeMail.

With KnowledgeMail, every Tacit user has a private profile, which is the long list of terms that characterize your recent interests. This profile is never shown to anyone else, not even your boss or the system administrator. Periodically, Tacit reviews your private profile with you, showing you the clusters of information that you seem to be interested in and recommending that you show these clusters to other knowledge users so they can learn of your interests, regardless of their job title. You show your clusters to others by moving parts of your private profile into a public profile. As the owner of the private profile, you are the only one who can ever move it into the public profile.

INFORMATION PATHWAYS AND EMPLOYMENT HIERARCHIES ARE DIFFERENT

When a user writes an E-mail, Tacit will suggest recipients who might be interested in that E-mail, based only on their public profiles. Most often, the sender will either choose none of the users proposed by Tacit, keeping the E-mail private, or all of the users proposed by Tacit, sharing his ideas with the entire group of interested users. If he chooses all of the users, the E-mail message becomes self-addressing.

Tacit's interface allows you to determine *why* different people are interested in the E-mail you're planning to send. First of all, the names of users proposed by Tacit are ranked in order by their expected interest in the message (not by their ties to you in the employment hierarchy). The sender can also tell how important each phrase within the draft is in selecting E-mail recipients. You can click on any person and see the color-coded terms that the particular person shares with your message. Or you can click on any term or any region of the E-mail and see the community of users who are particularly interested in that group of terms. In addition, Tacit rates the people you have addressed manually on E-mail, showing you how likely they are to be interested in the document. You may choose to remove some people from the distribution list if you know that they won't be very interested.

In learning why people across the employment hierarchy are interested in your E-mails, users are likely to create new information pathways. If, for instance, I learn that Sue used to sell software to Company X, she could become a valuable resource to me, even if she now works in customer relations. Without Tacit, I might never have met Sue.

KNOWLEDGE IS A PRODUCT

Tacit recognizes the value of knowledge, no matter how it's communicated. When employees are kept abreast of their co-workers' activities, they can present a unified front to customers and the competition. They also do their jobs more efficiently. KnowledgeSweep helps in this regard.

In addition to sharing knowledge through E-mails, Tacit sweeps through all of the employees' private knowledge looking for patterns of agreement. KnowledgeSweep is most often used with a search interface: One user searches for another user who has the type of knowledge that he needs. When KnowledgeSweep finds users with the desired knowledge, it informs them that someone else is looking for them. It does not tell the seeker that someone has been found. Each of the users with the desired information can choose on a case-by-case basis whether to respond to the request for knowledge. Since the users have control over which knowledge sweeps they respond to, they don't feel that their privacy is violated.

It's worth noting that, unlike concept mining, Tacit cares intensely about time. Your profile changes based on which set of words you use within a window of time. This helps improve the relevance of information you receive.

Business Applications

Tacit is useful across a wide variety of businesses, including pharmaceuticals, professional services, investment banks, energy, and high-tech companies. Within these businesses, Tacit can assist with selling, servicing customers, and forming relationships. For instance, an ad agency might receive a customer request for a television ad that features trained dogs. The ad agency runs this request through Tacit, and lets Tacit identify employees who would be most interested and knowledgeable about this concept.

As workers go about their daily projects, they don't and can't know everyone who might benefit from their work. Nor can they know everyone who might be able to help. The people who might benefit from their work, or help them with it, might not come into contact with them simply because the information and organizational hierarchies don't require it. It's up to you to make these connections for your employees.

Users of recommender systems (both for E-commerce and knowledge management) need explanations. If I'm going to forward an E-mail to Jill in accounting, I want to know why she's interested. Tacit explains why people will benefit from E-mails by highlighting terms of interest. Do you help explain why you're making recommendations?

When creating or using programs that monitor employee output, it's important to remember that employees should be in charge of their public profiles. Otherwise, workers will find a way to work around the system. And, more importantly, they won't benefit from the system's discoveries.

TACIT

RECOMMENDER(S): Text analysis (creates an interest model for each employee).

INPUT(S): Company documents and E-mail; public and private profiles; actions taken for individual E-mails.

OUTPUT(S): Suggested E-mail recipients for outgoing E-mail. Also notifies employees about co-workers with similar interests (from private profiles).

LESSON: *Optimal information flow doesn't necessarily correspond to predefined information or organizational hierarchies.*

PROCTER & GAMBLE

HOW DO YOU get the right information to the right people? That's the main challenge of knowledge management. With a company as big as Procter & Gamble, that challenge gets enormously difficult. Procter & Gamble sells more than 250 products to more than 5 billion consumers in 130 countries. And from its humble beginnings as a soap and candle company in Cincinnati, Ohio, Procter & Gamble now employs over 110,000 people worldwide. How are these employees supposed to know one another, let alone know what information to share?

The typical knowledge-management solution is to use keyword profile techniques. The employee registers her short- and long-term interests and the KM engine alerts her to any matches. There are two disadvantages to this approach:

1. It requires the user to create the profile. Many users are not willing to invest the time to create a profile, or to keep it up to date. Ironically, the busier the person, the less

willing she is to spend time on profiles that would make her job easier.

2. Keyword searches cannot tell how accurate, interesting, or suited to the tastes of the user the documents are. For instance, a beauty-care expert might want to learn about Cover Girl products in development, but is probably not interested in announcements about Cover Girl training sessions for new employees. Keyword search engines have a hard time making these distinctions.

Because keyword profiles are labor intensive and don't always reward vigilant profile updaters, Procter & Gamble sought something better. They decided to install a Net Perceptions for Knowledge Management solution, which uses collaborative filtering to recommend people and resources.

INFORMATION PATHWAYS AND EMPLOYMENT HIERARCHIES ARE DIFFERENT

Plugged into Lotus Notes or directly into the Web-based intranet, Net Perceptions for Knowledge Management studies the work and habits of employees. It can suggest documents that other employees have used or created based upon an employee's current task. It can also put employees in contact with each other when their interests dovetail—even if they work in different departments. Managers might find it helpful, too, to know what employees should undergo training together simply by studying the "knowledge communities" created around each employee. These communities often extend outside of traditional "organizational charts."

IDENTIFY EXPERTISE AND EMPLOYEE RELATIONSHIPS USING WORK BY-PRODUCTS

Best of all, collaborative filtering doesn't require employees to update their profiles. It adapts as their habits and interests change. When time is precious, employees won't have to spend hours searching for documents or experts that they know, or at least suspect, exist. Using collaborative filtering, they will recycle information rather than re-create it. And, if they're unable to find the perfect document, they can at least be directed to people who have been looking at similar documents. As a global corporation with knowledge workers in many different countries, Procter & Gamble employees might be hard-pressed to find just the right people they need to talk to otherwise.

So that employees don't feel uncomfortable contacting someone they don't know, Net Perceptions for Knowledge Management also includes an Explain key, which indicates the relationship employees share. For instance, the Explain key might say, "You've been looking at these four documents. The person you should contact has written one of them and has read all of the others." Armed with this information, employees can explain their reason for calling—and have a high degree of confidence that the call will be fruitful.

KNOWLEDGE IS A PRODUCT

Like people, information changes. Documents are created all the time. Sometimes they're revised. Sometimes new information comes out that makes earlier documents obsolete. When using a traditional bank of shared knowledge, information has a tendency to become out of date quickly. Rather than search through dated material, employees are more likely to do research on their own. With a dynamic knowledge-recommendation system like collaborative filtering, though, employees are much more likely to find the experts and documents they're looking for. After all, the recommendation engine knows them and their work. It's not searching in a vacuum; it's searching for nearest neighbors.

"By connecting a disperse staff with related interests or projects from around the globe, we feel confident that it will help us eliminate redundancies within our R&D activities and create better synergies between our best resources—our people," said John Roeder, vice president of Information Technologies at Procter & Gamble.

Companies like Procter & Gamble save time and money using

collaborative filtering. Not only does collaborative filtering limit redundancies, but it also creates profitable working relationships. Using collaborative filtering, employees with similar interests and responsibilities can not only share information on a onetime basis, but can establish the groundwork for future collaborations.

Business Applications

In global companies, where communication between divisions may not thrive due to distance and inconvenience, a dynamic knowledge base can make a world of difference. Costly scouting reports on the competition may be filed away on someone's computer in Berlin when they're needed ASAP in Philadelphia. Unless the database can recognize the relative usefulness of documents to distinct individuals, your employees may not find what they're looking for. They may not deem it worth their time even to try.

In addition to helping employees locate documents, help them find people, too. When doing this, it helps immensely if you explain *why* they should contact a particular person or expert.

PROCTER & GAMBLE

RECOMMENDER(S): Collaborative filtering.

INPUT(S): Time spent on documents, ratings.

OUTPUT(S): List of documents and people.

LESSON: *Expertise is only as valuable as your access to it. Don't just help people find expertise, help people find people with expertise.*

REFERRALWEB

I N THEIR ARTICLE "The Hidden Web," Henry Kautz, Bart Selman, and Mehul Shah reference a University of Virginia Web site called The Oracle of Bacon at Virginia. This site allows you to type in any actor's name (they have close to half a million actors listed in their database), and learn that actor's cinematic connection to Kevin Bacon. Because Bacon has been in a lot of movies, most actors are only a step or two away from him. Bing Crosby, for instance, acted in *Say One for Me* (1959) with Robert Wagner, and Wagner played a small role in *Wild Things* (1998) with Bacon. On average, any given actor is only 2.88 steps (or co-stars) away from Bacon. Why Bacon is the gold standard for this game is anyone's guess, but playing Six Degrees of Separation with Kevin Bacon has become an amusing time killer on long car rides.

In business, trying to find connections is not usually as fun as playing Six Degrees of Separation, but there's often more at stake. How do I find the person who knows the most about Starbucks' Japanese expansion efforts? Then how do I get him to take my call?

Kautz and his colleagues designed ReferralWeb with this expert-finding dilemma in mind. Using Alta Vista as a platform, the Referral-Web system allows users to find experts in any given field. First, ReferralWeb searches for Web documents that mention your name, then using links, co-authors, Netnews archives, and organizational charts, it establishes a social network for you. When you ask it to find an expert on Starbucks and Japan, it will not only return with experts, but experts who have the closest connection to you. Naturally, it helps if in your query you can name other experts you trust. That way ReferralWeb will refine its search even further.

With companies the size of small countries these days, you may not know everyone on your floor, let alone co-workers on the other side of the world. With ReferralWeb, you don't have to. The creators of ReferralWeb have developed prototypes for use within companies so that you can find the in-house experts you need (even if she's in Amsterdam) by mining intranet documents.

INFORMATION PATHWAYS AND EMPLOYMENT
HIERARCHIES ARE DIFFERENT

Experts are more likely to invest time and energy on questions from people they know, or at least people referred to them by people they know. And expert-seekers may want insider information about experts before contacting them. ReferralWeb finds relationships between workers in a company through a variety of sources, including the corporate directory, employee résumés, and the authorship of papers and technical reports in a company's database. The software also provides a graphical explorer that allows people either to explore their personal network or ask queries such as "Who are the personalization experts within three hops of me?" Once a user sees the result of the query, he can drill down to explore the relationship in more detail, evaluate which contacts and experts might be most appropriate to use (e.g., "He owes me a favor"), and make contact.

IDENTIFY EXPERTISE AND EMPLOYEE RELATIONSHIPS
USING WORK BY-PRODUCTS

Too often, expertise databases are filled with entries from people who exaggerate their own expertise. Often non-experts think they know more than they do ("I've been to Japan and I like coffee, so what is it you need to know?"). Real experts may decline to register their expertise either out of modesty or self-interest (many experts are already overwhelmed by advice-seekers, so why take out an ad in the yellow pages?). Instead of relying on self-declarations of expertise, ReferralWeb mines this information from work products.

Business Applications

The information people volunteer may not be as accurate or useful as the work they've done. ReferralWeb demonstrates how this information can be mined effectively using documents available to the public or just your company.

Finding experts is only half the battle; getting them to speak with you and assist you is the other. ReferralWeb makes it easy by listing people you know in common. Granted, some of these relationship pathways are going to be more tenuous than others (I worked with Bill, who wrote that paper with Sue, who heads Anne's department, who leads the Big Brother/Big Sister program with you), but the value of knowing your connections to everyone in your company is considerable. Team forming becomes a much easier exercise. Even social activities could benefit: using relationship charts to form golf foursomes, for instance.

REFERRALWEB

RECOMMENDER(S): Searchable database by relationship.

INPUT(S): All implicit—gathered from résumés, organizational directories, internal publications, and authors.

OUTPUT(S): Experts and personal connections.

LESSON: *Don't ask employees to volunteer their expertise. Mine work products instead—both for content and employee relationships.*

MITRE'S ORGANIZATION-WIDE LEARNING (OWL) SYSTEM

A RE YOU USING Microsoft Word as efficiently as you could be? Back when there were only a few dozen commands, probably. But now that the user's manual is as big as a telephone book, there are probably shortcuts you're missing and options you haven't considered. Is it worth your time to call the help desk at Microsoft? You may get some answers, but probably at the expense of your sanity. Besides, how is a customer-service rep going to know how *you* use Word?

What about using the Help menu on the toolbar? Where would

you begin? If you want to learn how to print envelopes, the Help option works. But the only way you're going to learn new techniques is by the Microsoft Office Assistant ("Clippy"), the annoying paper clip that pops up and makes suggestions. And, chances are, those suggestions will be for things you already know how to do.

Frank Linton at the MITRE Corporation developed a collaborative-filtering-based recommender system (OWL) that watches "over the shoulders" of employees as they use computer word-processing software and analyzes patterns of command use to figure out where user knowledge is deficient.

IDENTIFY EXPERTISE AND EMPLOYEE RELATIONSHIPS USING WORK BY-PRODUCTS

Modern word-processing systems, such as Microsoft Word, have a huge number of commands, many of which accomplish the same task. OWL uses the word-processing experience of other users to define the "norm" toward which users are trained.

OWL's recommender system consists of four steps:

1. Watching a broad set of Word users and recording which commands they used, and how often.
2. Analyzing this data to create expected usage levels for different commands.
3. Comparing actual user behavior with expected behavior.
4. Presenting recommendations to users in an unobtrusive way.

OWL found that the top 10 Word commands account for 80 percent of usage, the top 20 for 90 percent, and the top 100 for 99 percent. At the top of the list were File Open, Edit Paste, and File Save. Naturally, it gets far more job-specific the farther you head down the list. Of the 1,000-plus commands available in Microsoft Word, however, the average person used only 56, but different employees used very different subsets. Many employees, for example, used backspace as their only deletion command, not knowing about "select-and-delete" or "delete word," and as a result wasted considerable time.

INFORMATION PATHWAYS AND EMPLOYMENT HIERARCHIES ARE DIFFERENT

Unlike Clippy, OWL decided not to try to interrupt users with recommendations. For those of you who have received "It looks like you're trying to write a letter" a million times, this is a good thing. Instead, OWL provides users with an overview of different commands to be learned (and different reasons for learning them). The user is then free to explore these as he or she has the time, need, or inclination. Although they come from the entire pool of Word commands, they're the ones other users find most useful. It's reassuring to know that your colleagues implicitly vouch for the recommendations you're being given.

With OWL, managers benefit because employees help each other get more efficient at their work. Employees benefit because they can receive training without having to admit knowledge gaps. They also don't have to search across the company for the one person, or several people, who know the best time-saving techniques. They get training as they need it, on their own.

OWL updates users' recommendations every month—both to account for commands they now use and to reflect evolving knowledge in the community. Here, too, OWL demonstrates flexibility that Clippy doesn't. Its recommendations don't rush you, or repeat information you've already learned; they keep pace with you.

KNOWLEDGE IS A PRODUCT

As a product, knowledge should be quantifiable. OWL makes this happen. If you want to see where you stand in the general scheme of things, you can use the Skill-o-meter, which compares your knowledge of commands with the pooled knowledge of your colleagues. You can fine-tune that even more and see what commands people in certain departments or with similar job titles use.

Business Applications

OWL shows how recommenders must learn from and about the employee. Then they can recommend better ways to accomplish the tasks the employee routinely performs. Maybe more significantly, they can present new ideas that the employee would benefit from exploring. OWL's interface model is particularly good because it allows the user to choose which new idea to explore and when, rather than simply lumping commands into a recommendation list.

Your employees may be able to instruct each other—without so much as lifting a pen. And without risk of redundancies. How many training programs can make this boast?

MITRE

RECOMMENDER(S): Collaborative filtering (creates word-processing tutorials based on gaps in user knowledge).

INPUT(S): Implicitly gathered data from community of users, stored as a frequency profile (who uses which word-processing commands, and how often).

OUTPUT(S): Pulled suggestion list (user decides when and if to access recommendations).

LESSON: *Collaborative filtering not only sells products, it can sell new knowledge and training to your employees.*

Principle #6: Revolutionize Knowledge Management

Quick Tips

- Information pathways and employment hierarchies are different.
- Employees don't like to enter or update profile information. Period.

- Identify expertise and employee relationships using work by-products. The information people volunteer may not be as accurate or as useful.
- Keyword searches don't usually narrow down corporate documents effectively enough, so pair them with a recommender.
- If you let employees control what information they make visible to the company, they will be more inclined to let you automatically monitor their work products—including E-mail (Tacit).
- Protect privacy. If your employees don't trust a data-collection system, they'll find ways around it (Tacit). The same goes for your customers.
- In a global economy, companies need to address communication and collaboration across oceans. Recommenders can identify helpful co-workers, even if they're working out of Timbuktu (Procter & Gamble).
- Employees want a reason for contacting an expert they don't know. You can supply this by highlighting their shared interests (Net Perceptions for Knowledge Management) or by explaining the chain of personal connections that links them (ReferralWeb).
- Reduce redundancies by making the right documents readily available. Search functions need to incorporate the employee's interests and recent activity (through collaborative filtering) or react to specific input (such as ReferralWeb's expert search criteria).
- Helping employees make intracompany connections establishes the groundwork for future collaborations (ReferralWeb).
- Teach employees new tricks (MITRE's Microsoft Word functions). Don't force these learning moments on them, however. Let them integrate them at their own pace.
- Employees may not want to admit knowledge gaps. Automatic recommenders allow them to set up a

personalized training program and catch up to their colleagues without embarrassing themselves (MITRE).

Rather than spend money trying to locate experts and training outside your company, look within. Use recommenders to improve search functions, create a dynamic database, and facilitate collaboration. Don't trust serendipity to put people together (heart-valve designers and submarine engineers may not meet in the grocery-store checkout line); trust recommenders.

Interlude #6: Workplace Privacy

What kind of privacy can workers expect in today's workplace? Here in the United States, workers can generally assume that their managers are not listening in on their phone conversations unless they have been warned in advance. On the other hand, technology now allows us to determine how many keystrokes a worker uses per minute, per hour, per day, or how many calls a sales rep takes. Isn't it reasonable for you to know how productive your employees are? What about Internet interactions? Do you as an employer have the right to monitor the Web-surfing activity of your employees? Can you fire them if they are visiting the Playboy site when you're paying them to work for you? (What if they are looking for "marketing ideas" from Playboy?)

The answers to these questions are still evolving, but they have important implications for collaborative filtering in the workplace. After all, the knowledge-management application of collaborative filtering relies on the ability to know what documents employees have used, and how much they value them. This information is crucial in order to be able to recommend documents to other employees. Is it reasonable for a business to collect this sort of information about its employees? Can the employees be forced to participate even if they don't want to?

In general, businesses should be as concerned about the effect on employee morale as about legal issues. Employees expect to be treated with respect, and if they are monitored without their consent they will not feel respected. Employers should follow three steps to keep employees on board: (1) Communicate clearly about the data that is being collected and why it is being collected; (2) explain the benefits of collecting the data both to the company and to the individual employee; (3) don't do anything with the data other than what you've said you're going to do with it. Since collaborative-filtering applications offer direct benefits to employees, they will often be enthusiastic about participating as long as they understand that their privacy will be protected, and as long as you show that you are trustworthy with their data.

Use Communities to Create Content

> Meditation is not a means to an end.
> It is both the means and the end.
>
> —KRISHNAMURTI *THE SECOND PENGUIN
> KRISHNAMURTI READER* (1991)

> We are inclined to believe those whom we do
> not know because they have never deceived us.
>
> —DR. SAMUEL JOHNSON (1709–1784)

SOME OF THE TECHNOLOGIES we've profiled allow you to personalize content: Lands' End (My Personal Shopper), Clinique (Skin Typing), Mitchell (Calendar), and My Yahoo! (creating your own news and entertainment pages). These technologies save the information you enter so that it can be used at a later date. The best of these technologies learn more and more about your preferences so that they can make better recommendations.

Other companies we've examined have allowed employees to pool and access data for in-house purposes: Procter & Gamble (to reduce duplication of effort), Tacit (to mine your company's expertise—both private and public), and ReferralWeb (to discover connections among people). These companies gain a competitive edge by reusing content they've already created.

In this chapter we focus on commercial sites where the content is largely created by the user community. At Flutter.com, British gamblers can propose bets of their own choosing—anything from the outcome of an Arsenal/Liverpool soccer game to who will have the number one music single at Christmas. Epinions allows customers to weigh in on a myriad of topics (from Hoover vacuum cleaners to the First Bank of Massachusetts) so that customers can make informed buying decisions. Slashdot users provide running commentary on the quality and usefulness of articles. And, last, Expedia takes a page from some of the knowledge-management companies by mining already existing content to provide a helpful service (the cheapest airfares customers have found). As with the knowledge-management companies, relationships prosper on these commercial sites where information is both created and shared by customers.

The remarkable thing about the sites we profile in this chapter is that customers not only create free content, they actually value the content more than if the companies had created it themselves. Customers appreciate unbiased content, which is something only other customers can provide.

So how do you get customers to create content for you? It seems too good to be true. What's the catch? Well, for the most part, there is no catch. Customers genuinely like to contribute to the community. As long as the forum is respectable and the exchanges lively, customers don't hesitate to provide information or products entirely free of charge. In *The Cluetrain Manifesto*, Christopher Locke, Rick Levine, Doc Searls, and David Weinberger suggest that these forums can escape your control. In fact, to be useful, they *must* escape your control. The opportunity to create deep and effective interaction is what draws people in, and if they feel censored they will flee. The dialogue can be even more productive if you encourage your employees to weigh in. Be sure not to try to censor them, either (although you must be sure that they identify themselves as employees, not customers).

Although you shouldn't try to censor your customers, there are ways you can help facilitate their productivity and control the quality of their output:

1. Let customers create content for you.
2. Allow communities to edit and evaluate content.
3. Compensate customers for their input—in kind, pay, or prestige.
4. If you listen, they will come.

1. Let customers create content for you. "I have always depended on the kindness of strangers," says Blanche DuBois in Tennessee Williams' play *A Streetcar Named Desire.* Nowhere is that sentiment more in evidence than in today's on-line sites. In this chapter you'll see sites where customers create virtually all of the content. More often, you'll find customers creating valuable content with their reactions to content or products that you present—in the form of reviews. In both cases, customers are driven to contribute for two reasons. First, reviewing products or services allows people to act on their Good Samaritan impulses—without wasting too much of their time or energy. Second, people like to see their names in lights. Some people never get their fifteen minutes of fame. On the Internet, though, they get to see the product of their labors make it into print. It helps, too, that the Internet allows contributions to be stored indefinitely at virtually no extra cost.

2. Allow communities to edit and evaluate content. Some companies worry that if they invite customer feedback, they won't have any means to control its quantity and quality. They shouldn't worry so much. Customers can and will edit and evaluate the content their community creates.

Handing over the editorial reins is one of the best things companies can do. Customers will have a greater stake in the site, for one thing, because they know their voices are being heard. Customers also trust the opinions of other customers more than those of vested parties (like the host company or industry publications). After all, customers don't have an incentive to give biased reviews. Last, the host company won't have to pay for editors, so fixed costs go down. What's not to like?

Some customers may abuse editorial power by elevating bad content or rejecting good content, but sooner or later (usually sooner, given the speed of the Internet) the community will rein them in. Knowing that they've harmed other customers, not only the company, will help bring these renegades into line.

3. *Compensate customers for their input—in kind, pay, or prestige.* While customers may be willing to contribute content for free, it's important that you recognize their efforts. At this time, precious few companies are rewarding customers with monetary compensation. Sweepstakes are proliferating on the Web, but they're not tied to the creation of content. Customers don't feel like they've earned sweepstakes prizes. They'll appreciate them if they win, but in general sweepstakes don't encourage loyalty. Epinions, whom we profile in this chapter, is one of the first and the few to pay customers for their input. Even a small amount of pay can be a huge inducement for customers—not just in getting them to contribute more content, but also in getting them to create *better* content.

More often, customers are given status and/or privileges in return for the content they create. Customers love to be recognized for their opinions, and they love to know their opinions are being valued by others. Allowing the best and most frequent contributors a stronger ability to manipulate the opinions and actions of others is generally in a company's best interests. These contributors often know best what they and other customers want. Starring reviews is another way of identifying effective contributors.

Yet another way to compensate customers for their reviews is to allow them to benefit more from the reviews of others. We imagine forums where if you want to receive a valuable recommendation, you have to give one first. We expect to see more of these "pay-in-kind" models in the future.

4. *If you listen, they will come.* People like to vent. With the pro-

liferation of phone mazes, people often can't get someone to listen to their troubles. Since most retail stores hire minimum-wage workers, venting to them may be therapeutic on one level (releasing frustration), but you don't get the feeling that your opinions will result in reform. If your customers can't talk *to* you, they'll still talk *about* you—just somewhere else. Hate sites abound on the Web. At NorthWorstair.org, Ronald J. Riley skewers Northwest Airlines, in part because "NWA does not pay attention to customer complaints."

As much as people like to vent, they like to rave, too. When someone or something has bettered their life, people want to give credit where credit is due. It's important that they have an outlet.

In this chapter, we'll examine companies that depend mightily on the "kindness of strangers." At these companies' sites, customers not only provide the content, they often edit it too. In return, they get a vast collection of high-quality content, recognition of their effort and expertise, and, in some cases, innovative incentives.

FLUTTER.COM

F LUTTER" IS BRITISH SLANG for a small wager made for the sport of it. Flutter.com provides a forum where people can propose flutters and others can find and accept them. The bets cover a wide range of topics, with most of them being sporting events (a recent look showed nearly 2,000 soccer flutters pending). Other bets revolve around economic indexes, political events, and even the contents of the next day's newspaper. Yes, the clever flutterer can use his or her deep knowledge of the *Star* to propose a bet that the next day's cover will have a picture of Britney Spears, Geri Halliwell, or one of the Spice Girls.

What do the users of Flutter.com get? They get access to a wide variety of low-stakes bets more interesting than any bookie could conjure up. In a country that allows (and encourages) betting on almost anything, Flutter.com gives people access to the truly scarce wagering resource: people willing to take your bets. The site also serves as a trusted intermediary. In order to propose or accept a flutter, the user must have an account and enough money deposited to cover the bet. Flutter.com places wagered money in escrow (through the Royal Bank of Scotland) and serves as arbiter if the outcome of a particular bet is in dispute. In other words, users get a safe and fun place to bet.

And how does Flutter.com make a profit? Like bookies, they collect a percentage of the winnings from each bet (5 percent of the winnings, so a person who wins $100 gets only $95). Furthermore, Flutter.com accounts pay no interest; the company can earn returns on money being used for flutters or being held between them. And, to help encourage people to keep their money in the system, there is a redemption fee to get your money back out. From our perspective, it looks like Flutter.com makes out very well. They take a piece of the action, hold your money interest-free, and charge you to get your money back. So are people willing to pay this price?

The last time we viewed the site, on an uninteresting March evening, there were more than 5,000 pending flutter offers. This number doesn't include bets that have already been accepted, just those waiting for takers. And most of these bets were for events in the next few days. Apparently, the desire to wager overcomes any small concerns about the profit-taking of the bookie. This is not a site for "serious gamblers" seeking the best odds (some would refer them to the stock exchanges). In fact, bets are limited, and the amount of money a user can add to his account each month and quarter is also limited. While bets of up to £400 are allowed, few exceed £5, and many are much less.

LET CUSTOMERS CREATE CONTENT FOR YOU

At Flutter.com, customers generate all the content—and quite a diverse set of content it is! Flutter.com simply supplies the site, sets up bets into categories, and brokers the exchange.

ALLOW COMMUNITIES TO EDIT AND EVALUATE CONTENT

When we first visited the site, some of the flutters bordered on the truly bizarre. You could bet on whether aliens would invade Paris before July 1. The powers that be have reined it in a little since then—possibly over disputes as to whether or not aliens actually did invade Paris. Creative bettors still have some options, though. They can bet on whether there will be a white Christmas in London, who will win the MTV Europe Music Awards, and who will win the Booker Prize, for example.

COMPENSATE CUSTOMERS FOR THEIR INPUT—IN KIND, PAY, OR PRESTIGE

Customers are compensated for visiting Flutter.com, provided they win their bets! And, for many, the chance to frame and set the terms of the bet is compensation enough.

IF YOU LISTEN, THEY WILL COME

Flutter.com is a social site, but one built around content. Flutter.com's content is created by the community, and it is the center of the community. Thus far, the site has not needed sophisticated tools to match bettors with bets. A hierarchy of bets seems to suffice. In the future, however, we imagine that flutters may well be recommended—perhaps on the Web site, but perhaps by E-mail or mobile device. "Opportunities" that match the user's profile can pop up, allowing a better match, faster turnaround, and more action. Eventually, wireless access may even allow people at an event to propose and accept flutters efficiently. As a soccer match is tied, flutters will fly on which team and player will score the next goal. When the goal is scored, happy fans may also be enriched by the experience. Either way, Flutter.com as the gathering place will reap great rewards.

Business Applications

Encourage your customers' creative input. Run name-the-flavor competitions for new ice creams or beverages. Invite customers to vote for their favorite products. Give them space to write their reactions to your site or products. You don't have to create a new marketplace for customer interaction the way Flutter.com did, but recognize that customers can bring a lot of creative ideas to the table. They may come to your site just to see the ideas that other customers come up with. That's one of Flutter.com's main attractions: wondering what kind of bets people will propose.

FLUTTER

RECOMMENDER(S): Social navigation (number of open flutters indicates areas of interest).

INPUT(S): Flutters.

OUTPUT(S): Sorted tables of flutters.

LESSON: *The public can create more inventive products than even the best marketers.*

EPINIONS

SENDING COMPLAINTS to companies via E-mail: somewhat satisfying. Sending letters in to op-ed pages: okay, so long as they print it. Ideally, though, people want their opinions to be immortalized. If their reviews disappear into the ether, the effort it took to craft their comments is cheapened. That's where Epinions comes in.

Epinions recognizes the customer's desire to be heard. Epinions features more than 1 million comments and reviews in 30 different categories, ranging from electronics to travel. People come not only to comment and vent, but also to learn what other users have discovered so they don't repeat the same mistakes.

When John was buying a new minivan for his family, he visited Epinions. Nearly all the reviewers liked the Honda Odyssey, though some were disappointed that their dealers had pressured them to buy after-market stuff like leather seats. Almost everyone was thrilled with the Toyota Sienna, too, but one person from a cold climate said that the heating system didn't work well. Since John's from Minnesota, he decided to try out the Odyssey first. Unfortunately, the local dealer wasn't interested in selling the sort of entry-level minivan John's family wanted; they were only interested in selling vans with rust-proofing, sound-proofing, dealer-added leather seats, and other extras. One dealer told John that if he wanted a minivan like that "he should go ask Toyota." So he did. John and his family chose a particularly cold day to visit the Toyota dealer and had their kids sit in all of the different rows of seats. They didn't find any problem with the heating system. John went back to Epinions and noticed that other reviewers had disagreed with the first about the effectiveness of the heating system, so John and his family bought a Sienna. They've been through a tough Minnesota winter now, and can report that the heating system is just fine. Their kids love being able to control the heat for the rear seats themselves.

LET CUSTOMERS CREATE CONTENT FOR YOU

Magazines seldom accept reviews from individual readers because adding extra pages to the publication increases costs significantly. Also, by maintaining editorial control, the publisher retains the ability to ensure that large advertisers are not offended. As a result, readers have come to expect that automobile magazines and local newspaper reviews will be consistently favorable to automobile manufacturers. Readers are more apt to believe a stranger's opinion about a Ford Taurus than a magazine that displays ads for Ford. After all, the stranger isn't on Ford's payroll.

On the Internet, the user can choose to go anywhere with a single click of the mouse, while the advertisers have to go where the users are—unlike print publications. And, on the Internet, the cost of publishing information is nearly zero. That means that Internet sites like Epinions can publish millions of customer reviews.

By allowing customers to create their content, Epinions wins in several ways: It's cheaper, unbiased, and results in greater coverage (since staff writers can't possibly write as many reviews as Epinions users).

ALLOW COMMUNITIES TO EDIT AND EVALUATE CONTENT

On Epinions, each user creates a "web of trust" for himself. As the user reads reviews, he places the ones he likes into the category of trusted users whose opinions are weighed heavily by Epinions in forming recommendations for him. Others he places into the category of untrusted users whose opinions are ignored by Epinions. Over time, Epinions personalizes its recommendations for each user according to the web of trusted individuals. The more users rate reviewers, the better Epinions is able to serve them. Epinions generates tremendous loyalty as a result. When a user thinks about going to a Web site to get information about products and services, he knows that Epinions will be able to serve him immediately, whereas any other site would have to spend a long time learning about him before it would be able to offer equally good service.

Of course, like search engines, Epinions has to keep an eye on people trying to skew the system for personal gain. In the event that users try to plug their own products or otherwise violate the User Agreement, Epinions "tickets" them so that other users know they may not be trusted.

COMPENSATE CUSTOMERS FOR THEIR
INPUT—IN KIND, PAY, OR PRESTIGE

Epinions is one of the first Web sites to break the tyranny of the publisher and let anyone who has valuable information, no matter how infrequently, and no matter how small, to benefit proportionally by providing that information to the marketplace. In order to assure the best, unbiased reviews, Epinions lets users decide who should be compensated; that's Epinions' primary means of editorial control.

Epinions members who write reviews can get Eroyalties in several ways. First of all, they get $1 for every 100 visits by Epinions members. They can also earn Eroyalties through Income Share, which rewards timely, high-quality, and accurate reviews using an evaluation system that Epinions purposefully keeps vague to avoid fraudulent manipulation. Once they've accumulated $10 worth of Eroyalties, Epinions members can redeem these funds in the form of a check.

IF YOU LISTEN, THEY WILL COME

The sheer volume of reviews indicates that Epinions is scoring high marks in the listening department. One reviewer of Toro's Electric Blower discussed not only its ability to blow leaves, mulch, vacuum, and remove snow from cars, but also the way other Epinions reviewers have improved her life. Just that day she got tips for a sushi lunch from one reviewer. She also praised the entertainment essays of several other Epinion members. People at Epinions put care into their reviews (and into their responses to reviews). Epinions, in many respects, doesn't have to listen, because its customers do. Very well, we might add.

Business Applications

Even though Epinions doesn't reward reviewers extravagantly (the top reviews in the Auto category, for instance, receive roughly

1,000 page views a month, netting the reviewers $10), some incentive is better than none—considerably better. Reviewers want recognition for their efforts. They know that their opinions have value. Epinions sates this urge for recognition with Eroyalties, but also by ranking sites by their number of page views. Seeing their name ranked highly pushes reviewers to do their best, in part because they know that people have appreciated their input.

Customers like carrots. Coffee shops give you a free cup after you've bought ten and airlines give you free tickets after you've flown a certain number of miles. Are their ways you could be rewarding your best customers?

EPINIONS

RECOMMENDER(S): Pull-active collaborative filtering (users build web of trust themselves, instead of being paired automatically with nearest neighbors).

INPUT(S): Products and reviewers that users trust.

OUTPUT(S): Text reviews, aggregate score of products (five-star ratings), and predictions.

LESSON: *Creating content on your own can be costly. Valuable consumer input may be worth compensating for in cash, prestige, or in kind—because customers trust the opinions of other customers more than they trust yours, and by contributing they will feel more invested in your site.*

SLASHDOT

C CREATED IN 1997 by Rob "CmdrTaco" Malda and Jeff "Hemos" Bates, Slashdot's motto is "News for nerds. Stuff that matters." From the hundreds of submissions they get each day, Slashdot editors post articles (and links to articles) from elsewhere on the Net, with a brief intro by the submitter. On any given day you might find stories about sequels to the movie *The Matrix*, Intel Tualatin processors, or cloning sheep. The editors try to create an "omelet" of interesting pieces, ranging in form from articles, to book reviews, to interviews.

LET CUSTOMERS CREATE CONTENT FOR YOU

Once an article is posted, people start arguing over whether it is "right" or "interesting" or even "news for nerds." So not only do Slashdot members submit articles, they also create content by discussing the merits of the articles once they've been posted. In fact, it's hard to determine which Slashdot members value more: the comments or the articles.

ALLOW COMMUNITIES TO EDIT AND EVALUATE CONTENT

The thousands of daily comments written by Slashdot members are scored on a -1 to 5 rating scale, indicating how valuable they are. Users can then determine what level of comments to view. If they want to see all the comments, they choose -1. If they prefer to see only comments that have been rated highly, they can set the threshold to a higher number like 3 or 4.

Initially, Slashdot picked twenty-five people to rate comments. That proved to be too few, though, as the number of members grew. Now, regular Slashdot readers are occasionally selected to act as moderators. A moderator gets a small number of points (five) to add or subtract from the current score of a small number of comments. He or she can change the score of a single comment by five points, of five comments by one point each, or anything in between. No one moderator gets a huge ability to change a huge number of comments, thereby avoiding centralization of too much power. On the other hand, many individual moderators get a small amount of power. As moderators change comment scores up or down, they are likely to be seen by other readers, including other moderators. This introduces a version of the *first-rater* problem. The first-rater problem occurs when the first reader of a comment hates it and rates it poorly. As a result, no other readers may see the comment (or improve the score), even if it's a comment that many people would have liked to see. It's important to note, however, that moderation is not censorship because users can always choose to see all of the comments.

COMPENSATE CUSTOMERS FOR THEIR INPUT—IN KIND, PAY, OR PRESTIGE

If you post lots of articles on Slashdot and those articles are rated highly, you can earn "karma." Karma has two advantages: People with high karma get more moderation points (but this is capped to avoid too much centralization of power) and people with high karma get to post with higher-than-default initial scores, so their postings are more likely to be seen by others. Of course if their postings are bad, this increases the odds that the posting will be moderated down, which hurts karma!

IF YOU LISTEN, THEY WILL COME

Although Slashdot doesn't post every article submitted, they do post thousands of member comments. And they give each member his own page, which includes an author bio and a log of all his previous comments. Also, with the rating system, Slashdot ensures that members' comments are not only heard, they're evaluated. The result is that Slashdot members feel a proprietary stake in the site's content. Even if they're evaluated poorly, members will likely work harder to gain the respect of their peers.

Business Applications

Let the inmates run the asylum. Slashdot's members not only create their content, they edit it too. This works well in a focused community. Would it work for your customer base? Remember, you or your customers can bring in content from outside sources—at very little cost. If all your customers were in a room, what would they want to discuss?

SLASHDOT

RECOMMENDER(S): Statistical aggregation (from a limited subset of users who are given ratings points).

INPUT(S): Points and text articles.

OUTPUT(S): Ratings of articles (-1 to 5).

LESSON: *You don't need original content, or even editors, to be a trusted content site. Let the inmates run the asylum.*

EXPEDIA'S FARE COMPARE

H OW OFTEN do we hear about the person in the seat next to us on an airplane—you know, the one who paid half of what we did for the same flight? Airfares are complicated. Airlines set and change prices frequently to match demand, and attempt to get each traveler to pay as much as she (or her company) is willing. While airlines have recently begun to promise that they'll quote the cheapest fare for a flight, they are not obligated to tell customers that flying a day earlier (or later) may save them lots of money. The problem is, they have all the information but not the inclination.

Wouldn't it be nice if all of the customers could get together and compare notes? I'd like to ask "What's the cheapest going fare for a flight to Las Vegas?" and have other travelers tell me what fares they found, and how. Expedia.com's Fare Compare does exactly that. And better yet, it doesn't require members of the community to participate actively; it just remembers all of the fares people have found and makes them available when someone asks.

Joe tried this service when looking for tickets to Las Vegas. He thought he'd like to travel in May, and when he looked at some typical dates, the lowest fare was $330 round trip. He asked Fare Compare what low fares other Expedia.com customers found for Minneapolis to Las Vegas, and it came back with dozens of cheaper itineraries, including ones in May. When he narrowed down the search, he discovered that a small change in dates made a big difference in fare (mostly due to day-of-the-week pricing).

LET CUSTOMERS CREATE CONTENT FOR YOU

Expedia's database of flights and prices isn't created by their customers. In fact, Fare Compare is only one feature of Expedia's flight-reservation system. Expedia primarily routes customers to its Flight Wizard, which displays a standard reservation screen. You pick the dates, times, number of passengers, and any other preferences you have (business, first, or coach class; particular airline), and Expedia returns with your cheapest options, including an Expedia Bargain Fare. The Bargain Fare allows you to save up to 60 percent on the price of a ticket, but you have to be available to depart anytime between 6 A.M. and 10 P.M. (the airline chooses the time, not the customer).

So although Expedia's main database isn't generated by customers, the Fare Compare feature is. And since the customers who generated the information for Fare Compare have likely already purchased their tickets, they won't mind revealing the deal that they stumbled upon—provided, of course, that they remain anonymous, which they do. You could argue that the value of your seat goes down if the flight fills up, but that flies against the communitarian nature of Fare Compare.

ALLOW COMMUNITIES TO EDIT AND EVALUATE CONTENT

Expedia's Fare Compare acts automatically, so customers don't enter flight information themselves. They can't edit Expedia's displays, either, which is too bad because some of the fares shown are no longer available, due either to price changes or capacity controls. Customers can, however, evaluate all the bargains that their fellow travelers have so kindly discovered. In doing so, they will often follow links to look up fares, generating more data (and updating it) for the community.

COMPENSATE CUSTOMERS FOR THEIR
INPUT—IN KIND, PAY, OR PRESTIGE

A good travel agent may know fares to some popular places, but a good Web-based travel agency should know fares to lots of places, since lots of people request fare quotes. Simply remembering this information and making it available to customers is a tremendously valuable service. And valuable service is what on-line travel agencies need to provide. As airlines compete more aggressively both by promoting their own Web sites and by reducing and eliminating commissions, on-line travel agencies must justify the fees they charge (or the added advertising overhead) by serving customers better. Fare Compare is the type of service worth paying ticketing fees for—it still saves money over a "random" attempt at an airline Web site, and it saves time over systematic attempts to decipher the fare structure. Because Fare Compare generates its data implicitly (without any extra effort on behalf of customers), you could argue that compensation really isn't necessary or expected by Expedia customers. The Fare Compare service is compensation enough.

IF YOU LISTEN, THEY WILL COME

Expedia listens and customers come, but they may not buy. The system isn't a perfect lock-in. Customers could visit Fare Compare and then try to save fees by booking elsewhere (a historical problem among travel agencies). On the flip side, an unscrupulous airline might decide to quote a single low fare just to get "well listed" and then have that fare disappear. Even with all these limitations, Fare Compare is a valuable service that makes people want to visit Expedia.com and consider buying tickets there. As important, Expedia might become a membership service if the travel industry at large moves in that direction (which, we suspect, it might).

Business Applications

Expedia illustrates how customer purchases can create valuable search tools. How might you turn your customers' purchases into a useful search tool? Well, for one thing, you could create gift baskets based upon products that customers frequently ask to have wrapped. You could study popular combinations of products and pair them together. As long as the results of your data mining are displayed anonymously, customers won't mind that their purchases and experiences have been used to benefit others.

Oftentimes, the quality of editorial content is the differentiator between sites. Customers go to Expedia because of add-on services like Fare Compare. They may not fully appreciate the fact that Expedia can offer this service at virtually no extra cost (since the heavy work is done by customers), but we guarantee that Expedia enjoys the cost savings. And customers do appreciate the credibility that comes with knowing these fares were found by other customers, not someone with a stake in the process.

EXPEDIA'S FARE COMPARE

RECOMMENDER(S): Searchable database.

INPUT(S): Results of queries that customers have made (lowest fares).

OUTPUT(S): Sortable lists of data (by airline, fare, date, length of trip).

LESSON: *Customer input adds credibility to your site. And, as long as the results of their research are displayed anonymously and don't adversely affect them, they won't mind that their purchases are used to benefit others.*

Principle #7: Use Communities to Create Content

Quick Tips

- On the Internet, advertisers follow users. Web sites are in a better position than print magazines to offer unbiased reviews by customers—due to the cost of printing.
- Tap the creative genius of your customers. They can be a valuable and *free* addition to your marketing department (Flutter).
- Even when communities generate the content, you can make recommendations based upon their demonstrated interests. Let them know when suitable material or products are available (Flutter).
- Allowing customers to create content often results in cheaper and more trusted information, and greater coverage (Epinions).
- Allow users to create their own "web of trust." On content sites, this can be a list of people whose opinions they respect. On product sites, this might be brands they prefer or recommendations from certain nearest neighbors—given aliases to protect their privacy (Epinions).
- Reward your customers for quality content. Public recognition can mean a lot to your customers. Even if the reward is nominal it indicates that you value their contributions. Your customers will be encouraged to submit more (Epinions).
- The Internet has unlimited space at virtually no extra cost. Store individual reviews. Customers appreciate not only the access to data, but also the immortality of their work (Epinions).
- Spread out editing power, so that everyone is heard, not just the people who shout loudest. Editing engages customers and gives them a proprietary stake in the company or site (Slashdot).
- Anticipate the *first-rater* problem. If you allow customers to edit content, some good material may get slashed and

burned, unless you ensure it gets a second opinion (Slashdot).

- Even if you create your own database, you might be able to create a valuable search tool based upon what your customers do with that database—both their purchases and their queries (Expedia).

- Just because you provide a great service doesn't mean customers will complete the transaction with you. You need to find ways to lock them in: convenience, price, membership fees, to name a few (Expedia).

It's okay to depend upon the kindness of strangers. But it's better to reward them for their contributions. That way they'll keep coming back—both to visit and to provide content.

Interlude #7: Viral Marketing

As its name suggests, viral marketing works much like an infectious disease. If each customer convinces three other customers to buy your product, each of whom convinces three other customers, in a very short while you've got a hit on your hands. In his book *The Tipping Point,* Malcolm Gladwell describes the viral marketing phenomenon using a fun example: Hush Puppies. Hush Puppies were diminishing in popularity as its core market aged and moved on to other brands of footwear. Hush Puppies executives even contemplated putting the brand to sleep. Over a period of just a few months, though, trendy young singles in New York City began wearing Hush Puppies as sort of an ironic fashion statement. At epidemic speed, the fashion trend radiated outward from New York City, creating enormous—and unexpected—demand for the brand. This demand wasn't created by a traditional marketing campaign, using television or magazines to present an image of the brand. Not at all. The brand was reinvigorated almost exclusively by consumers themselves. Hush Puppies executives, most of whom are not young, single, and hip, probably could not have created this sort of demand for their product no matter what kind of advertising they did.

Some marketers are scared of viral marketing because it requires relinquishing control to customers. Viral marketing is hard to start, hard to control, and hard to measure. It can bite the hand that feeds it, as Hollywood well knows. When a Hollywood studio makes a movie that its focus groups project to bomb, the studio reacts in an unexpected way. Rather than cutting the opening-weekend marketing budget and thus cutting its losses, the studio will often launch a barrage of marketing just before the opening weekend. The rationale is that the studio knows that viral marketing is shortly going to be working against them: Everyone who sees the movie will tell their friends *not* to see it! The studio reacts by trying to get as many people as possible to go see the movie on the first weekend, grabbing as much revenue as it can, while it can. By contrast, a movie that the studio knows is going to be a winner is going to benefit from tremendous word-of-mouth advertising, so it doesn't need an artificial boost from first-weekend advertising.

There are ways, though, that the marketer can intentionally use viral marketing to his advantage. The trick to effective viral marketing is getting influential customers who really like the product to tell other customers. To do this you have to solve two problems. First, you have to identify influential customers. Companies like Microsoft hire campus representatives to identify well-connected people who can become on-campus influencers, since they know their employees don't have the on-campus status to start a virus. Second, you have to get those influential customers to communicate to other customers about your product. For Hush Puppies and other fashion items, this is easy: Customers communicate with each other through what they wear. With other, less visible products, you have to work harder. When Hotmail created its free E-mail service, it arranged for every E-mail message sent by Hotmail users to include an exhortation on the bottom of the message. The exhortation encouraged the recipient of the message to consider also signing up for Hotmail. In just a few months, this simple technique boosted Hotmail into heavyweight status. Hotmail now has one of the largest user bases of any E-mail system anywhere in the world.

PayPal is even more infectious than Hotmail—because in order to receive money, you have to join! With over 10 million users and new accounts growing by an average of 18,000 accounts per day, PayPal provides secure money exchanges on-line (through E-mail). In fact, over 1 in 4 auctions on eBay now use PayPal. With strong leverage (the ability to receive money, in this case), viral marketing becomes even more effective. Yes, PayPal still depends upon identifying influential customers and getting them to promote their product, but that effort is lessened by the incentive to be paid.

Researchers at the University of Washington have been studying ways that a collaborative-filtering database can be analyzed to predict which users are the influencers in the database. Once these users are identified, the traditional collaborative-filtering algorithm can help determine which influencers are most likely to favor your product. Then you can use preferential marketing tactics to encourage the influencers to sample your product. In fact, since you already know that if they sample it they will probably like it, and since you already know how many other customers they will influence to buy, you can even predict how much it is worth to you to convince each influencer to try your product! For instance, a moderately strong influencer who is likely to bring you twenty additional customers might warrant a 50-percent-off coupon. On the other hand, a very strong influencer who is likely to convince hundreds or thousands of other customers to buy your product might be worth VIP treatment. You could invite him to special training sessions or demonstrations, give him multiple free samples of the product, or otherwise help him to experience a product you are confident will sell—if only the right people hear about it.

With the number of marketing messages that people are exposed to, it's not surprising that they've developed immunities. They're aware of product placement in movies, they know snake-oil salesmen when they see them, and they might even suspect subliminal messages when they're not there. Consumers are already more willing to trust a friend than a marketing professional for advice about a movie or a car or a neighborhood. Viral marketing helps get the message out to these consumers, in a way they appreciate.

Turn Communities into Content

> What people say behind your back is your
> standing in the community.
>
> —EDGAR WATSON HOWE (1853–1937)

> ... individuals are realized only in and through communities,
> and ... strong, healthy, morally vigorous communities are the
> prerequisite for strong, healthy, morally vigorous individuals.
>
> —ROBERT N. BELLAH, FROM "COMMUNITY PROPERLY
> UNDERSTOOD: A DEFENSE OF 'DEMOCRATIC
> COMMUNITARIANISM,'" *THE ESSENTIAL
> COMMUNITARIAN READER*

I
N 1967, MARSHALL MCLUHAN sounded a warn-
ing with his prescient book *The Medium Is the Mas-
sage:* "Societies have always been shaped more by
the nature of the media by which men communicate
than by the content of the communication." He believed
that the world was becoming a global village, connected
by an electronic nervous system. The consequence, he
feared, was that culture would be wiped out and we
would all be reduced to a least common denominator that
would be defined by television.

More recently, Robert Putnam, author of *Bowling Alone: The Collapse and Revival of American Community* (1995), announced that American civil society was crumbling. He cited the decline of voter turnout, bowling leagues, bridge clubs, and fraternal organizations, among others. He also noted the deterioration of family bonds and trust in general. One of the reasons, he believed, was the technological transformation of leisure—particularly the proliferation of television watching.

Perhaps due to the corrosion of traditional clubs (like bowling leagues), people are seeking out other people in record numbers on the Web. While we won't try to defend television, we believe the Internet can and is helping to develop global communities that feature lots of interpersonal interaction and trust. Rather than being communities of geography or employment, they are instead communities of interest. Sure, some of the people on the Web are only interested in shouting into the void (chat rooms, in our experience). Many more, though, are eager to make lasting connections. The problem is: How do they find people whose company they'll enjoy?

Some dating services charge as much as $5,000. Not because they do exhaustive research or have such high fixed costs, but because upper-class singles want some assurances that they'll be matched with people in a similar tax bracket. The Paris metro used to charge more for first-class cars, even though they were the exact same seats as coach. Why? To assure riders of a certain class of companions. Elitism of this sort can be ridiculous, but the message here is important: People are willing to pay a considerable amount of money to be placed in clubs, even when there's no assurance that they'll like the people in these clubs. As America learned from *Who Wants to Marry a Millionaire,* not everyone with money is a catch or even a good seatmate. There are Rick Rockwells everywhere.

The desire to find people you like is incredibly strong. Until recommenders came around, though, you had to rely more on serendipity. That's all changed. Recommenders are now being used to help people find clubs and compatible people within those clubs.

Recommenders are also being used to form new clubs. After

all, if there are enough people who share your interests, why shouldn't you have a club of your own?

While you're probably aware of the ways people congregate on the Web (chat rooms, bulletin boards, portals, games, etc.), what may not be clear is how this affects mainstream retailers. Why should retailers care about creating interest communities among their customers? Well, for one thing, remember Paco Underhill's refrain from "Principle 3: Maintain Excellent Service Across Touchpoints": *The more contact with customers, the more they buy.* This guideline extends to customer/customer contact. After all, customers can help each other navigate your site and find items of interest. Simply congregating at your site has tremendous value. One of the main reasons people go to Amazon is for the communities that gather there.

Imagine you own a camping store. Your customers may want to meet to discuss rappelling gear or what to bring on a six-day canoe trip. Without encouragement, they probably won't. If they had some assurances that the topic and the people would suit them, they might agree to meet at your store for a cup of hot chocolate and an hour discussion. You probably spend thousands, if not millions, of dollars on advertising just to get customers into your store. Starting an interest community is far cheaper. Recommenders can help you match people together who share the same interests, increasing the likelihood that the group will continue meeting.

In this chapter we'll explore several of the most popular interactive sites (AOL, eBay, and gaming sites like MSN.zone and OKbridge). From them, you will learn how technology plays a role in putting people together (and keeping them together). You'll also see firsthand the value of creating interest communities.

Here are a couple of tips for turning communities into content:

1. Social = sticky.
2. Hosting a community leads to viral-marketing opportunities.
3. Your customers may be your best sales- and servicepeople.

1. *Social = sticky.* There's a reason why there are *The Rocky Horror Picture Show* revival houses around the country. The people who go to these typically late-night showings have seen the movie tens, if not hundreds, of times. Why do they keep showing up? Because they like the movie? Yes. But that's not the heart of it. People go to *The Rocky Horror Picture Show* to see other people. Fans of the movie dress up like the characters in the movie (the hump-backed butler, the cross-dressing villain, and the like). They also shout out responses to virtually every line in the movie and sing along with the songs.

People like to be with people who share their interests—even interests as unusual and narrowly defined as *The Rocky Horror Picture Show.* In some cases, *especially* with interests this unusual and narrowly defined.

2. *Hosting a community leads to viral-marketing and recommender opportunities.* A viral marketer must analyze the potential customer base in a new way: looking for communication and persuasion paths. Viral marketing depends on getting your product into the hands of those whose use will "infect" many others. That requires identifying the types of customers who will evangelize and those who have the authority to compel use by others. Once the target customers are identified, the viral marketer must figure out how to induce those users to adopt the product, often by making it free or cheap for early adopters.

Creating a cohesive community may be the best marketing dollars you've ever spent. Talk about a persuasion path. Take eBay, for instance. eBay takes every opportunity to put their customers together. You might think that the buying and selling exchanges would be enough. Not nearly. They have bulletin boards, a café where people can chat, and even a library (which might provide material for discussion). eBay is now a place where mini-businesses, not just collectors, camp out. And these havens allow evangelical customers the opportunity to recruit others.

Furthermore, the types of customers who are likely to start a new discussion thread or schedule a chat may well be the same ones who have the personality and connections to be effective evangelists. You want these people on your site—not on your competitors'!

3. *Your customers may be your best sales- and servicepeople.* When people get together to talk at your site, they'll inevitably discuss your products and services. They may not only raise service problems, they may also be able to suggest solutions. Sometimes these solutions will help you to improve your products, but even more often they will help satisfy other customers. Businesses can save big money by channeling the support power of their customer, as companies ranging from Oracle and Microsoft to tiny one-product consumer-goods manufacturers have learned. Of course you may also find that customers help lead others to your products and services. Free support, *and* free sales help!

Portals and other sites where people congregate make money another way, too. Wherever people spend a lot of time, there are many opportunities to advertise. In addition, we've seen a movement toward premium groups and clubs where you have to pay for certain features. Fantasy football sites on newspapers, for instance, often charge for player or injury updates. Either way, you benefit from having customers be the content.

No, Americans aren't bowling together anymore and television is mostly mindless entertainment, but the desire for human interaction hasn't diminished. People don't like to be alone. The Internet has allowed people to make connections that they never would have before. People in small Wyoming towns can meet people in Madrid who share their interests. Internet users are not confined by region, race, economic status, or gender. On-line, what matters most is what you have to contribute: products, actions, opinions, humor—the possibilities are endless!

AOL CHAT AND INSTANT MESSAGING

D OES AOL TIME WARNER own the world yet? If not, it will soon. With over 135 million subscribers to its entertainment empire (Time Inc., HBO/Cinemax, AOL, Time Warner Cable, etc.), AOL Time Warner knows something about creating communities. And mergers, we might add.

In the early days of Internet service providers, it was a bit murky who would come out ahead (or even alive). Through its advertising blitz, omnipresent free CDs, and brand-building strategy, AOL overcame the limitations of its servers. Customers today would need Prozac to put up with the hours of busy signals and tortoise-like navigation that AOL first offered. Loathed and loved, AOL has grown considerably since its inception in 1985. AOL now boasts over 31 million subscribers. Their 2001 second-quarter revenue stood at a cool $2.1 billion, up 13 percent from the same quarter the previous year.

If they haven't already, AOL can pop the cork. They won. And not just in the United States, we might add. AOL International offers on-line services to 16 countries in 8 different languages and claims over 6 million customers. The numbers abroad are skyrocketing.

On their Web page, under the category "Who We Are," AOL advises visitors that it "seeks to build a global medium as central to people's lives as the telephone or television." Now, that sounds a bit ambitious, but who are we to argue? In 1996, AOL users spent 12 minutes on-line a day. Now they spend nearly 70 minutes.

Two of the main reasons for AOL's success are their chat rooms and their Instant Messaging service. They may not be as revolutionary as the telephone, but they have, in fact, changed the way people communicate.

Chat Rooms

Chat rooms are virtual meeting places where people come together to "talk" by typing messages. AOL is the king of chat, providing thousands of chat rooms on every imaginable topic. Tens to hundreds of thousands of people worldwide gather in these chat rooms during peak hours (which are becoming around-the-clock as AOL becomes increasingly international). Why are they there? The answer can be found in the three C's: Communication, Companionship, and Courtship. We have long known that people like the chance to tell their story, to be heard. They even often like the chance to hear others tell their own stories. Chat rooms provide a safe and convenient place for people to engage in conversations on a wide variety of topics, including topics too sensitive or embarrassing to discuss among "real-world" friends. Chat-room companions can be a supportive community, and, if they are not, you can change rooms or simply ignore the people you don't like (removing their messages entirely from your view of the conversation).

Instant Messaging

Instant Messaging (IM) provides a complementary service to chat. It combines a directory of "buddies," an awareness service, and a low-effort, high-context communication channel. IM users have a window that keeps track of which buddies are on-line and whether they've been active recently. With just a couple of clicks, you can send a message to a buddy instantly. The buddy may see it right away, or he may finish other tasks and get back to you later. When both participants are actively using IM, it becomes like a private chat channel, with the added feature that users can be aware of other users outside the channel. When participants are paying attention to other things, it becomes a lightweight form of E-mail, keeping the context of the conversation active and supporting a faster turnaround than full-fledged E-mail offers, but also restricting its users to smaller and simpler messages.

IM has become a huge hit. At first it was being used primarily socially, to help friends keep in touch in virtual on-line space. IM features have been added to gaming environments (such as the Microsoft Network's game zone, zone.msn.com) to help players find favorite opponents or teammates. Soon IM spread into offices, with employees using it both as a quick source of assistance and as a tool to help determine when to arrange telephone and in-person contact. (One side effect is that many offices have had to restrict the use of free IM services since they send unencrypted information over the Internet.)

SOCIAL = STICKY

America Online long ago recognized that the masses didn't want an Internet service provider; they wanted a place where they could communicate with people. By providing virtual gathering places and forums for communication, AOL became not only an enormously popular service, but also an extremely sticky one. After all, as organizations as diverse as fraternities, churches, and gangs have long realized, how likely are you to leave your friends? The fact that most AOL users have E-mail sent to their AOL address and maintain an AOL directory of E-mail addresses makes it even harder to leave.

HOSTING A COMMUNITY LEADS TO VIRAL-MARKETING AND RECOMMENDER OPPORTUNITIES

In our early days after founding Net Perceptions, we spent some time studying AOL chat rooms in the hopes of finding a "killer recommender application" that would help people locate discussions that interested them. We imagined a system that could mix subjective evaluations of people with analysis of content. Try though we might, however, we had a hard time finding the content. More than 90 percent of the chat rooms we visited, no matter what the labeled topic, degraded rapidly into "courtship behavior." Within minutes of joining a chat, we were sure to see someone asking for "ages and sexes" of the discussants, or perhaps specifically asking whether there were any participants of "interest." We quickly learned an important lesson: People were in chat rooms not to find information, but to find people. And many of them needed to anchor their discussion in a physical description of their companions (even when that physical description is untrue, as they frequently are).

We never built that recommender application, but had we done so, it would have been easier than we'd expected. We didn't need to know anything about topics, it turns out. If we'd simply detected the conversation partners people liked and disliked, that would have allowed us to use collaborative-filtering techniques to find other partners they might like or dislike. Note the irony that in this case, the "neighbors" who share your taste may be really bad partners, even while they are really good sources of recommendations.

IM also provides the core of a recommender community. Many of the early collaborative-filtering systems directed recommendations through preexisting social channels. In other words, users either explicitly identified the people whose recommendations they trusted, or they explicitly identified people to whom they wanted their recommendations directed. A community of IM users has built-in associations among people. Anyone on a buddy list is likely to be more trustworthy than the average user. High levels of discussion are also likely to indicate compatibility. As far as we know, as of this writing none of the IM providers are using this social-network information to form recommender communities, but it seems obvious that one day they will do so (hopefully with the consent of the participants). At that point, service providers will be able to direct information, advertising, offers, and other personally selected content to users based on the reactions of their IM pals. Suddenly, IM moves from being a money-losing way to get customers to being a revenue-enhancing way to target marketing.

YOUR CUSTOMERS MAY BE YOUR BEST SALES- AND SERVICEPEOPLE

Not surprisingly, AOL has vigorously guarded its IM system, preventing competitors from routing messages and awareness information between their networks and AOL's. AOL happily provided free access to its IM system, but not within its competitors' sites and services. In this way, they capitalize on their fundamental edge (which is the critical mass of people they have) to become the obvious choice for many users seeking an ISP and Internet community. Rather than leave this community, customers who appreciate these services will likely recruit friends and family members instead.

Chat rooms and IM are also for self-contained support communities. From helping other users with the technicalities of using the chat facilities (e.g., teaching newcomers how to ignore someone and how to express emotion textually) to guiding people to other interesting content, the presence of a community of users has drastically reduced the number of people AOL would otherwise need to pay to support their extensive system. Indeed, AOL may have once taken this too far. A number of "volunteers" who moderated chat areas were being told just when and how to "do their job." Some of these people complained that they were being treated like employees, and hence deserved minimum wage rather than free AOL service. The moral: Community members may sell and service on your behalf, but not if they're kept on a leash.

Business Applications

Many large sites have discovered the power of chat rooms to bring people to live events and to give them a chance to air their opinions. Public radio stations such as Minnesota Public Radio have on-line "soapboxes" where people can sound off, sometimes leading to airing their views on the radio. CNN regularly hosts chats with news reporters and news makers. You can arrange discussions with experts or new-product designers, or simply organize forums where people can discuss the products, services, and topics that interest them.

Consider how to incorporate Instant Messaging. Lands' End uses it as a way for customers to bring friends along on trips to the virtual store, or to contact sales reps in the middle of an on-line shopping trip. AOL uses it to foster community. And, in the future, we imagine that the personal connections made will lead to highly accurate recommendations.

AOL

RECOMMENDER(S): None.

RECOMMENDER OPPORTUNITY: AOL could recommend on-line chat rooms and discussion partners based on information such as what participants say, how long they typically chat, and who is on their buddy list.

LESSON: *If people connect to others through your site, they'll become loyal to it, and thereby to you.*

eBAY

L IKE AOL, eBay is an on-line pillar. People spend more time shopping on eBay than any other site, according to Media Metrix. With 34 million registered users and $5 billion in annualized gross sales for 2000, eBay has grown exponentially since its launch in 1995. Now, in addition to auctions, eBay offers fixed-price trading through Half.com. eBay Stores extend eBay's presence even more—allowing sellers to set up customized shops in the friendly confines of eBay.

At first glance, eBay's infrastructure doesn't seem all that impressive. All they do is offer a venue for buyers and sellers to meet. In the process, however, they've created a tremendous sense of community. This is because eBay has worked hard to engender trust among strangers. They were founded under the following principles: "We believe people are basically good. We believe that everyone has something to contribute." For eBay to succeed, people have to be good. Otherwise, buyers wouldn't send money for products they haven't seen to people they haven't met.

People are understandably very nervous about buying something on the Internet. Traditional retailers who create physical stores are generally considered trustworthy because of the expense of setting up operation and their accessibility to customers who want to complain. And, among traditional retailers, stand-alone stores sit a notch above mall stores in terms of perceived reliability. On-line retailers who have their own Web site are much less expensive to set up than traditional stores, and slightly less accessible, but they still require that someone sign up for an URL and go to the trouble of building a Web site. eBay retailers just have to sign up for an account and— *voilà*—they're in business.

Since most transactions on eBay take place between the buyer and the seller, the buyer has to have some way of trusting that products will actually come to him, and the seller has to have some way of trusting that payment will actually come to him. eBay could solve this problem by acting as an intermediary between the buyer and the seller, but this would dramatically increase eBay's overhead. eBay would have to manage not only the flow of money in all of its various forms, but also the flow of physical goods. Furthermore, many of the challenges in eBay transactions are not created by disagreements over whether money was actually sent or whether goods were actually received. Most of these problems arise from disagreements about the quality of the goods received. For instance, if I promise to sell you a bike and the bike arrives with rust marks, you might be very disappointed. On the other hand, I might feel that I've lived up to my promise to sell you the bike that was pictured, in as-is condition.

eBay overcomes these problems by having buyers rate and express their opinions about the sellers with whom they do business. The rating system is quite simple. You just give the seller you interacted with a positive (+1), neutral (0), or negative (-1) rating. eBay ID cards then allow you to view a summary of the most recent information about eBay members: the number of positive, neutral, and negative comments they've received over the past week, month, and six months, and whether there have been any bid retractions. By scanning this information, you can make a decision about whether the seller is trustworthy. At the bottom of the page, you can also read the comments by buyers who have done business with this seller. New buyers can decide whether to do business with the seller based not only on the statistical summary but also on the specific problems previous buyers encountered. For instance, if all of the problems were with late delivery and you don't need the item for several weeks, you might be willing to wait.

Naturally, sellers aren't the only ones who should be scrutinized. To be equitable, eBay also lets sellers rate buyers. One problem with these buyer and seller score sheets, however, is that as people disagree about problems, they may rate each other badly without sufficient cause. eBay attempts to address this problem by allowing members to respond to complaints written about them. For instance, a seller who is accused of shipping products late might respond by saying that he shipped as soon as the check cleared, but the first check bounced.

Another problem, hard to get around, is that eBay sellers who earn a bad profile fairly can just create a new profile and quit using the old one. This behavior leads buyers to seek out sellers who have an extended history with eBay. The longer the history, the more trust the buyer will have. This creates a significant challenge for new sellers, however, since buyers have no incentive to trust them.

SOCIAL = STICKY

Judging from the number of positive transactions listed next to each buyer and seller, eBay is extremely sticky. For some, eBay is borderline addictive. There is almost no end to the number of tempting products for sale there at any given time. And eBay veterans get an adrenaline rush from the possibility of getting these items for cheap.

The fact that eBay users get together off-line indicates that their connection isn't strictly professional. On their Community page, eBay indicates that some users plan vacations together, get together for picnics, organize grassroots movements, and even help each other with home repairs. eBay's bulletin boards and chats at the eBay Café help to cultivate this communal spirit.

HOSTING A COMMUNITY LEADS TO VIRAL-MARKETING AND RECOMMENDER OPPORTUNITIES

eBay's viral aspect comes from all the people who say "I bought on eBay" or "I'm selling it on eBay." You've probably heard these comments from friends, neighbors, and even celebrities. Jay Leno, for one, sold a celebrity-autographed motorcycle on eBay to benefit the victims of the World Trade Center attacks.

eBay recommends buyers and sellers through its rating system.

These recommendations (and the actions of influencers like Leno) give customers the confidence to buy or sell on eBay. eBay could, however, take it a step farther (or even several steps). They could, for instance, recommend buyers and sellers who are endorsed by people you've endorsed.

Despite clear category distinctions and search functions, eBay's vast collection of goods can be daunting. Customers might not think to investigate glass chess sets, and yet that may be exactly the kind of thing they want. Using items they've clicked on or bid on, eBay could assemble a pretty impressive collection of their interests. Recommendations generated by people who share their interests could really help customers navigate eBay's many wares.

An incredible feature of viral marketing is the way it builds on itself. With each transaction, eBay members gain confidence in the rating system—leading to more frequent transactions. The more eBay buyers and sellers rate each other, the greater the confidence of *new* buyers and sellers, too. They see high member ratings, and they have some assurance that they'll be satisfied with their sale or purchase. We call this the *Vortex Effect*. Once rating systems reach a critical mass, they create a black hole in which no sales can escape to your competitors.

YOUR CUSTOMERS MAY BE YOUR BEST SALES- AND SERVICEPEOPLE

eBay allows customers to create their own stores on its site, provides a library of articles on topics like "Caring for Your Jewelry" and "Autograph Authentication," and has granted over $2,500,000 to non-profit organizations. It's no wonder eBay's customers are devoted. At eBay, customers go so far as to form "neighborhood watch" groups to protect against misuse or etiquette violations. On one occasion, we recall hearing, an active eBay customer got divorced from her husband. In the settlement, her husband kept the computer. This woman's on-line friends took up a collection to buy her another computer (on eBay, we believe) to get her back into the community. Talk about salespeople!

Business Applications

Clearly defined rating systems are a good way to recommend products, or people, to your customers—especially if they include detailed comments. Ratings and comments help remove fear of the unknown.

Customers can rate people just as easily as they can rate products. They can rate employees they have contact with, other customers, or the competition. These ratings might not only serve to identify your strengths and weaknesses more clearly, they may also give other customers the confidence to buy. You could, for instance, use customer ratings of your call-center operators to do a better job of matching callers to operators who have served them well.

eBAY

RECOMMENDER(S): Statistical aggregation (takes into account time frame, number of sales, rating scale, text comments).

INPUT(S): Ratings and comments of sellers and buyers.

OUTPUT(S): Colored stars, indicating level of trust engendered by sellers.

LESSON: *The Vortex Effect: The more sales and ratings you have, the more sales and ratings you get.*

GAMES

F THE PROLIFERATION of fantasy sports across the country is any indication, Americans are into games and gaming. How else can you explain over 200,000 MSN gamers on an average Monday afternoon? They're playing MechCommander2, You Know It! Pop Trivia, and classic staples like chess, bridge, and backgammon. And, of course, they're gambling with on-line blackjack, roulette, and craps (hopefully for fun, but at least some of them for money at offshore on-line casinos).

Americans like to game—both for the competition and for the camaraderie. There is an endless array of games to choose from on-line, almost all of them multiplayer. Most games have chat facilities and some have convention cards to help communication. Players seem to have as much fun bantering back and forth as they do testing their game-playing skills. The games are so popular that entities like the American Contract Bridge League now sanction on-line games and award master points, which formerly were reserved for in-person bridge games and tournaments.

The problem with on-line game sites, however, is making introductions. Most people know what games they like to play, but when they first join a community like MSN or OKbridge, they don't know who they'd like to play with. They know that there are literally thousands of people playing games at any given time. With so many people, they can reasonably assume that someone out there is the perfect partner for them. But how do they find him or her?

When John first started playing bridge on MSN, he had a very hard time finding tables he could play at without getting attacked or having partners leave. The MSN community has a set of rooms of different skill levels and a large number of tables in each room. At the table, players negotiate styles of play and their preferred bidding conventions. John is a good, but not expert, player, which puts him in the largest category of players. Finding suitable partners was very hard, though, because he didn't understand the esoteric language. Partners would shoot out a stream of characters like "SAYC + RKC 3124 + ud signals okay, pd?" and he'd have no idea what they meant.

Even once you figure out the shorthand and realize the correct answer is "No way!" finding someone who is able to bid and play the way you bid and play is still a challenge. Many players bounce from table to table looking for a good fit.

SOCIAL = STICKY

Right now, on-line game communities can be *very* hard on new players, criticizing them so harshly that they never come back.

Other new players choose to play only against robots. Robots are silent and tolerant, but they don't play very much like other humans. Playing against robots is like hitting a tennis ball against the wall: After a while, it gets boring.

Once people find good partners, however, they are often loath to leave gaming sites. On the introductory page for players who are considering signing onto OKbridge, one player tells how were it not for OKbridge she "never would have met the wonderful man who is going to be my husband." The two of them played over 3,000 hands together. Their bridge game suffered as they fell in love, but, having endured some bad games, they feel like their love can handle anything.

With the exception of the introductory phase, these on-line gaming communities are so successful that neighborhood bridge centers are suffering. Their patrons are often old and leery of going out at night (especially in Minnesota winters); MSN and OKbridge provide the social outlet they desire without the hassle.

HOSTING A COMMUNITY LEADS TO VIRAL-MARKETING AND RECOMMENDER OPPORTUNITIES

Although OKbridge has a Friends List where you can store names and locate players you enjoy playing with and MSN provides a similar search option, they both could benefit from recommenders. First, a more detailed match could be made on syntactic criteria, like what bridge-bidding systems you play. Second, that match could be combined with taste criteria, like what other people you've enjoyed playing with. For instance, some people at about John's level in bridge have enormous patience for very slow play, which he can't stand. Others very much like yelling at their partners when things go badly. This group sometimes likes a partner to yell back and sometimes doesn't. A collaborative-filtering system would result in a lot more marriages and a lot less friction.

YOUR CUSTOMERS MAY BE YOUR BEST SALES- AND SERVICEPEOPLE

If you ever do make it to a neighborhood bridge center, you're almost certain to find players championing OKbridge—even though they've elected to play at the bridge center on that particular night rather than on-line. They applaud the flexibility. The $99 yearly fee is well worth it, you'll hear time and again. After all, you can play 24/7.

If you've met any diehard bridge players, you know they're behind the improvements on sites like MSN and OKbridge. They won't hesitate to complain. Discussions happen all the time on MSN about how games work, demystifying the shorthand, and even identifying sore sports and "cheaters" who leave games they are going to lose (depriving the winner of the credit).

Business Applications

There's a reason why reunion organizers hand out name tags and arrange a wide array of activities: Just putting people together isn't enough. You need to help people make connections. All the bells and whistles in the world (like the advanced graphics and bidding systems on MSN and OKbridge) won't necessarily result in content customers. Make sure you don't ignore the human element. Nobody likes to stand on the dance floor all alone no matter how good the band.

GAMES

RECOMMENDER(S): None.

RECOMMENDER OPPORTUNITY: Gaming sites could recommend partners and opponents based on analysis of playing style, satisfaction with past partners and opponents, and game-specific preferences.

LESSON: *For some sites, the social element is as important to customers, if not more important, than the content, products, or services.*

Principle #8: Turn Communities into Content

Quick Tips

- Instant messaging (IM) may not be the next telephone, but it's close. It's lighter and faster than E-mail and has found tremendous success in many venues: social, gaming, intra-office, and commercial (AOL).
- Remember the three C's: Communication, Companionship, and Courtship. This is what drew most people to the Internet initially. Don't underestimate the value of these offerings. If you don't consider your site a "social" site, you're missing a big opportunity (AOL).
- Buddy lists can generate highly effective recommender communities (AOL).
- Customers can rate people just as easily as they can rate products. They can rate employees they have contact with, other customers, or the competition. These ratings might not only serve to identify your strengths and weaknesses more clearly, they may also give other customers the confidence to buy (eBay).
- Give the people who get rated an opportunity to respond. The resulting discussions will be much richer than just the statistical averages (eBay).
- Customers will find a way around punitive measures (i.e., banishment from a site or bad reviews). They may simply enter under a new profile. Customers will help police their community if you give them the opportunity to do so, either through ratings and reviews or by more direct measures (eBay).
- If your site's intent is to put people in touch with each other and they wind up preferring the company of robots, you need to improve your service (Games).
- For first-timers on social sites, the learning curve for shorthand is steep. Try to make your site more hospitable to newcomers (Games).

- Allow visitors to keep track of people they've enjoyed playing and socializing with. You might even provide encouragements to build social networks, the way MCI tried to encourage users to enlist friends and family members with discounts (Games).

People use the Internet not because they want the company of robots, but because they want to communicate with other people. For some companies and sites, people connecting with other people is their entire business. Fostering interest communities on your site, however, will pay dividends even if your products and services don't necessitate customer/customer interaction. Barnes & Noble University is a prime example of this. Hundreds of thousands of book buyers now congregate at Barnesandnoble.com to discuss literature. Do the math. Can you afford not to create interest communities?

The Future of Collaborative Filtering and Recommender Systems

We are drowning in information and starving for knowledge.

—RUTHERFORD D. ROGERS

It wasn't raining when Noah built the ark.

—HOWARD RUFF

The future we see for recommenders revolves around bringing them into the light. By that we mean outdoors. You've seen how recommenders have revolutionized Internet marketing. We envision recommenders moving out more into the public and the bricks-and-mortar sphere. The tools are already in place: mobile phones and wireless PDAs, interactive kiosks, smart cards, and software agents. And the incentives are just too tempting to ignore.

A new generation of more accurate, time- and location-sensitive recommenders is also on the horizon. These recommenders will incorporate some of the cutting-edge techniques you've seen on display here—namely, confidence measures, user thresholds, and combination recommenders. We'll also discuss some that are just emerging, like footprint technologies and temporal recommenders.

Extrapolating from what we've seen in other industries, we also imagine that some colossal battles will be waged over the ownership, use, and storage of customer-purchase histories. Who comes out ahead will largely depend on who gets there first.

Bringing Recommenders into the Light

Software Agents

At their simplest, software agents are autonomous programs that scan parts of the Internet and collect information that might be most interesting to a user. For instance, a user might have an agent that watches the Microsoft Web site for new patches to Windows 2000 and notifies him when patches are made available. (In fact, Microsoft provides such an agent with Windows 2000.)

Software agents are willing to scan enormous numbers of documents without complaint, looking for those that are interesting to a user. News agents can watch what articles you read and find commonalties in pieces you like. As new articles come in, their ability to predict your reactions will improve. We've found that they're not as effective as other humans (and collaborative filtering) in forming predictions, but they're tireless and they travel well. These agents will consume every bit of information that comes in and provide limitless opinions.

At present, agents do have several weaknesses:

1. Some of them are not able to learn from users.
2. As the number of software agents increases, it may be hard for users to select which ones are best for them.
3. Agents generally have information only about the content of an item and not about actions other users have taken with that item.

Agents will be combined with recommenders in the future in several ways. For one thing, recommenders will help users select agents that will be most useful for them. Agents will also be used to help fill in the gaps in collaborative-filtering systems. Since software agents are so industrious, they are happy to rate everything, even the most unpopular items, so that there are opinions to use when you need a recommendation. Your nearest neighbors may turn out to be software agents in disguise.

Wireless and Mobile Devices

Businesses are focusing on being available wherever, whenever, and however their customers want to interact with them. One consequence is the emergence of M-commerce (mobile-commerce) platforms to provide customers with the ability to buy what they want from mobile phones or wireless PDAs. These devices allow businesses to reach out to customers in their cars, at a friend's house, on the beach, and just about anywhere else.

Although mobile devices are convenient because they can be taken anywhere, they do have limitations. With limited memory, small screens, and small keyboards, traditional navigation and search interfaces don't work. It's simply too cumbersome for mobile users to have to scroll through reams of material or enter a long list of search terms.

That's where recommenders come in. Recommenders can limit the number of items a customer needs to see on each page. If a customer is presented with the options she will most appreciate, she won't have to scroll through product after product. For instance, if a user is interested in jazz music, her handheld can have the names of jazz albums she is most likely to be interested in purchasing, along with information and reviews of those albums. When she is in a store thinking about buying an album, the most important information will be at her fingertips.

Recommenders can also be used in voice interfaces where the limiting factor is low bandwidth rather than the size of the screen on the device. We all know the frustration of waiting for a faceless voice to read us the choices from a list so we can press a number on our phone. In the future, voice interfaces will be connected to recommenders so best choices are presented early. For instance, 777-FILM presents information about movies showing in area theaters. In the Twin Cities there are hundreds of movies showing at any given time, and navigating through the list of possible movies takes ten to fifteen minutes. A recommender could immediately present you with the five movies you'd be most interested in viewing based on movies you've liked in the past.

Wireless devices will soon know where you are, so they can display movies at the theater nearest to you. They'll also be able to present offers for stores when you're approaching them.

As a marketer, this may sound great: You can reach people anywhere, anytime. On the other hand, as a customer, it may sound like a nightmare: Are you going to be bothered wherever you go? Bear in mind that these technologies can be set up to allow customers to pull recommendations when they want them. Customers might even be able to "sell" the opportunity to disturb them by suggesting, for example, that they receive a minimum of one dollar or 10 percent off before they consent to receive advertisements on their cell phone or PDA.

Kiosks

Imagine going into your local movie store, swiping your membership card, and getting suggestions for movies you might like to rent based entirely on your past purchases. You can say if you didn't like one in the past, and that information will be incorporated into your recommendations. Your recommendations might also include movies that aren't the highest on your list but are being offered at a discount because the store has ten in stock. At the point-of-sale terminals in stores, the coupons that are printed won't be just for products that are willing to pay to get cross-promoted (for example, if they buy Coke, give them a coupon for Pepsi), but will be for products the consumers might not even know they would like, including the examples we've seen of surprising recommendations in call centers (like GUS).

To date, kiosks have been employed mainly for search purposes, but it won't be long before they're promoted to recommender status. One day they may be as omnipresent as ATMs.

Smart Cards

Today, stores retain customer-purchase histories and preferences. As customers go from store to store, there might as well be a firewall between their identities at each store. Naturally, stores don't want to relinquish their customer information, because that would enable their competitors to offer comparable service and recommendations. And, as a result, they might lose their customers. Customers, on the other hand, would benefit from a competition between stores for the right to recommend products. With smart-card technology, they may get that chance.

In the near future, a customer could have a smart card that knows every jazz album she owns and how much she likes each one. When she goes to a jazz store, she could swipe the smart card at a kiosk and get recommendations for CDs. She'd get different recommendations from every store she visits, based on inventory and the type of recommendation system used. Stores would be able to compete freely for customers based on both inventory—as today—and on the quality and speed of their recommender system. Our shopper might choose to go to a particular jazz-music store because it does the best at helping her find music she likes. If another promising store springs up, or if she's out of town, she would still be able to access her information using the smart card. Better yet, since all of the preferences of a consumer for thousands of products can fit in a few tens of kilobytes of storage, our jazz shopper could use her smart card in any number of venues, not just music stores.

The Next Generation of Recommenders

Footprints

Have you ever wondered how other users navigate a Web site? Now you can find out. Early work in social navigation provided visible *read wear* and *edit wear* to let people viewing electronic documents know how actively those documents had been used (just as many students learn the trick of finding good books in a library by looking for worn ones). More recently, Web browsers have been augmented with trails—little footprints that help you see where other members of your community have been. Along with these subtle techniques, a variety of applications are providing interfaces that allow you to talk with other people on the same Web page or on a closely related one. These systems either leave messages behind (perhaps questions waiting for an answer) or set up a live chat.

A number of experimental footprint systems have been designed for special-purpose applications. A group in Sweden has built an on-line grocery where you can see other people shopping, and even join them in "recipe rooms" to see what recipes are popular. The irony is that Swedish grocery shoppers rarely discuss their buying in person. The same group is now working on techniques to put footprints and messages in real space, not just on the Internet. As you carry your PDA or cell phone around a shopping mall or city, you'll be able to tell where your community members have been and see the messages they left behind.

Parametric Search

We are beginning to see the emergence of systems that combine recommender systems with traditional search systems. A search for "soccer" on Amazon.com returns 2,219 results in Books. As a youth-soccer coach, John has purchased about a dozen youth-coaching books from Amazon. When he needs a new soccer book, it would be wonderful to get a list of the best two dozen, based on the books he's purchased in the past. His current non-keyword recommendations suggest only two soccer books, along with children's books, science-fiction books, scientific non-fiction books, and computer-science books. These are all interests of his, but they're *not* what he's interested in right now!

Future systems will combine what is called "parametric search" with recommenders. In these, you enter your desired criteria along a set of dimensions. The system searches the catalog for items that fit your desires and ranks the returned items according to how good you are likely to find them. The parametric search allows you to produce a subcatalog that is tailored to your current information need. The recommender allows you to search through this smaller catalog for the items that will be most interesting to you from the ones that fit your need. The recommender and the search system are perfect matches for each other: One understands your long-term tastes and interests, and one searches for items that fit your current need. Together, they find what you're looking for (and nothing else).

Temporal Recommenders

Have you ever been low on eggs or milk and not realized it until you got home from a trip to the grocery store? Temporal recommenders could remind you of products you may be low on, or out of, based upon how frequently you buy those items and when you last purchased them. Instead of making shopping lists at home, you could do it on a store's Web site and be reminded of these items when you got to the store. Your purchase histories and shopping lists could even be merged with those of family members or friends so that you don't both wind up buying a twenty-four-pack of toilet paper.

We also anticipate temporal recommenders that predict changes in your taste. For example, a temporal recommender might learn that your wine tastes are evolving and use the pattern of evolution to match you against more experienced wine drinkers. Then the recommender could suggest wines to help develop your palate. Similar techniques exist across the arenas of education and training—recommending what you need next, not what you just finished (no matter how good it was).

We haven't seen many temporal recommenders—yet. But, like parametric searches, temporal recommenders are mindful of short- and long-term needs. They're too promising not to succeed.

Confidence Measures

As their exposure to recommenders grows, customers may want some assurances before acting upon a recommendation. Marketers should be able to supply, either explicitly or on request, a set of confidence measures—starting with a prediction. For instance, Moviecritic.com shows a target with each prediction; the closer the arrow is to the center of the target, the more likely the prediction is accurate. Buyers may be skeptical of confidence measures they don't understand, though. They may think the store is pushing them to make a buying decision. One way to increase buyer confidence—and thereby sales—is to give explanations for the recommendations. The explanations might be in terms of the products, other people, or past experience with the recommender. For instance, one explanation might be: "You liked *Star Wars* and *Star Trek*. Everyone else who liked those two movies also liked *The Matrix*. That's why we're predicting you'll like *The Matrix*." Explanations of this type help users understand how the store is working on their behalf and help them overcome their inertia to make a purchase.

Thresholds

As we saw with Slashdot, some marketers will choose to put users in charge of their recommendations. For instance, a store might let a user choose a threshold at which to have television shows recommended to her. If the show's prediction is four stars for her, the customer could request that her TiVo record the show. If the prediction is three stars, the customer might request that it be listed along with all the other three-star programs and sent in an E-mail once at the beginning of the week. If the prediction is five stars, the customer might want to be paged an hour before the show.

Ownership, Use, and Storage of Customer-Purchase Histories

Security and Storage

As we mentioned in "Interlude #5," Microsoft's .NET provides a way for people to store information on servers at a central location. They can then access this information from wherever they are. A customer may choose to upload his preference information to .NET and just identify himself to a store with a smart card, giving the store permission to access his preference information temporarily. In this way, the information can be completely portable, no matter how much storage it eventually requires. This approach raises important privacy issues, though, since the customer may not trust the .NET server company to hold his preference data. The temptation for the company to make use of the data for marketing or to resell the data to others will be powerful. Even if the people currently running the store promise not to share the data, the customer must worry about what will happen if the company is bought by someone else, or goes bankrupt, as happened with Toysmart. One solution may be for the customer to use a service that stores only encrypted data in the .NET server. The only way the information can be decrypted is with a password provided by the customer. This way, the .NET server company (say, American Express) holds the data but has no way to make use of it.

Even if a customer encrypts her preference information, she still has to reveal this information to individual store owners if she wants to benefit from their recommender systems. The jazz store has to know what music the customer has liked in the past in order to recommend new titles to her. One radical alternative is that the customer may be able to run the recommender in her handheld computer. In this case, the customer would download a program along with a large amount of anonymous recommender data from a third-party recommender company. She would load the program and data onto her PDA and get recommendations directly from the PDA. The PDA could ask the store about its inventory to be sure the recommendations are only for products that store sells. Of course, the store could refuse the request, but at the cost of losing the customer. The customer could share her preference information with the third-party recommender company in a way that would guarantee that the information was completely anonymous. This technique requires new recommender algorithms and powerful PDA devices, but research on these designs is already under way. Brad Miller, also a Net Perceptions cofounder, is working on these issues for his Ph.D. at the University of Minnesota.

Recommender Coalitions

Recommender communities, or coalitions, are bound to form. Holders of customer preferences and purchase histories will talk with other entities about ways to share and maximize the value of that knowledge. (Of course these coalitions raise important privacy questions.) Many of these coalitions will be among non-competitors who have mutually beneficial information. For instance, music sites will be able to advise moviemakers about the types of music that a film's target audience is most interested in listening to. Once this sort of sharing takes place, lines will get drawn in the sand pretty quickly. In some cases cooperation will win and competitors may share information equally. In other cases we imagine a coalition will form with the intent of shutting out another group.

Recently, three of the top four airlines and all three top U.S. automakers have formed separate coalitions. The airlines started a ticket site (Orbitz); clearly they want to try to own the business of selling tickets. This is not a recommender problem, just an example of the power of coalitions to compress competitive boundaries. In the auto industry a coalition formed to negotiate with the supply chain. In recommenders we will see similar pressures. Companies will want to keep popular recommenders to themselves, since they provide a competitive advantage. On the other hand, economies of scale encourage companies to get together and share all the preferences to give the best possible recommendations. Antitrust legislation doesn't say anything about recommendations and preference sharing, just pricing, so it's a bit premature to guess how things will come out.

ASPs

Application service providers (ASPs) will arise to provide third-party recommenders to competitors. These companies will collect data from a group of companies and disseminate recommendations back to all of the companies. Companies will pay for the recommendations and be rewarded for the preference data they contribute, much like the DoubleClick Network. Over time, these ASPs will strive to create vortexes of information within a domain, so they have so much preference information that anyone who wants to sell products in the domain simply must share their preference information. Not to be a part of the vortex would be like a Greek farmer not coming to the agora. There will be considerable conflict among the ASPs who want to own the information, the companies they serve, and the consumers who see the information as their own.

The Ratings Race

As customer-preference information becomes centralized in the hands of recommender coalitions and ASPs, attackers will try to pollute preference bases with bogus ratings to get their products preferred by more customers. Naive attacks in which a large number of positive ratings are put in for some products won't work, because the recommender will just form neighborhoods of people who all like those products. More sophisticated attacks will be more successful, such as polluting a recommender system with millions of fake "users" who all say they like a random collection of items in addition to very strongly liking the item in question. Recommender systems will explore identity systems, systems that detect random preferences, and other techniques to combat these problems. Over time, more and more sophisticated offensive and defensive systems will evolve. If defensive systems are unable to adapt to the attacks rapidly enough, social and legal approaches will likely be used to protect the recommenders from attack.

Afterword

Marketing has sometimes gotten a bad name for trying to get people to buy things or listen to pitches for things they don't want. With collaborative filtering, marketers present items that customers *do* want. Marketers become welcome assets and even prognosticators, not irritants.

With smart cards, software agents, parametric searches, and more wireless applications on the horizon, we envision a golden era of marketing. Marketers will be able to reach customers how and when they want to be reached. And marketers themselves will find it hard not to be tempted by the new level of personalized offers and services.

What follows is a day in the life of a marketer (Marshall) in the not-too-distant future:

6:00 A.M.

Marshall wakes up and remembers he needs to pick up a present for his son's thirteenth birthday. He jots down the name of several of Justin's CDs from the rack by the stereo. On his laptop, Marshall types in the names of the CDs. Based on these titles, and the fact that Marshall needs these CDs tonight, CDs.com suggests to him six other CDs that his son might like. Each of these is in stock at their local retail store, where CDs.com offers to hold them for him. He chooses two, making sure they're appropriate for a thirteen-year-old.

8:00 A.M.

Marshall arrives at work, grabs a cup of coffee, and goes through his E-mail. The E-mail is sorted in order from most important to least important, as predicted by his recommender, based both on the contents of the E-mail, and on what other people who have received the E-mail have done with it.

One E-mail describes how the customer loyalty campaign has flourished since Marshall decided to pair the most valuable customers with service people who have served them well in the past—based on length of calls, personality matches, and sales records. Marshall has approved a bonus plan for top workers who are consistently chosen by the software to provide service to the best customers (because they do the best job!).

10:00 A.M.

Scanning a memo, Marshall notices that the percentage of conversion to sales has doubled in the last year because the new recommendation software is working so well. Stores using recommendation software are doing double the upsell over stores using the old cross-sell approach. With a projected $10 million increase in revenues per month, Marshall approves a planned rollout of the recommendation software.

11:45 A.M.

At lunch, Marshall takes the waiter's advice and orders the hot turkey sandwich. The gravy tastes like it's come out of an industrial-sized can and the turkey is sliced thin like deli meat. He's learned his lesson: No more rolling the dice with recommendations from untrusted sources.

12:30 P.M.

Marshall gets back from lunch and decides to surf the Web for a few minutes. His recommender notices idle time and suggests he place an order for a pearl necklace for his wife. The pearl necklace has been selected based on his wife's purchases as one she'll love, and the recommender has been watching for the right time to get it for several months. Right now the price of pearls is down because of oversupply, and with their fourteenth anniversary coming up in a few weeks, Marshall decides to pull the trigger.

2:00 P.M.

Marshall looks over manufacturing plans at his company's Ohio factory. Since his recommender predicts the new Fuzzy Chandler wizard puppet will sell many more copies than had originally been planned, Marshall retargets an additional factory to produce the Fuzzy Chandler puppets. He increases plans for revenues for the quarter accordingly.

3:00 P.M.

Since he will soon be going out of town on a business trip, Marshall investigates social outings with his family. His recommender suggests a package of VIP tickets to a Broadway show, dinner for four, and parking, all at a special price since he is such a valued customer. It's a new show but sounds like something he'll like, and he accepts after checking his family's calendar.

4:00 P.M.

Marshall starts a campaign for the Fuzzy Chandler puppets simultaneously on the Web, at call centers, and in-store at kiosks and cash registers. He sets the date of the campaign to coincide with a big marketing push. He approves a budget request to send free puppets to the 1,000 opinion leaders predicted by the software to have the highest combination of (a) influence in the marketplace and (b) probability of liking the new product.

5:00 P.M.

For an upcoming business trip, Marshall's recommender suggests a different hotel than the default one his company usually books. This hotel costs a little more per night, but it is famous for its spas to help execs recover from jet lag, and since the hotel would really like his business they're willing to match the business rate at his usual hotel.

5:30 P.M.

Marshall stops by the music store on his way home. Based on his purchase history with CDs.com and this particular retail store, Marshall is offered a coupon for 20 percent off on a jazz CD by a new artist he has heard of but never listened to. He buys the two CDs for Justin and the jazz CD for himself.

7:00 P.M.

Marshall goes to dinner with his family at the restaurant his recommender suggested. The restaurant is nearly invisible from the street, so he wonders if he ever would have discovered it on his own. Everyone in the family agrees it's their new favorite restaurant in the city. They love the quaint ambiance, the tropical plants, and the pepper-crusted steaks.

10:00 P.M.

Marshall gets home from the show with his family. He takes a minute to appreciate how well his day went. He purchased presents he's confident his wife and son will love, he enjoyed a wonderful dinner and a lively show, and he dramatically increased his company's revenues—all thanks to recommenders. He toasts the brave new world with a scotch. It's a single malt he's never tried before—but one he's sure he'll like.

Acknowledgments

This book is a direct result of the wonderful experience we had in the creation and ongoing success—despite the ups and downs of the e-commerce marketplace—of Net Perceptions.

First, we'd like to thank the other co-founders of Net Perceptions: Brad Miller, the "lead Ph.D. student" of GroupLens research and Vice President of R&D of Net Perceptions; Steven Snyder, the CEO and visionary leader; and David Gardiner, who introduced us to Steven at his Ph.D. graduation party, and who was our first and most passionate "user advocate."

The people who made the technology real—taking our research-quality code and turning it into industrial-strength products—are crucial to Net Perceptions' success. The development team includes too many hardworking, disciplined, brilliant people to mention all by name, but the first few stand out. Lee Gordon, Paul Algren, and Jim Hanlon, who all knew each other as top coders at Cray Research, were the first developers to join Net Perceptions, and continue to be among the best software people we've ever worked with. We learned more about building great software from Lee, Paul, and Jim—and their many teammates—than from all the books about software we've ever read.

Dan Frankowski, John Rauser, and JJ Jenkins were the members of the software team who contributed especially valuable insights through memorable philosophical conversations, afternoon juggling sessions, and thoughtful discussions about the future of recommender technology.

The members of the Net Perceptions research team were invaluable in helping us explore the opportunities for recommenders. Valerie Guralnik worked on the ways understanding time could improve recommendations, Filip Mulier and Mike Ekhaus worked on the item-item algorithm (the best algorithm known for recommendation), and Tom Nurkala directed the research group. We also acknowledge our deep debt to Paul Bieganski for his active mind, creative thinking, and willingness to tell us we were wrong when we were!

Bringing a disruptive technology to market required the insights and understanding of many business leades. We have been very lucky over the years to have visionaries on our board of directors who understood the challenges and opportunities we faced. First and foremost is Ann Winblad, who has been there from the beginning with her wisdom, intelligence, and directness. We also owe a debt for insights from Will Lansing, John Kennedy, Vern Raeburn (and his wife, Dottie Hall, a marketing whiz), Michael Gorman, and Brian Jacobs.

We have also been fortunate to work with many brilliant businessmen and -women. Don Peterson, the new CEO, has brought renewed energy and commitment to customers to Net Perceptions, and we thank him for carrying the torch. Tom Donnelly, the CFO, brings levelheaded financial wisdom and a passionate cut-the-crap style. We thank Steve Larsen for teaching us about high-tech marketing, George Moser for showing us the ropes on the sales side, Steve Vantassel for sharing his understanding of the retail business, Lee Gerdes for his vision of how "data" will change the enterprise in every way possible, Patty Hamm for her efforts to make Net Perceptions a welcoming and fun place to work, Jon Ebert for his marketing expertise from California trade shows to the Far East, and Sang Kim for his vision of how recommenders could change the knowledge management world. Last but certainly not least, we thank Theresa Anderson for her careful attention to detail that kept us out of trouble on too many business trips.

We also thank all the customers, too many to name, who led the charge in "crossing the chasm" of recommender systems from academic idea to practical tool. Without your vision, confidence, creativity, and hard work, recommenders would be yet another idea sitting on a shelf in the laboratory waiting for someone to dust it off and put it to use!

We are proud that collaborative filtering is a triumphant example of academic research being transferred into industrial applications. We particularly want to thank Paul Resnick for helping to start it all, for being one of the deepest thinkers we know, and for being a good friend and colleague through the years.

More than a score of students helped explore and develop this technology. The first to believe were Danny Iacovou, Mitesh Suchak, and Pete Bergstrom, who built the first GroupLens system at Minnesota and MIT back in 1993 and 1994.

The two of us spent an all-out Hack Week in 1995 with Paul Resnick, Brad Miller, Jon Herlocker, David Maltz, and Mark Claypool. We are thrilled to have Brad back in our lab now, where he is exploring the next generation of community recommenders. Jon became our second "lead Ph.D. student," oversaw the creation of MovieLens, and continues research on recommender systems as a professor at Oregon State University. Dave is now co-founder and Director of Engineering at AON Networks. Mark is currently a professor at WPI, where he explores innovative ideas for combining collaborative filtering with other types of information filtering, among other research interests.

After Hack Week, our research group blossomed. Badrul Sarwar earned a Ph.D. developing innovative techniques for collaborative filtering of very large and sparse domains. Ben Schafer explored the diversity of recommenders in e-commerce for his Ph.D., leading him to design interfaces for contextual customer needs. Brent Dahlen built the first version of MovieLens; Tom Zielund did our first controlled user study; and David Leppik studied partitioning items to form better neighborhoods. Mark O'Connor developed our recommender for groups. Nathan Good helped us learn when to mix intelligent agents into a recommender community; and Al Borchers brought a wealth of mathematics skill to help us develop and evaluate new algorithms. Irfan Ali studied how outbound e-mail brings users back; Hannu Huhdanpaa built DBLens, a collaborative filtering engine on a commercial database; and Tim Tian studied search and indexing interfaces for news recommendations. Joe Morin and Kien Quan built a new experimental recommender, and Patrick Baudisch helped us design text-content recommenders. We've been remarkably fortunate to have worked with many talented undergraduates on this project, including George Atendido, Tim Lee, Hae Young Kim, Gabirel Aguirre, Mary Bernadette Garza, Josh Chu, Adam Shearer, and Ammon Hall. And many students working on other projects spent time offering help and advice, particularly Ed Chi, now a well-known information visualization researcher.

Today our research group is as strong as ever. Brad Miller is joined by Cathy Guetzlaff, who contributed her passion and energy to the NetP knowledge management product. Ph.D. students Sean McNee, Dan Cosley, Mamun Rashid, and Prateep Gopalkrishnan have brought new energy into the project and are busily inventing the next generation of recommenders. Tony Lam has been invaluable in developing and maintaining the research infrastructure that makes this work possible, and Istvan Albert has recently joined us to help manage the lab.

Of course, keeping such a talented group fed and well-equipped takes money, and we're particularly grateful to the National Science Foundation for its support of much of our work through six different grants through the years.

Many other researchers have been working in the area of recommender systems. Pattie Maes helped spread the word about collaborative filtering through the Ringo system and later through Agents, Inc./Firefly Networks. Loren Terveen and Will Hill collaborated on some of the most innovative recommenders we've seen, and have been valuable colleagues. We're thrilled that Loren recently joined us here as a professor at Minnesota. Ken Goldberg's joke recommender Jester combined serious research with jovial content. Henry Kautz's ReferralWeb helped pave the path from recommenders to knowledge management. Lyle Ungar has been exploring very interesting applications of fundamental statistics technologies to recommenders. Jack Breese wrote the most thorough comparison of recommender techniques to date. Tom Malone's early work on the Information Lens inspired GroupLens. Even the name GroupLens is a tribute to his work! Hal Varian had the vision to see how important this field would become, and to invite the field to Berkeley for its first workshop (which he and Paul Resnick organized). At that workshop we met Marvin Weinberger, who first helped us see the commercial potential of this technology.

All of these people have, through their work and personal contact, shaped the field and us. Their experiences fueled our ideas and we hope this book may give them new ideas to keep the cycle going.

As professors, we've had immense support from our colleagues in making this work a success. We particularly want to thank our colleague John Carlis, who shares our lab, our ups and downs, and generously shared his ideas about databases and writing (not to mention basketball and racquetball) over the years. George Karypis, a world expert on data mining, collaborated with us on some collaborative filtering algorithms and developed what may be the best publicly available collaborative filtering software. Our colleagues at the University of Minnesota, both in Computer Science and across diverse fields helped us in uncountable ways from critiquing our ideas to sending us students. Our department heads during and after the founding of Net Perceptions—Ahmed Sameh, Yousef Saad, and Pen-Chung Yew—were remarkably flexible at letting us balance the opportunity to bring our technology to the world with our academic responsibilities. Our technology transfer office, headed by Tony Strauss, made it possible for us to build a company, keep research going, benefit the university, and keep everything legal.

Without the encouragement and help of our editors at Warner, this book would still be on the "someday" list. Susanna Einstein saw the wonderful article "The Art of the Sleeper" Malcolm Gladwell wrote in the *New Yorker*, and called to talk us into writing the book. Her ideas and vision helped form the direction and scope of the book. Zach Schisgal carried us through the bulk of the writing, helped us keep our focus, and helped us find Eric Vrooman. Sandra Bark carried us through copyediting and into production.

The two of us particularly want to thank Eric Vrooman, whose contribution was incredible. He was not merely a wordsmith, but combined the skills of a professional writer with the energy to invest countless hours learning all about recommender systems so he could help us craft ideas, experiences, and anecdotes into a coherent whole.

Finally, we want to include some personal thank-yous. John would like to thank his wife, Maureen; his children, Eric, Karen, and Kevin; and his parents, John and Mary; all of whom have put up with years of his "playing around with computers." Joe thanks his wife, Ellen, for unfailing support even when she needed it more, and he hopes this book will one day make sense to his son, Ben, who today can only ask why we didn't prominently feature Elmo.

Index

HF 5415.32 .R54 2002

Riedl, John.

Word of mouse

GAYLORD S